HISTORICAL DICTIONARY

The historical dictionaries present essential information on a broad range of subjects, including American and world history, art, business, cities, countries, cultures, customs, film, global conflicts, international relations, literature, music, philosophy, religion, sports, and theater. Written by experts, all contain highly informative introductory essays on the topic and detailed chronologies that, in some cases, cover vast historical time periods but still manage to heavily feature more recent events.

Brief A–Z entries describe the main people, events, politics, social issues, institutions, and policies that make the topic unique, and entries are cross-referenced for ease of browsing. Extensive bibliographies are divided into several general subject areas, providing excellent access points for students, researchers, and anyone wanting to know more. Additionally, maps, photographs, and appendixes of supplemental information aid high school and college students doing term papers or introductory research projects. In short, the historical dictionaries are the perfect starting point for anyone looking to research in these fields.

HISTORICAL DICTIONARIES OF ASIA, OCEANIA, AND THE MIDDLE EAST

People's Republic of China, Third Edition, by Lawrence R. Sullivan. 2016.
Israel, Third Edition, by Bernard Reich and David H. Goldberg. 2016.
Nepal, Second Edition, by Nanda R. Shrestha and Keshav Bhattarai. 2017.
Burma (Myanmar), Second Edition, by Donald M. Seekins. 2017.
Yemen, Third Edition, by Charles Schmitz and Robert D. Burrowes. 2017.
Chinese Economy, by Lawrence R. Sullivan. 2018.
Malaysia, Second Edition, by Ooi Keat Gin. 2018.
Tajikistan, Third Edition, by Kamoludin Abdullaev. 2018.
Postwar Japan, Second Edition, by William D. Hoover. 2019.
Iraq, Third Edition, by Beth K. Dougherty. 2019.
Democratic People's Republic of Korea, Second Edition, by James E. Hoare. 2019.
Chinese Environment, by Lawrence R. Sullivan and Nancy Y. Liu. 2019.
Saudi Arabia, Third Edition, by J. E. Peterson. 2019.
Republic of Korea, Fourth Edition, by James E. Hoare. 2020.
Tibet, Second Edition, by John Powers and David Templeman. 2020.
Chinese Culture, by Lawrence R. Sullivan. 2020.
Syria, Fourth Edition, by Omar Imady, David Commins and David W. Lesch. 2020.
Afghanistan, Fifth Edition, by Thomas H. Johnson and Ludwig W. Adamec. 2021.
Lebanon, Second Edition, by Tom Najem and Roy C. Amore. 2021.
Palestine, Second Edition, by Ilan Pappe and Johnny Mansour. 2021.
Chinese Communist Party, Second Edition, by Lawrence R. Sullivan. 2022.
Laos, Fourth Edition, by Martin Stuart-Fox and Simon Creak with Martin Rathie. 2022.
Taiwan (Republic of China), Fifth Edition, by John F. Copper. 2024.
Financial System in China, by Lawrence R. Sullivan and Nancy Y. Liu-Sullivan. 2024.
Thailand, Fourth Edition, by Gerald W. Fry. 2024.
New Zealand, Fourth Edition, by Janine Hayward, Richard Shaw, Lara Greaves, and Claire Timperley. 2024.
Azerbaijan, Third Edition, by Zaur Gasimov. 2026.
Artificial Intelligence in China, by Lawrence R. Sullivan and Nancy Liu-Sullivan. 2026.

Historical Dictionary of Artificial Intelligence in China

Lawrence R. Sullivan and Nancy Liu-Sullivan

BLOOMSBURY ACADEMIC
NEW YORK • LONDON • OXFORD • NEW DELHI • SYDNEY

BLOOMSBURY ACADEMIC
Bloomsbury Publishing Inc, 1359 Broadway, New York, NY 10018, USA
Bloomsbury Publishing Plc, 50 Bedford Square, London, WC1B 3DP, UK
Bloomsbury Publishing Ireland, 29 Earlsfort Terrace, Dublin 2, D02 AY28, Ireland

Cover design: Chloe Batch
Cover image © iStock.com/Muhammad Asroful Umam

A catalog record for this book is available from the Library of Congress.

ISBN: HB: 979-8-7651-4563-0
ePDF: 979-8-7651-4565-4
eBook: 979-8-7651-4564-7

Series: Historical Dictionaries of Asia, Oceania, and the Middle East

Typeset by Deanta Global Publishing Services, Chennai, India

Dedicated to the creators of artificial intelligence (AI) without whom this book could not have been written.

Contents

Preface

Artificial intelligence needs to be smart, not human.

Origin Unknown (2018)

Defined as computer systems performing tasks that normally require human intelligence, artificial intelligence (AI) has been described as the basis of a "fourth industrial revolution" with profound effects to science, industry, and various aspects of society. Rooted in philosophical and technological developments dating back to ancient times in both the West and China, AI has emerged as a powerful force transforming basic relations between humankind and machines, with the latter acquiring a capacity to "learn" from vast amounts of data, providing decision-makers in business and government unprecedented powers of analysis and prediction in various realms from stock market prices to disaster relief to military and geopolitical strategy. Following years of rejecting AI technology and tools largely promoted in the former Soviet Union, the People's Republic of China (PRC) switched gears in the 2010s, calling for applications of AI throughout the economy, especially industry, and society with a goal of becoming a global leader by 2030. Containing more than 150 separate entries that describe the multiple facets of AI in general and applications in the PRC specifically, this *Historical Dictionary of Artificial Intelligence in China* includes a reader's note, list of acronyms and abbreviations, map, chronology, introduction, glossary, appendix, and bibliography. Serving as a one-stop source for readers from academia, business, and the sciences, this volume gives special attention to the individual scientists and entrepreneurs in the West and China responsible for major developments and advances in AI technology along with developments in ancillary fields such as science fiction and films that influence elite and popular opinion on the frequently opaque world of AI.

Reader's Note

The Romanization of Chinese language words used in this dictionary is the *Hanyu pinyin* system developed in the People's Republic of China (PRC) in the 1950s and also currently used in the Republic of China on Taiwan. Chinese terms and phrases generally unknown to the Western reader are italicized along with newspapers, book titles, and major policy reports and decisions. In Chinese and East Asian culture, generally, the family name comes first preceding the given names. In order to facilitate the rapid and efficient location of information and to make the book as useful a reference tool as possible, extensive cross-references have been provided in the dictionary section. Within individual entries, terms and names that have their own entries are in **bold** the first time they appear. Related terms which do not appear in the text are indicated as *See also*. Conversion of Chinese currency, the *yuan* and abbreviated as CNY RMB, to the US dollar is 7:1.

Acronyms and Abbreviations

AAPI	application programming interface
AES	advanced encryption standard
AGI	artificial generative intelligence
AGV	automated guided vehicle
AI	artificial intelligence
AIGC	artificial intelligence generated content
AIHK	artificial intelligence association of Hong Kong
AIR	Institute for Artificial Intelligence Research
AISC	artificial intelligence supercomputer center
AIoT	artificial intelligence of things
AMRS	automated mobile robots
AR	augmented reality
ARMS	autoregressive models
AV	autonomous vehicle
AWS	Amazon web services
BCI	brain-to-computer interface
BGI	Beijing Genomics Institute
BIGAI	Beijing Institute for Generative Artificial Intelligence
BMI	brain-machine interface
BYD	build your dreams
CAAI	China Association for Artificial Intelligence
CAC(1)	Cyberspace Administration of China
CAC(2)	China Association of Automation
CAM	continuous automated monitoring
CAS	China Academy of Sciences
CASS	China Academy of Social Sciences
CCB	China Construction Bank
CCP	Chinese Communist Party
CCTV	China Central Television
CMA	China Meteorological Administration
CNCB	China National Center for Bioinformation
CNGB	China National Gene Bank

CNN	convoluted neural network
CNY	China *Yuan*
CPU	central processing unit
CRISPR	clustered regularly interspaced palindromic repeats
CRM	customer relations management
CSRC	China Securities Regulatory Commission
CT	computer tomography
CV	computer vision
DCIM	data center infrastructure management
DNA	deoxyribonucleic acid
DUV	deep ultraviolet light lithography
ESA	European Space Agency
EUT	expected utility theory
EUV	extreme ultraviolet lithography
EV	electric vehicle
FM	foundational model
GANs	generative adversarial networks
GE	genetically engineered
GNP	gross national product
GPS	global positioning system
GPT	generative pre-trained transformer
GPU	graphic processing unit
HFT	high frequency trading
HH	Hodgkin-Huxley
HIT	Harbin Institute of Technology
HKMA	Hong Kong Monetary Authority
HKPC	Hong Kong Productivity Council
HRL	hierarchical reinforcement learning
HSSS	hierarchical state space search
HTN	hierarchical task networks
ICBC	Industrial and Commercial Bank of China
IoT	Internet of Things
IP	Internet protocol
IPRAI	Institute for Pattern Recognition and Artificial Intelligence
ISO	International Organization for Standardization
LIDAR	light detection and ranging
LIME	local interpretable model-agnostic explanations
LLM	large language model
LRD	long-range dependencies
LSTM	long short-term memory
MAS	multi-agent system

MATL	Microsoft Asia-Pacific Technology Co.
MCMC	Markov Chain Monte Carlo
MIIT	Ministry of Industry and Information Technology
ML	machine learning
MOE	Ministry of Education
MOST	Ministry of Science and Technology
MPS	Ministry of Public Security
MSS	Ministry of State Security
NASA	National Aeronautics and Space Administration
NDA	National Data Administration
NDRC	National Development and Reform Commission
NLP	natural language processing
NPC	National People's Congress
OECD	Organization for Economic Cooperation and Development
OP	operations research
PLA	People's Liberation Army
PoW	proof-of-work
PRC	People's Republic of China
QAI	quantum artificial intelligence
R1	reasoning one
RAG	retrieval augmented generation
R & D	research and development
REID	re-identification
RGV	rail guided valuation
RLGT	reinforcement learning for generative tasks
RNA	ribonucleic acid
RNN	recurrent neural network
RRAM	resistive random-access memory
RSA	Rivest-Shamir-Adleman
SAIC	Shanghai Automotive Industry Corporation
SAIS	Shanghai Academy of Artificial Intelligence for Sciences
SAR	Special Administrative Region
SCIO	State Council Information Office
SCM	supply chain management
SCS	social credit system
SHAP	Shapley additive explanations
SIIO	State Internet Information Office
SMR	small modular reactor
SOE	state-owned enterprise
SQL	structured query language
SVM	support vector machines

Synbio	synthetic biology
TB	terabyte
TBM	transformer-based model
TD	temporal difference
TSMC	Taiwan Semiconductor Manufacturing Corporation
TWAS	The World Academy of Sciences
UAV	unmanned aerial vehicles
UQ	uncertainty quantification
VAE	variational autoencoder
VPN	virtual private network
VR	virtual reality
WAIC	World Artificial Intelligence Conference
XAI	explainable artificial intelligence
5G	fifth generation

Chronology

Artificial Intelligence in China and the World: Ancient to Modern

976–922 BCE Chinese mechanical engineer Yan Shi, during the Zhou Dynasty (1046–256 BCE), creates a human-like automata capable of walking on its own accord, with internal organs constructed of leather and wood to mimic a human being.

406 BCE Daoist philosopher Lie Yukou formulates a myth of creating intelligent beings with capabilities surpassing humans.

5th–4th Centuries BCE Greek philosophers Plato (428–347 BCE), Aristotle (384–328 BCE), and others inaugurate the study of logic and formalistic reasoning, such as Aristotle's syllogism, with *The Elements* by Euclid (circa 300 BCE) providing a model of formal mathematical reasoning. Greeks also produce the Antikythera Mechanism, a proto-computer operating with bronze gears and cogs used to predict the positions of the planets and the occurrence of eclipses of the sun. Sacred statues in Greece and in Egypt were believed to possess real minds capable of wisdom and expressing emotions.

9th Century Persian mathematician Al-Khwarizmi develops the algorithm.

1088 Su Song, a hydro-mechanical engineer in Kaifeng, China, during the Song Dynasty (960–1279), constructs an astronomical clock tower housing automata mannequins that perform various tasks, such as demonstrating wind direction.

13th Century English philosopher Roger Bacon creates male head composed of brass or bronze that was said to be able to answer any question.

1495 Leonardo da Vinci invents robotic knight consisting of a suit filled with gears and wheels connected to an elaborate pulley and cable system allowing for independent motion without human intervention.

1500s Swiss inventor and physician Paracelsus formulates idea of an "artificial man" known as "homunculus."

16th–18th Centuries Western philosophers Thomas Hobbes (1588–1679), Rene Descartes (1596–1650), and Gottfried Leibniz (1646–1716) postulate that all rational thought can be construed as systematic on a level with algebra and geometry with study of mathematical logic essential to all thought. Descartes further develops a mechanical view of the human mind with physical systems governed by natural laws while Leibniz constructs a universal calculator, known as the Stepped Reckoner, for performing the four basic arithmetic functions.

1642 Blaise Pascal (1623–1662) in France invents first mechanical calculator known as the Pascaline.

1684 Creation of chain rule in calculus postulates that any change in one variable reverberates throughout a chain of multiple variables, a concept which has subsequent impact on machine learning (ML) and the development in artificial intelligence (AI) of backpropagation and neural networks.

1748 Philosopher David Hume (1711–1776) develops epistemological concept of induction that would become basis of supervised learning.

1763 Posthumous publication of notes by Thomas Bayes (1701–1761) laying out Bayes' Theorem of inverse probability, that is the probability distribution of an unobservable variable which later is known as inferential statistics.

1800 Swiss mechanician Henri Maillardet builds an automaton in London known as the "Draughtsman-Writer" with large-scale memory capable of producing elaborate sentences and poems.

1818 Mary Shelley publishes *Frankenstein.*

1820 Charles Babbage (1791–1871) develops the concept of an "Analytic Engine" for carrying out complex arithmetic processes though the actual machine is never built.

1854 George Boole (1815–1864) publishes *The Laws of Thought* with Boolean algebra, creating the fundamental concept of binary logic involving ones and zeros subsequently employed in modern computers.

1860–70s Samuel Butler of England publishes *Erewhon* as a utopian science fiction novel along with the essay "Darwin Among the Machines" portraying machines as a kind of "mechanical life" undergoing constant evolution with the dire prospect of machines supplanting humans as the dominant species.

1912 Leonardo Quevedo (1852–1936) of Spain invents the first chess-playing machine, considered by some as the first functional computer, along with the construction of machines to solve real and complex roots of polynomials.

1913 Bertrand Russell (1872–1970) derives mathematical truths from logical principles and introduces a novel notational system for symbolic logic that is subsequently employed in the first AI systems. Creation of Markov Chain by Russian mathematician Andrey Markov as a stochastic process describing a sequence of events in which the probability of each event depends solely on the state attained in the previous event, not in past history.

1920s German mathematician and philosopher David Hilbert (1862–1943) declares that all mathematical reasoning can be formalized.

1921 Czech playwright Karel Capek (1890–1938) introduces the term "robot" in play entitled *Rossum's Universal Robots* (*R.U.R.*).

1929 Robot named *Gakutensoko* is developed in Japan.

1936 British mathematician Alan Turing (1912–1954) publishes "On Computable Numbers" and along with Alonzo Church (1903–1995) develops the concept that any form of mathematical reasoning can be mechanized, which leads to the invention of the "Turing Machine" with a capability of executing instructions and manipulating symbols. During World War II, Turing and the team at Bletchley Park in the United Kingdom develop the Colossus electrical mechanical device for breaking German Enigma machine military codes.

1940s Considered the "father of information theory" and the "information age," Claude Shannon (1916–2001) is the first to describe Boolean gates essential to all digital electronic circuits which become the foundation for AI. First discussions take place of neural networks as an idealized form of artificial neurons.

China and the World: 1945–2025

1945 ENIAC machine employs computer architecture storing data and program in the same memory as developed by American physicist John von Neumann (1903–1957), who also establishes Game Theory.

1950 Alan Turing publishes "Computing Machinery and Intelligence" and devises the "Turing Test" or "Imitation Game" as the first proposition in the philosophy of AI while Claude Shannon develops a jury-rigged mechanical mouse. In the fictional novel entitled *I, Robot*, Isaac Asimov explores robots, humanity, and existence with tales of robots going mad and secretly controlling the world.

1951 First machine with neural networks capable of learning developed by cognitive and computer scientist Marvin Minsky and Dean Edwards.

1952 Arthur Samuel develops a computer program to play checkers.

1955 Allen Newell and Herbert Simon develop the concept of a "logic theorist" as manipulation of symbols is considered the essence of human thought that leads to the development of computer software capable of executing logical proofs and solving mathematical theorems. Geoffrey Hinton, known as the "father of artificial intelligence," employs neural networks to simulate the human brain.

1956 Workshop on AI convened by John McCarthy is held at Dartmouth College in New Hampshire with financial support from the US government as research on AI is recognized as an academic discipline. Inauguration of revolution in cognitive science involving symbolic AI, generative linguistics, computationalism, and functionalism along with emergence of reinforcement learning in AI.

1957 Invention of the perceptron as the first functioning neural network by Frank Rosenblatt.

1958 John McCarthy creates LISP as the first programmable language for AI.

1959 Arthur Samuel coins the term "machine learning," describing the capacity of computers to make predictions and decisions based on the analysis of data sets. "General Problem Solver" algorithmic program is developed while IBM produces 7090, the first computer employing transistors.

1961 First industrial robot is employed in a General Motors automobile assembly plant.

1960s Development of fuzzy logic and so-called soft computing tools such as Bayesian networks outlining probabilistic graphical models and stochastic modeling in which random variables are employed to estimate the probability of different outcomes over time along with development of computer vision. Invention of robotic arms for industrial production.

1966 First "chatterbox" psychotherapist called Eliza is introduced by Joseph Weizenbaum using a natural language processing computer program to imitate a human therapist. Soviet mathematician Alexey Ivakhnenko publishes "Group Methods of Data Handling" establishing the foundations of deep learning.

1970 First facial recognition system unveiled at Osaka Exposition in Japan. Release of film *Colossus: The Forbin Project* that portrays takeover of the world's advanced weaponry by super intelligent computers.

1972 Publication of the fictional novel *Cyborg* by Martin Caidin that inspires television programs featuring bionic men and women.

1974 United States and United Kingdom halt financial support of AI, beginning the first "winter" of investment in AI lasting until 1980.

1977 Release of first in a series of *Star Wars* movies with portrayals of amiable and talkative droid robots R2-D2, C-3PO, BB-8, and a slew of others.

1979 American Association of Artificial Intelligence established.

1980 John Searle formulates the "Chinese Room Argument" challenging the idea that computers can have genuine understanding or consciousness, so named for the notion of translating the Chinese language without a total understanding of the meaning of the words.

1981 Japanese government renews AI investments based on success of so-called expert systems employing "if-then" rules that emulate decision-making ability of human experts to solve complex problems. Introduction of the IBM personal computer.

1981 Fifth generation computers developed in Japan.

1982 Development of backpropagation for the training of neural networks composed of multiple layers of artificial neurons with billions of parameters. Release of the film *Bladerunner* featuring android "replicants" largely indistinct from real human beings and roaming the earth with superior strength and knowledge developed by the private Tyrell corporation.

1984 Release of first of several *Terminator* movies featuring a human-like cyborg powered by a neural net processor with superior strength and intelligence.

1986 First driverless car built in Germany. Gigantic neural networks are created composed of millions of neural layers and billions of parameters interconnected to mimic the human brain with capability of performing intricate tasks such as image recognition and complex decision-making including autonomous vehicles. Recurrent Neural Networks (RNN) are developed with capability to analyze large data sets that vary over time similar to human language along with Convolutional Neural Networks (CNN) to study multidimensional grid-like data such as visual images.

1987 Alacrity Solutions established as a strategic management advisory system.

1988 Machine learning applied to decision theory as temporal difference (TD) learning algorithm is developed employing differences between predicted and actual rewards to update future predictions as a core concept in reinforcement learning.

1990s Second "winter" for AI investments follows the 1987 stock market crash in the United States.

1990 Neural networks are employed to recognize handwritten notes.

1994 CASP is set up to study the biological field of protein folds.

1997 Development of Long Short-Term Memory (LSTM) as a type of neural network in deep learning that uses gates to process and retain information and is employed in advertising and stock market prediction. In a game of chess, IBM Deep Blue computer defeats reigning world champion Gary Kasparov.

2001 Steven Spielberg film *A.I. Artificial Intelligence* is released portraying a childlike android capable of love.

2002 Improved performance of ML from deep learning. Focus on artificial generative intelligence (AGI) by American companies including Google.

2003 Human DNA successfully mapped.

2006 Stanley Kubrick film *2001: A Space Odyssey* features human-like computer named "HAL." Amazon develops AWS cloud computing with generative AI solutions capacity harnessing both large language models (LLMs) and foundational models (FMs).

2010 DeepMind founded in London, United Kingdom, by Dennis Hassabi and others, bringing an interdisciplinary approach to building artificial generative intelligence (AGI) systems. Microsoft employs Azure Machine Learning platform to support fine-tuning and deployment of large language models.

2011 IBM introduces Watson computer with capability of answering questions posed in natural language along with a set of AI assistants. Google Brain is established while a deep learning artificial intelligence research team led by Andrew Ng combines open-source ML research with information systems and large-scale computing resources that is subsequently incorporated under Google AI. Advances in supervised learning lead to voice recognition systems and translation apps while AlphaGo harnesses deep neural networks to master traditional Japanese game of *Go*.

2012 "Father of AI" Geoffrey Hinton and others debut AlexNet, a Convolutional Neural Network (CNN) model that represents a breakthrough in deep learning and computer vision. Chinese company Baidu attempts to hire Geoffrey Hinton.

2014 Google acquires DeepMind. Astrophysicist Stephen Hawking warns against possible deleterious effects of AI.

2015 December: OpenAI is founded by Sam Altman and others as a nonprofit company for development of safe and beneficial AGI to serve humanity.

2016 China's National Development and Reform Commission (NDRC) issues an Internet+ Artificial Intelligence Three-Year Implementation Plan.

2017 August: Spurred on by advances in AI in the West, especially the United States, China announces *New Generation Artificial Intelligence Development Plan* involving a major commitment to developing various fields of AI with a goal of becoming "the world's primary artificial intelligence country" by 2030 with planned investments totaling $142 billion. Google develops transformative architecture for large language models (LLMs) to assist computers to better process how humans communicate.

2018 AlphaFold employing AI to design protein structures is developed by DeepMind.

2019 China issues *Guidelines for the Construction of the National New Generation Artificial Intelligence Open Innovation Platform.*

2020 Fully 47 percent of robotic manufacturing worldwide occurs in Japan. Deep neural networks created to synthesize genomic segments are employed by AlphaFold. China issues *National New Generation of Artificial Intelligence Standardization Guidance.*

2021 China announces *New Generation of Artificial Intelligence Ethics Code.*

2022 China issues regulations requiring registration of all AI algorithms developed in the country. **May:** DeepMind introduces Gato as a deep neural network for a variety of complex tasks including engaging in dialogue, controlling robots, and playing video games with a capacity to perform multiple tasks at the same time. **November:** American nonprofit company OpenAI begins launch of a series of generative AI chatbots culminating in GPT-4 with the capacity to write stories, poems, essays, tweets, and computer code.

2023 Chinese company Alibaba Cloud releases *Tongyi Qianwen* large language model. **November:** Safety Summit on Artificial Intelligence convened in the United Kingdom issues the *Bletchley Declaration* on the safe development of AI signed by 28 countries including China, India, the United States, and the European Union with concern expressed of potential misuse of AI by terrorist organizations and cyber criminals. Chinese government declares that all algorithms are blocked with developers subject to punishment.

2024 China invests $6.1 billion in construction of large-scale data centers for the planned eight regional computing hubs in the country and announces *Artificial Intelligence+ Initiative to Integrate AI and Industry* and *Action Plan for Information Standard Construction.* **May:** China rolls out large language model based on President Xi Jinping Thought. **June:** In a speech at the National Science and Technology Conference, President Xi Jinping outlined goals of making the PRC a "technological powerhouse" by the year 2035. **October:** Dennis Hassabi and John Jumper of DeepMind are awarded the Nobel Prize in Chemistry for their work in developing AlphaFold protein structures database while Geoffrey Hinton and John Hopfield are awarded the Nobel Prize in Physics for their work in statistical physics. **December:** Chinese research laboratory DeepSeek releases open-source large language model produced at substantially lower cost and utilizing less advanced computer chips with capabilities equal to or superior to more expensive models developed by major high-tech firms such as Meta and OpenAI.

2025 February: International AI Summit convened by France and India in Paris issues declaration on inclusive and sustainable AI development with the United States and the United Kingdom refusing to sign the agreement. **April:** Study session of the CCP Politburo focused on promoting the healthy and orderly development of AI indicating that China and the United States have reached a point of no return in building bifurcated AI systems as Xi Jinping emphasized the need to seize the initiative and gain the advantage in the AI field with breakthroughs in fundamental theories, methods, and tools while employing AI to lead a paradigm shift in scientific research and accelerate technological innovations and breakthroughs across various fields. Nvidia Corporation CEO Jensen Huang declares PRC AI capability is close behind the United States. **May:** Newly elected Pope Leo XIV, an American, identifies AI as one of the main issues facing humanity, saying it poses challenges to defending human dignity, justice, and labor.

2030 Official target date for China to become a global leader in the development of AI.

2026 February: AI-driven humanoid robots perform dance routine with live actors in Chinese Lunar New Year televised performance.

Introduction

> Artificial intelligence or alien intelligence?
>
> *Origin Unknown* (2018)

Pick up a newspaper, turn on the television, or do a computer search on Google or YouTube, and one of the most popular topics will inevitably be the rapid development and enormous global impact of artificial intelligence (AI) including in the People's Republic of China (PRC). While rooted as far back as ancient times, especially in the emergence of key mathematical tools such as algorithms in ninth-century Persia, AI is primarily a post-World War II phenomenon catapulted to prominence by the invention of the computer and the creation of the Internet. Promoted by governments, private companies, and innovative entrepreneurs creating a tidal wave of AI tools applied to multiple realms of science, economy, and society, the PRC has emerged as a major player intent on becoming the global leader by the year 2030. Initially reluctant to embrace the new technology which was denounced by Chinese officials as a "pseudoscience" up to the late 1980s, the country performed a total flip-flop when confronting major AI advances especially in the United States. Announcing an all-out effort beginning in 2017 to master the complex technology, AI tools were perceived as a panacea to a low productivity economy with applications to various social realms including health care and crime prevention while ensuring political and social stability. While the benefits have been substantial, most notably in the major breakthrough achieved by the DeepSeek chatbot in late 2024, multiple problems have emerged mainly concerning intrusions into personal privacy by the creation of large-scale data sets and abuses of human rights by mass government surveillance enhanced by sophisticated AI systems serving the political interests of the ruling Chinese Communist Party (CCP).

History

Developing along separate but parallel paths, the intellectual and technological groundwork of AI emerged in Chinese and Western civilizations as early engineers conceived of human-like automata and philosophers examined the realms of logical and formalistic reasoning that would over the centuries shape the content of AI systems and applications. Fascination with artificial creatures exhibiting human qualities, often with superior strength and intellectual faculties, was shared by innovative speculations from the ancient Zhou and Song dynasties of China to the mechanical marvels produced by Roger Bacon and Leonardo da Vinci in medieval Europe. Similar developments in the theoretical arena came from philosophies as divergent as Chinese Daoism with its focus on the relationship of humankind and nature to the mathematical inclinations and formalistic reasoning of ancient Greeks and the modern thinkers of the European Renaissance.

Spurred on by early inventions such as mechanical calculators along with dramatic transformation of mathematics by the creation of calculus, the Bayesian theorem of inverse probability, Boolean binary logic, information theory, and symbolic logic, among others, the march from a purely human to an artificial though human-made intelligence proceeded into the modern era supplemented by science fictional accounts featuring a utopia of benign robots or a dystopia of rogue computers and alien technological creatures. Major turning points in this seemingly ineluctable process occurred during and immediately after World War II led by Alan Turing and John von Neumann involving development of computers with memory storage capacity as the first machines utilizing neural networks were constructed in the 1950s. Following a workshop on AI convened at Dartmouth College in 1956, a virtual revolution occurred in cognitive science involving symbolic AI, generative linguistics, and computationalism along with emergence of reinforcement learning and creation of the perceptron as the first fully functional neural network to mimic the human brain. Also developed were early versions of machine learning and construction of robotic machines for utilization in industrial facilities with Japan and then the Republic of Korea becoming important participants in the AI revolution. Despite setbacks occurring in two AI "winters" in the 1970s and 1990s brought about by withdrawal of financial support primarily by the United States, progress continued in fits and starts with development of key AI components. Included were large language models (LLMs), natural language processing (NLP), computer vision (CV), artificial generative intelligence (AGI), and facial and voice recognition as governments and businesses generated the big data sets subject to analysis and pattern recognition by increasingly sophisticated AI algorithms. Application to multiple fields includes business, commerce, and science including medical drug discovery, weather forecasting, military strategy, and space exploration while science fiction portrayed the benefits and especially potential dangers of AI dominated by humanoid robots (killer and savior terminators alike) and rogue computer systems (HAL 9000).

In the case of the PRC, the initial rejection of all things associated with AI reflected a general distrust of modern science in the political revolutionary ideology of CCP leader Mao Zedong (1949–1976), especially during the radical Cultural Revolution (1966–1976) and a specific association of the technology with the "revisionist" crimes of the pariah Soviet Union. Making a dramatic turnabout to embracing the necessity of developing modern science and technology inaugurated in 1978–1979, Chinese leaders opened the door to scientific innovation that gradually legitimated work on the components of AI, especially computers, with prominent Chinese scientists, most notably Qian Xuesen, initially trained in the United States, becoming leading advocates. With dramatic developments of powerful chatbots such as ChatGPT and other AI systems particularly in the United States, the PRC made AI a priority of national development especially in 2017 with explosive growth of AI companies and AI tools that elevated the industry to global standards in many realms most evident in the advanced chatbot R1 released by the Chinese firm DeepSeek in late 2024. Stay tuned!

AI: Components and Challenges

Mimicking the human brain with its 100 billion neurons and approximately 1000 trillion synapses in terms of cognitive capacity and creative intelligence is no easy task. While the most advanced LLMs used to power chatbots such as ChatGPT4 feature enormous computing power compared to previous versions with reputedly one trillion parameters, the current state of AI is still considered "narrow," excelling in specific tasks of data processing but falling short of humans in creativity, emotional intelligence, and an ability to adapt to novel situations and still nowhere near the capacity for superintelligence that would exceed the best human minds. Comparing an artificial neural network with the human brain is based on the assumption that artificial neurons are comparable to biological ones, whereas in reality, 1,000 of the former are required to simulate the behavior of a single biological neuron, with chatbots trained to predict what word comes next in a sequence generating a capacity to make conversation and write text similar to human beings. Drawing from the vast amounts of data available on the Internet, LLMs rely on NLP to function and when combined with the separate domain of computer vision, can accelerate diagnostics, improve accuracy, and minimize human error and bias in multiple realms from, among others, drug discovery to stock price prediction to weather forecasting. With innovations such as transfer learning accelerating the development of new LLMs piggybacking on earlier models without having to reinvent the wheel, AI progresses in an upward trajectory, allowing individual enterprises and entire countries, such as the PRC, to leapfrog toward new and perhaps unfathomable phases of technological achievement but with challenges of intrusion on privacy and the possibility of uncontrolled rogue AI systems wreaking economic and social havoc.

A

ACCELERATED PRODUCTION (*JIASU SHENGCHAN*). Defined as the utilization of **machine learning (ML)** and **neural networks** engaged in **deep learning** to optimize the manufacturing process, accelerated production involves enhanced data collection and analysis and improved decision-making in the creation of **smart technology** in factories. Major beneficiaries of applying artificial intelligence (AI) to increasingly complex manufacturing processes include improved quality control, **predictive maintenance**, and enhanced **supply chain** orders and production line planning organization along with reduced expenditures. Replacing traditional manufacturing with its heavy reliance on cumbersome and time-consuming data collection methods prone to human error and generally unavailable for real-time application, accelerated production generates large reams of data for immediate use. Employing computer **software** to automate data processing and analysis, the technology provides production management personnel with real-time insights and actionable information enabling the making of informed decisions both quickly and accurately, especially in new and more increasingly complex manufacturing sectors involving sophisticated product development and fabrication such as electronics and **semiconductors**. Able to detect and report potential problems in production such as defects in materials and equipment malfunctions, the production process is optimized with lower costs, less downtime in production lines, and reduced wastes of raw materials.

In an industrial sector that has traditionally suffered from low levels of **productivity** mainly as a result of the highly bureaucratized system of central economic planning pursued from 1953 to 1978 under the influence of the Soviet Union and the often misinformed economic ideas of Chinese Communist Party (CCP) Chairman Mao Zedong, the current government of the People's Republic of China (PRC) is strongly attracted to accelerated production as an effective means for catching up with the more advanced industrial economies in the West and Japan. Incorporated into the ***Artificial Intelligence Plus Initiative to Integrate AI and Industry*** enacted in March 2024, accelerated production is a central component in national efforts to develop an AI-driven industrial sector with the Ministry of Industry and Information Technology (MIIT) taking the lead in the implementation of major policies. Plans include the establishment of a system of industrial parks, 178 national high technology zones, and 45 national advanced manufacturing clusters with special emphasis on integrating information technology and manufacturing. Singled out for the development of accelerated production are **electric vehicles (EVs)** and EV charging stations, **energy** production, especially electric power, life sciences, and health care, including **medical imaging** devices, diagnostics, and **drug discovery** with the first drug fully generated by AI currently undergoing clinical trials. Driven by the country's large and highly profitable pharmaceutical industry, heavy investments are planned in various realms of AI including the Medlinker online medical advisory platform similar to **ChatGPT**. Accelerated production is also slated for introduction to the expanding **space exploration** industry and **quantum computing** technology as the entire high technology sector has already reported a 7.5 percent increase in added value along with similar plans for the burgeoning service sector of the national **economy**. *See also* BIG DATA AND DATA SETS and DATA CENTERS.

ADVERTISING AND MARKETING (*GUANGGAO, YINGXIAO*). Employed in generating commercial advertisements and evaluating performance of various marketing methods, artificial intelligence (AI) can both create and curate advertisements while also providing large **data sets** for predicting consumer behavior and assisting in such critical marketing processes as dynamic pricing and optimizing digital advertising. Most revolutionary is the capacity of AI tools to personalize and customize particular ads and to steer spending on ads to specific, segmented audiences through various electronic and **social media**. Whereas admen in previous years were saddled with such laborious tasks as producing spreadsheets for optimizing ad spending, AI has taken over much of these routine efforts, freeing up admen to concentrate on the more creative side of the business in which AI complements but does not substitute for humans in the overall advertising and marketing sector. Along with analyzing and providing recommendations for improving the performance of ads, AI tools can also spot mistakes that could harm potential customers and perform critical customer relations management (CRM) functions as demonstrated by the highly successful American company Salesforce which generates 200 billion AI-driven predictions a day.

In the case of the People's Republic of China (PRC), AI in advertising has become mainstream with digital marketing employed to create a personalized **customer service** experience with widespread AI-generated content, especially in the hyper-competitive field of **e-commerce** led by **Alibaba**.

Employed are various forms of **augmented reality (AR)** combining real-world and **computer**-generated three-dimensional content to create an immersive experience that transcends traditional shopping, along with virtual livestreaming which broadcasts live video to an audience often with interactive elements. Producing massive amounts of data that facilitate consumer insight discovery, media planning, brand tracking, and ad impact evaluation, AI tools have also made copywriting and ad designing an in-house process with concomitant cost reductions for major Chinese **companies**. *See also* SENTIMENT ANALYSIS.

AGRICULTURE (*NONGYE*). A vital sector in the global **economy** and in the domestic economies of many developed and developing nations, agriculture has undergone dramatic changes with the introduction of artificial intelligence (AI) in such realms as precision farming, crop monitoring, yield prediction, **supply chain** optimization, and sustainable resource management. Equipment and new inventions employed in AI applications to **smart** farming practices include satellites, **drones**, unmanned tractors and rice transplanters, **computer**-driven irrigation systems, soil sensors, AI-based greenhouse **robots**, and vertical agriculture. In the case of precision farming, critical resources such as water and fertilizer are targeted for specific crop areas with varying needs that can result in reducing waste, improving crop quality, and increasing overall yield. Similar benefits can be achieved with AI crop monitoring systems and **software** with **algorithms** employed to analyze crop images that identify diseases and pests early on, enabling timely intervention thereby preventing widespread damage and reducing excessive pesticide use along with enhanced soil monitoring. In terms of yield prediction, AI can analyze historical data and potential **weather** patterns to predict crop yields with greater accuracy allowing farmers to plan their operations more effectively and optimize resource allocation while also employed to manage livestock, optimize feeding programs, and improve overall herd management. In the case of supply chain management, AI can analyze market trends and predict demand, helping farmers to make strategic decisions about crop selection and pricing with AI-powered systems managing inventory, tracking shipments, and ensuring timely delivery. Benefiting the environment, sustainable practices facilitated by AI include more rational crop rotation, minimal tillage, and cover cropping along with optimizing irrigation systems, reducing water usage, and promoting water conservation as analysis of available **data sets** makes for more informed decisions and environmentally friendly farming practices. When combined with **Internet of Things (IoT)** sensors that monitor soil moisture levels and weather conditions, algorithms can decide in real time how much water to provide to crops. Also available are autonomous crop irrigation systems designed to conserve water while promoting sustainable agriculture and farming practices with AI in smart greenhouses optimizing plant growth by automatically adjusting temperature, humidity, and light levels based on real-time data. While human observation of agricultural conditions is limited in accuracy, **computer vision** models can monitor soil conditions to gather accurate data necessary for combating crop diseases and using the data to determine crop health with sensors that detect growth conditions, triggering automated adjustments to the environment. Aided by AI, utilization of **synthetic biology** is also employed offering transformative solutions for enhancing crop resilience, **productivity**, and sustainability by accelerating the design and optimization of genetic circuits, enabling the creation of smart crops, self-monitoring, adapted, and responsive technology, that can dynamically respond to changing environmental conditions. Overall, these innovations are essential to meet global challenges such as climate change, population growth, and resource scarcity that threaten the sustainability of the global food system as AI significantly overcomes the many disadvantages of traditional farming with substantial cost savings generated by the new wave of digital automation.

International **companies** involved in the application of AI to agriculture include, among others, Gingko Bioworks, a leading synthetic biology platform that designs and builds organisms for various applications such as agricultural bio-stimulants; Amyris, focusing on developing sustainable ingredients and products using synthetic biology; Bayer and Syngenta, emphasizing crop breeding and biopesticide development; Precigen, using genetic engineering and synthetic biology to develop new crop varieties and improve plant traits; Pivot Bio, a developer of microbial inoculants for enhancing nitrogen fixation in plants, reducing the need for chemical fertilizer; and John Deere, producer of the CN spraying device that distinguishes crops from weeds.

The largest agricultural sector in the world employing 40 percent of the country's workforce, the People's Republic of China (PRC) is leveraging AI and synthetic biology to enhance greater efficiency, higher yields, and self-sufficiency in ensuring food security for a population of 1.41 billion. Utilized to accelerate breeding, optimize resource use, develop innovative crops with enhanced traits like stress tolerance and yield, and open up unused land to crop production, the new technology plays a role in engineering crops with specific features and improving agricultural practices including highly automated greenhouses and vertical farming facilities. Major examples include precision farming and smart agriculture with AI-powered platforms like the "Agriculture Brain" employed by **Alibaba** utilizing **big data** to help Chinese farmers optimize planting, irrigation, seed selection, and fertilization, leading to higher yields and reduced resource use; smart greenhouses with AI-powered environmental control systems regulating temperature, humidity, and other factors to create optimal growing conditions, improve crop quality and yield; agricultural robots used for such critical tasks as planting, weeding, harvesting, and monitoring crops, reducing labor costs and improving efficiency with AI-equipped drones performing tasks like spraying pesticides, fertilizing, and monitoring crop health along with the BeiDou satellite system providing imagery used for cropland **mapping** which integrated with remote sensing and geographic information systems provide farmers with precise information used for plowing, weeding, harvesting, pest control, and monitoring crop health; and AI-powered supply chain optimization used to predict demand, optimize inventory levels, and streamline **logistics** for agricultural products, reducing waste and improving efficiency including **blockchain**-based food traceability to track agricultural products throughout the supply chain, enhancing transparency and food safety. Also deployed in livestock management is AI-powered pig farming with AI systems used to track pigs, monitor their health and behavior, and optimize feeding, improving animal welfare, and reducing costs along with **facial recognition** for livestock to identify individual animals, enabling personalized feeding and monitoring for signs of illness or distress. With fish constituting a major portion of the Chinese diet, AI-driven fish farms, so-called "blue farming," have been developed in fresh lakes and coastal seas to monitor water quality, optimize feeding, detect diseases, and manage fish populations in aquaculture, improving efficiency and sustainability as AI-powered feeders dispense feed based on fish behavior and appetite, reducing waste and improving feed efficiency. Chinese companies applying synthetic biology in agriculture include Anhui Huaheng Biotechnology (AHB) and BASF Agricultural Solutions collaborating on developing bio-stimulant products with Changing Biotech a leading player in microorganism-based protein development and Shandong Shunfeng Biotechnology Company developing genetically engineered crops with improved traits.

"AI WASHING" (*RENGONG ZHINENG XIDI*). Defined as a deceptive **marketing** tactic promoting a product or service by overstating or distorting the role of artificial intelligence (AI), AI washing is pursued by **companies** wanting to appear as operating with cutting-edge technology in an appeal to consumers. Various forms of the practice include claims of utilizing AI when in actuality employing less sophisticated technology, overstating the efficacy of existing AI tools employed by the company, hyping nonexistent AI solutions to extant problems, and the bolting of an AI **chatbot** onto a non-AI operating structure. Prevalence of AI washing stems in part from the lack of a commonly accepted definition of AI and the generally loose definition of the concept that feeds such deceptive practices. AI washing also consists of glossing over or simply ignoring the deleterious effects of AI technology on the environment, especially the potentially deleterious impact of the enormous **energy** demand of the technology with **laws and regulations** aimed at deterring the practice in developed economies, especially the United States.

With 4,500 recognized AI **companies** in the People's Republic of China (PRC) and many more firms claiming to be involved in some aspect of AI, AI washing is a persistent problem with firms and individuals engaged in the practice subject to the regulatory authority of the Cyberspace Administration of China (CAC). Public cases in which accusations of AI washing were brought against a Chinese company include Xiao-i Cognitive Intelligence Corporation based in Shanghai with headquarters in the Cayman Islands and a stock listing on the NASDAQ. Founded in 2001, the company has been sued by shareholders for overstating its AI capabilities and ability to compete in the global AI market. Fully 80,000 AI-related companies in the PRC have halted operations in recent years with AI washing apparently a common practice. *See also* ANTI-FRAUD.

ALGORITHMS (*SUANFA*). Defined as a set of instructions to be followed in calculations and other similar **mathematical** operations, algorithms are a central component in artificial intelligence (AI) serving as a program that tells **computers** how to learn and operate autonomously. Algorithms employed in AI are generally very complex, composed of large sets of rules determining the steps taken by a computer in its ability to learn and by taking in **training** data that enhances the learning process. Supplied by developers, the data employed by the algorithm is either labeled or unlabeled with three types of learning—**supervised**, **unsupervised**, and **reinforcement learning**—with dozens of subcategories and the differences between the various types determined by how the computer is trained and how it functions. So-called K-nearest algorithms deal with data points in close proximity that are mapped to demonstrate relationships, while **neural networks** consist of a collection of AI algorithms that mimic the human brain. Major uses of AI algorithms include data entry and classification, advanced or **predictive analytics**, search engines such as **Google**, **virtual assistants** such as Siri produced by Apple, **robotics** assembly, and **autonomous driving** vehicles. While algorithms always generate the same output for a given input, AI is capable of changing output based on new inputs. Algorithms are also used to sort data or find the shortest path between two points, with AI tools used for classification and regression. In the case of **Google** DeepMind, the company's latest AI project known as Alpha Evolve combines the coding skills of its Gemini AI model with a method for testing the effectiveness of new algorithms and an evolutionary method for producing new designs. Coming up with more efficient algorithms for several kinds of computation, including a method for calculations involving matrices, improves on an approach called the Strassen algorithm that has been relied upon for more than 50 years by reducing the number of calculations required to produce a result. Applications include enhancing scheduling tasks inside **data centers**, sketching out the design of **computer** chips, and optimizing the design of the algorithms used to build **large language models (LLMs)**.

Employed in all facets of AI development in the People's Republic of China (PRC), algorithm developers operate under substantial state **regulation** embodied in the *Algorithm Recommendation Regulation* enacted by the Chinese government in 2022. Major provisions require that service providers shall not use algorithms to impose unreasonable restrictions on other Internet information service providers or hinder or disrupt the normal operation of the Internet information services legally provided by them. Service users are also to be explicitly informed of the use of recommendation services and offered an output, but they must also be allowed to view keywords used by algorithms to profile individuals and be given an opportunity to remove the tags. An algorithm registry has also been created requiring algorithms that can affect public opinion or "have social mobilization capabilities" to provide basic information on the algorithm and conduct algorithm security self-assessments. In terms of ideological controls, algorithms in the PRC must reflect the "core values of socialism," while any unregistered algorithms will be blocked, with developers subject to punishment.

ALIBABA. A prime **e-commerce** company and global leader in cloud **computing** services in the People's Republic of China (PRC) founded by Jack Ma (Ma Yun) and currently headed by Eddie Wu, Alibaba is devoted to employing artificial intelligence (AI) to transform e-commerce by providing a more personalized experience for its millions of customers. Major AI developments include the multilingual Tongyi Qianwen ("unified thousand questions") **chatbot** and other innovations to enhance **customer service** experience by handling common inquiries and enabling businesses to develop their own generative AI programs and solutions. A **large language model (LLM)** trained on vast amounts of data and introduced in 2023 by Alibaba Cloud, the chatbot is an **open-source model** with several billion **parameters** and multiple cutting-edge AI tools such as **transformer**-based **neural networks** employing **natural language processing (NLP)** capable of handling sequence-to-sequence tasks and long-range dependencies (LRD) that describe how statistical dependence between two points decays over time. Other functions include a coding copilot that generates content such as code or images while also checking for errors in complex programs with 90,000 enterprises utilizing the service nationwide. Also pursued is the integration of AI into major Alibaba services such as Taobao online shopping making available customized product recommendations; the Tingqu smart speaker device which drafts summaries of meetings and creates personalized schedules; Tongyi Wanxiang for generating images; and Modelscope as a service platform for providing hundreds of pretrained generative tools on the cloud platform. Unique features of these services include utilization of **augmented reality (AR)** offering customers a visual search for products with an interactive function that allows a virtual "try on" of clothes. With **supply chain** management a major challenge to online shopping websites, Alibaba has also developed the Rookie (*Cainiao*) **logistics** arm for optimizing warehouse operations employing AI-driven **robots** and automated systems for the management of inventory, packing, and shipping especially during peak demand periods such as the annual Singles' Day (November 11), China's biggest daily shopping event. As delivery of millions of packages daily requires precise logistics planning, Alibaba employs AI to analyze traffic patterns, **weather forecasting**, and historical data to determine the most efficient delivery routes, speeding up delivery times, and reducing fuel consumption and operational costs.

Extending AI capabilities beyond its core business operations, Alibaba is involved in urban management through the City Brain project, an initiative that aims to create **smart** cities by using AI to optimize traffic flow, improve public safety, and enhance urban planning. In the city of Hangzhou, the home base of Alibaba in Zhejiang Province, the project was first implemented with AI systems analyzing data from traffic cameras and sensors to manage traffic lights, reducing congestion and improving emergency response times. Also pursued is the development of AI for environmental monitoring that analyzes data from various sources, including satellite imagery and **Internet of Things (IoT)** devices, to monitor air and water quality, assisting city authorities to promptly address environmental issues, and promote sustainability. Integrating AI into its e-commerce platforms, logistics operations, customer service, and urban management projects, Alibaba has enhanced business efficiency as the technology continues to evolve with the company issuing more advanced chatbot versions following the release of the breakthrough technology by the Chinese company **DeepSeek** in December 2024. *See also* BAIDU.

ANTI-FRAUD (*FAN QIZHA*). Development of artificial intelligence (AI) technologies has had a substantial impact on fraud detection and prevention in business and **finance** in a variety of ways, especially fraudulent activities that are increasingly difficult to detect using traditional rule-based systems. Employing **machine learning**–based **algorithms** to analyze vast amounts of **data sets**, patterns, and anomalies indicative of fraud can be identified in real time, allowing **companies** and financial institutions to take immediate remedial action, reducing potential losses and unnecessary costs. Learning from the data over time improves predictive capacity to spot suspicious customer behavior, such as sudden large purchases and transactions, while also allowing firms to adapt to new threats such as online scamming and other nefarious methods to gain illicit monetary benefits. A major development in the future of AI in financial fraud detection is the integration of blockchain technology that provides a secure and transparent ledger that can be used to store transaction data and with other similar technologies will enable financial institutions to better track and detect fraudulent activities even in complex networks.

In the case of the People's Republic of China (PRC), AI tools have been employed against increasingly sophisticated fraudsters that themselves employ available AI tools to reap illicit financial gains at the expense of unknowing victims. While many local authorities in the country have formed so-called AI police squads in an effort to deal with **telecommunication** scams and other increasing fraudulent activities, their criminal counterparts have resorted to using **deep fakes** and face-swapping AI technologies that manipulate voice and facial images to cheat unsuspecting people of their wealth. With increases in scamming and other fraudulent activities in the country's robust banking sector, institutions such as the giant Industrial and Commercial Bank of China (ICBC) have also come to rely on various AI anti-fraud tools as human oversight alone is simply incapable of tracking such highly sophisticated methods. *See also* CRIME AND CRIME PREVENTION.

ARTIFICIAL GENERATIVE INTELLIGENCE (*SHENGCHENGSHI RENGONG ZHINENG*). A subset of artificial intelligence (AI) also known as generative AI or gen AI, artificial generative intelligence (AGI) has the capacity to create new content based on a learning process that includes images, text, music, video, and code. Employing **large language models (LLMs)** to learn from and mimic vast amounts of data, AGI generates new content in response to specific prompts by the user, a process facilitated by AGI systems understanding **pattern recognition** and structures of their **training** data which enables the delivery of new content. A product of improvements in **transformer**-based **neural networks** developed in the early 2020s including **ChatGPT** and various text-to-image and text-to-video services, AGI is employed across a variety of industries and commercial sectors including **finance**, **marketing**, art, writing, product design, and fashion while also employed to formulate crisis action plans for the **military** and production plans for industry. Potential problems of AGI utilization include potential misuse in cybercrime and **deep fakes** and large-scale losses in **employment** in major economic sectors. Capable of learning complex subjects including art, biology, chemistry, human and programming languages, AGI takes such inputs as audio, code, images, and videos and creates new content for these modalities. In the case of ChatGPT, **natural language processing (NLP)** is employed in multiple ways to simulate human-like conversations, image generation to create new real-world-like images, video generation employing **deep learning** methods that forge new footage based on previous frames, speech generation used for **text-to-speech** conversion, **virtual assistants**, and voice cloning, and, so-called "jasper campaigns" creating content tailored to various types of communication channels. The different types of generative AGI models include generative adversarial networks (GANs), variational autoencoders (VAEs), autoregressive models (ARMs), recurrent **neural networks** (RNNs), **transformer**-based models (TBMs), and **reinforcement learning** for generative tasks (RLGTs). A potentially powerful tool for streamlining the workflow of creative artists and musicians, engineers, researchers, and scientists, AGI is the focus of major global **companies** such as Amazon, **Google**, Meta, and **Nvidia**.

While the People's Republic of China (PRC) considers AI as a key factor to becoming a global player in the **economy** and the military, the country has been less receptive to AGI, seeing the technology as posing a potential threat to national security and social-political stability. With the Chinese government pursuing policies of censoring and controlling the content of the Internet, access to chatbots released by **OpenAI**, Google, and Meta has been blocked, while the first major PRC-based chatbot, Ernie.Bot by **Baidu**, faced major delays in release and confronted major regulatory hurdles and state controls imposed in 2023 specifically aimed at AGI, as all LLMs must register with the government **algorithm** registry, meet truth and accuracy requirements, and reflect the "core values of socialism" along with stringent and heavily detailed standards on input training data developed by the technical working group TC260. Development based on unregistered **foundational models** is explicitly forbidden, preventing foreign **open-source models** from operating in the PRC and effectively discouraging smaller companies or entrepreneurs from venturing into this space. Cases of Chinese firms experiencing a censorious state regime include iFlytek whose AI-powered educational tablet evidently produced a passage criticizing former Chinese Communist Party (CCP) leader Mao Zedong, resulting in penalties imposed on employees and suppliers. Also imposed was a block on Internet access to Hugging Facc, a major open code repository where developers can access and work on many generative AI models collectively, yet another indication that in the PRC under the leadership of **Xi Jinping**, maintaining state control over cyberspace is often a higher priority than developing cutting-edge AI.

ARTIFICIAL INTELLIGENCE PLUS INITIATIVE (*RENGONG ZHINENG + CHANGYI*). Approved by the People's Republic of China (PRC) at the governing National People's Congress (NPC) in March 2024, the *Artificial Intelligence Plus Initiative to Integrate AI and Industry* is a strategic plan to accelerate the adoption of available artificial intelligence (AI) technologies across various sectors of the Chinese real **economy**. As a legacy of the state-controlled central economic planning system adopted from the Soviet Union in the years 1953–1978, research institutes were organizationally separated from ministry-run production facilities with little or no integration of newly developed products into the real economy. Aimed at breaking down this silo-like bureaucratic structure that still persists, the *Initiative* contains various proposals for incentivizing Chinese firms, both state-owned enterprises (SOEs) and private **companies**, to integrate AI into core business operations with an overall goal of increasing **productivity** at notoriously low efficiency firms, especially in heavy industry, and improving product quality as a way to enhance international competitiveness. Primary focus is on the development of **large language models (LLMs)** "with Chinese characteristics" as productivity tools in the country's many traditional industries through vertical integration and creation of digital industry clusters along with the creation of an AI infrastructure including **data centers** and new **energy** projects. Emphasis is also given to luring investors along with cultivating the necessary talent and skills required by AI technology as AI in China contributed 500 billion CNY ($69 billion) in 2023, involving a reported 4,500 enterprises. Major corporate promoters of the *Initiative* include prominent AI players such as iFlytek as the PRC attempts to deal with the problems created by the cutoff of various high technology components, such as advanced **semiconductors**, from the United States.

AUGMENTED AND VIRTUAL REALITY (*ZENGQIANG, XUNI XIANSHI*). Utilizing **machine learning (ML)**, augmented and virtual reality (AR and VR) enhance human perception of the real world with applications to a wide range of activities such as gaming, shopping, and entertainment. While AR enhances the real world with digital information through mobile devices such as smartphones or tablets, often employed in manufacturing and industry, or with hands-free glasses or headsets, VR removes users completely from the real world, fully immersing them in a virtual world using a head-mounted display or headset and employed in such sectors as health care, architecture, and **education**. In the case of AR, content spans multiple senses including visual, auditory, and olfactory by combining real and virtual worlds, real-time interaction, and accurate three-dimensional images of virtual and real objects. Seamlessly interwoven with the physical world, augmented reality alters a person's perception of a real-world environment, whereas virtual reality substitutes the real-world environment with a completely simulated one. A primary value of augmented reality is the way components of a digital world are blended into the user's perception of the real world not by simply displaying data but by integrating immersive sensations that are perceived as natural parts of an environment. Utilizing **software** apps and hardware such as special AR glasses, the technology overlays digital content onto the real-life environment and objects with filters that alter the appearance of a person or object in a photograph with games that blend real and virtual systems. Invented in the early 1990s, functional AR and VR systems were developed in **military** laboratories in the United States and then extended into commercial activities such as education, communications, medicine, and entertainment. Widely adopted in various economic and entertainment sectors in the People's Republic of China (PRC), augmented and virtual reality contributed an estimated $8 billion in revenue in 2024. Popular venues employing the technology include virtual museums and popular shopping malls with **e-commerce** companies such as **Alibaba** offering its "Buy+" technology. *See also* VIRTUAL ASSISTANT.

AUTOMATED REASONING (*ZIDONG TUILI*). A subfield of artificial intelligence (AI), automated reasoning is fundamental to generating **computer** programs capable of employing mathematical logic and reasoning to answer questions about what any system or program will do or will never do. Connected to the fields of theoretical computer science and philosophy, automated reasoning allows computers to engage in automated reasoning completely, or nearly completely. Developed subareas of automated reasoning include automated theorem proofs and the somewhat less automated but more pragmatic subfield of interactive theorem proofs and automated proof checking as a form of guaranteed correct reasoning under fixed assumptions. Additional topics include reasoning under **uncertainty** and so-called nonmonotonic reasoning which allows for conclusions based on new information and serves as an essential component in AI. Historically, the development of formal logic played a major role in the field of automated reasoning that led to the development of AI with formal proofs in which every logical inference is checked back to the fundamental axioms of **mathematics** with all intermediate logical steps supplied, without exception. There is no appeal to intuition, even in cases where the translation from intuition to logic is routine, such that a formal proof is less intuitive and less susceptible to logical errors. Major tools and techniques of automated reasoning include classical logic, fuzzy logic, calculus, Bayesian **inference**, reasoning with maximum entropy, that is selecting a probability distribution with the largest remaining uncertainty, and many less formal ad hoc techniques. Reflecting the enormous strength of mathematics in Chinese history and contemporary society, automated reasoning has been the subject of numerous **conferences** and workshops in the People's Republic of China (PRC) since the 1990s at prominent **education** institutions such as Nanjing University and at the Joint Center for Mathematical Research of Peking University. Ongoing research is also conducted at major **research institutes** such as the Automated Reasoning and Cognition Center in the western city of Chongqing with concentration on intelligent **algorithms** and **software**, automated reasoning, reliable computing, numerical solving of nonlinear differential and algebraic equations and their applications.

AUTONOMOUS DRIVING (*ZIDONG JIASHI*). A cruial technology for realizing the development of self-driving autonomous vehicles (AVs) including automobiles and trucks, artificial intelligence (AI) is essential to creating the innovative memory and storage of vast amounts of data necessary for a vehicle to be truly autonomous. Relying on tiny cameras and miniature laser systems, AVs are made continuously aware of the surrounding environment by identifying and classifying information which is fed into the **computer** control of the vehicle, making possible split-second decisions based on a detailed understanding of the driving environment. For a vehicle to have the capacity to be driven without human user control, an extensive amount of **training** must be undertaken for the installed AI network to perceive and digest the information necessary to come up with a safe and secure decision in any potential traffic situation. Upwards of 300 million lines of code with more than one terabyte (TB), one trillion bytes, of storage along with memory bandwidth of more than one TB per second is needed to support the computational performance necessary for autonomous driving platforms. Relying on a continuous, uninterrupted stream of data and instructions, real-time decisions are made based on complex **data sets**. Success of early AVs is largely the result of vehicles repeatedly taking the same route, learning every detail of the route with high-resolution **mapping** serving as a key component of the self-navigation system. Once there is less reliance on needing to recognize the route, the attention of the onboard computer is directed to monitoring traffic patterns and detecting the presence of pedestrians and other potential real-time hazards, with the operational range of most AVs restricted to specified routes of operation.

Aggressively pursuing the development and deployment of AVs, the People's Republic of China (PRC) has opened 20,000 miles of national roadways to driverless vehicles and issued 16,000 licenses for AV operations, with major cities such as Wuhan in central China fielding a fleet of so-called "robotaxis" (*jiqiren chuzuche*). Major Chinese **companies** involved in producing AVs and essential AI components include 19 automakers, most prominently BYD, NIO, SAIC, and foreign-owned Tesla, and high-tech firms such as **Baidu** and **Huawei**, with Didi, WeRide, and Pony.ai as operators. Conducting initial development of the **software** at companies located in Silicon Valley in the United States and carrying out initial road tests in California from 2013 to 2022, production and personnel were shifted back to the PRC, with the heavy emphasis on the production of **electric vehicles (EVs)** facilitating the introduction of AV technology. Current plans call for AVs to constitute 20 percent of the total automobile fleet in the PRC by 2030.

AVIATION (*HANGKONG*). A technology uniquely suited to the rapidly developing and constantly changing demands of the aviation industry, artificial intelligence (AI) has a profound impact on multiple aspects of commercial and private airlines, enhancing performance and efficiency while addressing key safety issues. Most evident in the commercial arena is the utilization of AI tools such as **predictive analytics** to handle flight delays by analyzing real-time data on potentially disruptive **weather** conditions and snarled airport operations, with more efficient updates of departure times and rebooking of customer flights when necessary. Also achieved is better management of fuel consumption and emissions, with AI technology optimizing flight plans and traffic routing, with **machine learning (ML)** employed to maximize airline revenue management, avoiding such money-losing phenomena as half-empty cabins while also reducing the risk of overbooking. With automated inventory management, AI **algorithms** analyze usage patterns and aircraft maintenance schedules, making for less wasteful storage of spare parts while relying on **predictive maintenance** to identify potential equipment failures before the fact and a reduction of flight disruptions. Utilizing **facial recognition** powered by AI, passenger check-in, immigration processing, and baggage handling operations are streamlined, along with optimizing crew scheduling, yielding concomitant reductions in labor costs and expediting aircraft design and certification procedures utilizing AI **software** and **robots**.

Applied to the rapidly growing aviation industry in the People's Republic of China (PRC), AI tools have become a favorite of the nine major airlines companies, especially in terms of improving customer experience that for years suffered from constant flight delays, disruptions, and poor in-flight service. Examples include the state-owned China Eastern Airlines, which has employed AI to handle huge amounts of data in tailoring airline services for individual consumers, with the airline's data lab unit attempting to solve problems before they occur by allowing customers to give better instructions and feedback on their in-flight experience. By automatically classifying thousands of complaints, solutions are recommended to help frontline customer relations staff, with China Eastern Airlines fielding 41.6 complaints per million passengers. AI-related technologies have also been deployed at major airports, with Beijing Capital International Airport launching a facial recognition system for security checks in April 2018, a practice now employed at 70 national and regional airports. *See also* MILITARY APPLICATIONS.

B

BACKPROPAGATION (*FANXIANG CHUANBO*). A fundamental **algorithm** component of artificial intelligence (AI) to train artificial **neural networks**, backpropagation serves as the core mechanism in **machine learning (ML)** for adjusting the weights of a network based on the error between its predicted output and the desired output that essentially allows AI to learn from mistakes and improve its accuracy over time. The primary function of backpropagation is to calculate the gradient of error with respect to the network weights, which indicates the degree to which each weight should be adjusted to minimize error. In the forward pass stage of the process, data is fed through the neural network to generate output, while in the backward pass stage, the error between the predicted output and the actual target is calculated with the error propagated backward through the network, allowing each neuron to adjust its weights accordingly. Vital for the **training** of **deep learning** models, backpropagation is composed of complex neural networks with multiple layers, with a capacity to learn intricate patterns from large **data sets** and an essential ML technique. Necessary to achieve the optimization of artificial neural networks, backpropagation facilitates the use of gradient descent algorithms to update network weights, which is the method by which deep learning models are able to "learn."

Actively developing and utilizing backpropagation to advance AI capabilities, the People's Republic of China (PRC) has invested heavily in the technology in various AI applications including **facial** and **voice recognition**, **natural language processing (NLP)**, and machine translation. Impacting the use of backpropagation are various **regulations** imposed by the Chinese government on data collection, along with controls over sensitive applications involving anything challenging the "core values of socialism," along with ethical considerations involving invasion of **privacy**. Major challenges include limitations due to restrictions on access to high-end **computing** hardware such as advanced **semiconductors**, especially by the United States, which is crucial for developing sophisticated AI models. Extensive data collection practices in the PRC also raise concerns about potential misuse of data in AI training, as face recognition systems powered by backpropagation are widely deployed for public security purposes and mass **surveillance**, often against potential political opponents and vulnerable ethnic minorities such as the Uighurs from Xinjiang Province.

BAIDU. The largest Internet search engine provider in the People's Republic of China (PRC), Baidu (meaning a "hundred times") was an early adapter of artificial intelligence (AI) beginning in 2010 with "Baidu Brain" as its core AI technology engine employing **machine learning (ML)**. Accessed by one billion electronic devices and 544 million active users in the PRC, Baidu offers a full AI stack, including AI chips, a **deep learning** framework, **natural language processing (NLP)**, knowledge graph, **speech recognition**, **computer vision (CV)**, and **augmented reality (AR)**, while operating with an **open-source** AI platform. Most prominent is the AI **chatbot**, Ernie.Bot, with several iterations since its introduction with approximately 300 million users in the PRC including **robots** capable of understanding voice commands and reading written words. Also available is Baidu.Core providing online **marketing** and non-marketing services and Baidu.Cloud employing an AI cloud platform to serve approximately 85,000 businesses. Committed to making every user a potential developer, Baidu AI tools enable users with little or no knowledge of coding to create their own **artificial generative intelligence**-powered chatbots for specific functions integrated into their websites. Collaborative efforts by Baidu include work with **telecommunication** giant **Huawei** and the American firm **Qualcomm** to develop AI-powered **smart** phones and other devices while the Baidu Apollo program for **autonomous driving** has been offered for free to Chinese automakers. In the medical field, Baidu deep learning is employed to detect cancerous cells in the human body with computer vision employed to provide better diagnosis of disease. A pioneer in **foundation models**, Baidu has been an innovator in data exploration and **accelerated production** while Baidu Baike is an online encyclopedia, Baidu Tieba a keyword discussion group, and iQIYI for video streaming. *See also* ALIBABA.

BIG DATA AND DATA SETS (*DA SHUJU, SHUJUJI*). A large and complex collection of information that is difficult to manage and analyze, big data has a symbiotic relationship with artificial intelligence (AI) as big data constitutes the basis of learning and decision-making by AI tools which employ large data sets to perform cognitive tasks such as generating texts or making recommendations based on **pattern recognition**. With **training** on specific data sets, AI acquires expertise on subject matter ranging from business and **finance** to medical diagnostics to **weather forecasting**, automating complex steps and processing with a goal of identifying major but sometimes subtle patterns in the data and generating actionable insights making for faster and more accurate decisions. Employed in all phases of data collection, storage, and retrieval, AI can handle highly diverse sets of data spotting common human errors while alerting the user to anomalies or unexpected patterns. Applied to business and commercial affairs, AI can anticipate and capitalize on emerging trends in industry and **marketing** by analyzing reams of information on consumer behavior and personalizing and optimizing performance of digital marketing campaigns with enterprises leaning on big data to train AI **algorithms** that in turn analyze, understand, and dissect data sets. Advantages include a capacity to extract more value from data sets and to generate statistical models and detect patterns different from traditional rules-based approaches that follow explicit and often highly restrained instructions as big data provides the raw material by which **machine learning (ML)** can derive new insights. Disadvantages include the tendency of big data sets based on historical material to perpetuate biases and suffer from poor quality while bringing major disruptions, including potential reductions in **employment**, to the workplace.

In the case of the People's Republic of China (PRC), big data and data sets have been attractive to both state and commercial interests with the National Data Administration (NDA) established in 2023 to collect and centralize the massive reams of data collected by various agencies in the country while also unifying industry data standards, facilitating data sharing across bureaucratic agencies and social and economic sectors, and streamlining data **regulations**. With a government highly concerned with issues of national security and social stability, big data has been employed to strengthen and centralize **surveillance** of the population, most notably in extensive use of **face** and **voice recognition** technologies. On the economic front, China has integrated big data functions into its prevailing **industrial policy** of promoting key, high-value, and high technology sectors by adopting a three-year *Data Element X* plan stressing the importance of high-quality data, enhanced data circulation, and data security with applications to the predictive power of analysis as opposed to the prevailing backward-looking practice of many Chinese users. Sectors singled out for enhanced application of big data include **transportation**, **logistics**, and the life sciences, with major data sets such as the Health and Nutrition Survey and data set archives managed by institutions such as New York University Libraries in Shanghai. *See also* DATA CENTERS.

BILIBILI. A popular video-sharing website and **social media** network in the People's Republic of China (PRC), Bilibili, commonly known as "B station," was launched in 2009 targeting the younger generation in the country, offering long-term, in-depth videos, many of which contain artificial intelligence-generated content (AIGC). Also offered is the Coeus self-developed cloud-native artificial intelligence (AI) platform for data processing and model **training** serving a wide range of uses including **advertising**, **natural language processing (NLP)**, speech-making, image **training**, and **e-commerce**. An **open-source model**, Bilibili is concerned with the inability of users to distinguish between real and virtual content and the inadvertent spread of misinformation, such as videos with virtual singers mimicking real pop stars. Adopting a policy of clearly labeling AIGC, a practice also adopted by its major video competitor Douyin (literally "shaking sound"), the Chinese mainland version of TikTok, the two **companies** are devoted to protecting user **privacy** rights as stipulated by enhanced **regulations** issued by the Chinese government. With a reported 200 million users in 2024, Bilibili estimates that AIGC, as the most popular offerings, will constitute 25 percent of its video offerings by 2026.

BIOCOMPUTING (*SHENGWU JISUAN*). Reflecting advances in neuroscience, biocomputing involves construction of biological **computers**, or mini brains, employing active neurons and brain tissue that mimic the structure and main functions of the human brain. A potentially invaluable tool for research, especially of certain human diseases, this invention will make possible the computational performance of the best computers with the **energy** efficiency of the human brain. Consisting of three-dimensional cultures of cerebral tissue, biocomputers are a product of three major technological innovations in the fields of electrophysiology, artificial intelligence (AI), and brain organoids, with potentially enormous reductions in energy consumption from 10 megawatts for supercomputers to 20 watts for the human brain. In terms of electrophysiology, the major challenge involves finding a noninvasive system for communicating with cerebral organoids, where multiple electrochemical signals occur every second in a small mass of tissue culture. In the absence of such signals, cerebral organoids remain inoperative, unable to construct the three-dimensional structures necessary for nerve tissues to function, as brain mechanisms require more than a simple electrochemical signal. True memory involves the reorganization of neuron networks and the intervention of other brain cells, including microglia, the immune system of the brain. Further development in AI is also necessary, as brain tissue cultures produce large volumes of data that require interpretation, which recent advances in **algorithms** are able to meet. Last is the necessity of increasing the scale of brain organoids beyond the current brain tissue cultures, which contain a maximum of 15,000 neurons. Any increase in scale requires protection against oxygen deprivation, with each cell connected to oxygen and nutrients similar to the performance of the bloodstream in a living organism.

While microfluidics can provide the perfusion in which oxygen-rich blood is provided to body tissue, this process has yet to be transposed to cerebral organoids comparable to the brain size of a mouse. Constituting a merger of biology with computer hardware, biological computers may help explain how the brain manages to process incomplete information while revealing the mechanisms of such human disorders as dementia and Asperger's syndrome. Initial applications of the technology include teaching brain cells on a chip to play ping-pong, developed by the DishBrain project at Monash University in Australia.

Actively engaged in the field of biocomputing, various approaches and applications have been pursued in the People's Republic of China (PRC) including "brain-inspired" AI research involving the development of neuromorphic chips which are designed to mimic the operations of biological neurons. Also pursued by Chinese scientists are advances in DNA computing involving the creation of programmable DNA-based gate arrays capable of performing complex computations with potential applications to the classification of molecules and solutions to **mathematical** problems. Exploring the use in biocomputing of brain organoids, major projects in the PRC involve connecting brain-on-chip biocomputers to electronic devices that employ human neurons to control **robots** with future applications to brain-computer interfaces along with potential **drug discovery** and improved analysis of biological data. Like other countries engaged in biocomputing research, the PRC faces ethical considerations regarding the use of brain organoids and the potential for self-awareness in these systems along with the need for **regulations** to handle sensitive data. Related fields experiencing significant growth and development in the PRC include bioinformatics with substantial **publications** and researchers in such areas as **genomics**, proteomics, and computational modeling along with studies on metabolic networks, computational neurobiology and biological manufacturing.

BIOTECHNOLOGY (*SHENGWU JISHU*). A ubiquitous presence in biology and the life sciences especially during the 2020s, artificial intelligence (AI) including statistical-driven **machine learning (ML)**, **big data** analytics, knowledge discovery, and **natural language processing (NLP)** have had a transformative impact on biotechnology, especially in the realms of **drug discovery**, food security, health care, clean water, and clean **energy**, along with enhanced management of agricultural and forest lands. Heavily dependent on data storage, filtering, analysis, and sharing, major biotechnology **companies** maintain huge data sets that are required for complex tasks of chemical analysis, **genomic** sequencing, and enzyme studies, all of which require AI **software** and digital computation. Major areas of biotechnology with substantial application of AI include agriculture, forestry, medicine, animal breeding, and bioinformatics that involve utilizing **computer** technology to collect, store, analyze, and disseminate big data.

In the case of the People's Republic of China (PRC), interest in biotechnology employing AI has focused on achieving innovations in medicine and health care, especially cell and gene technology, along with **synthetic biology** and bioengineering. Also pursued is a focus on reading, writing, and editing the human DNA utilizing ML and cloud **computing**. Examples of international biotechnology collaboration involving AI include the Japanese pharmaceutical giant Takeda, which in conjunction with Fudan University in Shanghai, has established a Digital Innovation Academy in the PRC. Priority goals aim to utilize the advantages of both Takeda and Fudan to engender development of patient-centric digital therapies and commercial transformation, gain research insights into the development of digital health care products and solutions while cultivating talent for the digital health care industry in the PRC. The Academy also aims to combine efforts to develop innovative topic studies and conceptual models ranging from screening and diagnosis to treatment with AI solutions essential to these studies.

BLETCHLEY DECLARATION (*BULAIQIELI XUANYAN*). An agreement reached at the Artificial Intelligence Safety Summit convened at Bletchley Park in the United Kingdom in November 2023, the site of the famous codebreaking operation in World War II, the Bletchley Declaration addresses the challenges and opportunities posed by artificial intelligence (AI) while focusing on securing public safety and protecting against the potential misuse of the technology by criminal gangs and terrorist organizations. Participants included representatives from 28 nations, including the People's Republic of China (PRC), the European Union, India, and the United States, along with **computer** scientists and technology leaders with India taking a leading role in formulating concrete proposals. Emphasis was on so-called "frontier AI" in reference to highly sophisticated **artificial generative intelligence (AGI)** models with potentially dangerous capabilities. Major proposals for increased regulatory scrutiny included guaranteeing personal **privacy**, dealing with historical biases, and protecting intellectual property rights. *See also* INTERNATIONAL GOVERNANCE.

BLOCKCHAIN TECHNOLOGY (*QUKUAI LIAN JISHU*). Providing a decentralized, immutable, and transparent ledger, blockchain technology in combination with artificial intelligence (AI) offers solutions for various industries by enhancing efficiency, scalability, and security. Ensuring the data integrity and trust crucial to AI applications, blockchain serves as the storage location for the **algorithms** that process and analyze large amounts of data identifying patterns, making predictions, and automating processes. Examples of the synergistic application of the two technologies include health care with patient data stored on a blockchain protecting data **privacy** and security; **supply chain** management with blockchain tracking products and ensuring authenticity, while also optimizing **logistics** and predicting potential supply disruptions; assisting in detecting fraudulent **financial** transactions with blockchain providing a secure and transparent record of transactions; and automating **smart** contracts on blockchain making for faster and more efficient transactions. AI tools have also been instrumental in enhancing blockchain performance by strengthening security and improving consensus mechanisms and scalability which, in turn, increase trust in AI-based decisions and predictions. In the case of the People's Republic of China (PRC), convergence of AI and blockchain technology has led to the development of smarter, more efficient blockchain solutions. Included is the adoption of the consensus mechanism known as proof-of-work (PoW), where network participants solve complex mathematical problems to validate transactions and add new blocks to the chain, securing the network and rewarding participants while reducing **energy** consumption and increasing transaction speeds.

BRAIN-TO-COMPUTER INTERFACE (*NAOJI JIEKOU*). A technology that enables the human brain to communicate by thought alone with external devices including **computers**, brain-to-computer interface (BCI) employs artificial intelligence (AI) in multiple ways by detecting and then converting brain signals into digital commands with applications to health care, **robotics**, and other neurophysiological discoveries. Operating with BCI noninvasive wearables such as headbands, earphones, and **smart** glasses, or more invasive brain implants with sensors that translate brain waves into instructions and text, AI contributes to BCI by providing real-time feedback from improved efficiency of **training**, emotional recognition in real time, cognitive screening by digitizing screening tests, synthesizing speech when the user silently mimics sentences, and predicting the intent of a speaker. Utilizing motor and sensory tools embedded in the devices, AI-enhanced BCI improves the quality of patient care and rehabilitation in health care, improves worker **productivity**, and accelerates the performance of **robots**. Major problems and challenges include long-term **training** periods, maximizing real-time feedback, and the need for less invasive technologies such as near-infrared spectroscopy.

Utilization of BCI employing AI has expanded rapidly in the People's Republic of China (PRC) with major applications in health care, especially for physical rehabilitation and treatment of debilitating diseases such as Parkinson's, epilepsy, and depression. Focusing on cognitive enhancement,

Chinese researchers at institutions such as the Neural Engineering Laboratory at Tsinghua University aim at merging AI with natural intelligence, as Chinese firms such as Brain Company in Hangzhou and We-Linking Medical Technology experiment with new technologies, such as implanting microprocessors in patients to better control seizures and control wheelchair movement, with industry-wide forums convened in the PRC. Recent developments include the development of a brain-on-chip at Tianjin University, which combines brain organoids with a neural interface chip used to train a robot to perform various tasks, along with implants into the brain of a monkey to control robotic arms. Controlled experiments have also been conducted in Chinese primary and secondary schools with BCI headsets on students monitoring attention span and mental concentration in the classroom. Ethical standards for BCI use have also been promulgated for minimizing harm, with continuing debate among Chinese BCI developers over the advantages and disadvantages of noninvasive versus invasive methodologies. Commercialization of BCI in the PRC is expected to produce a future market value of $16 billion, with plans for major clinical trials of the technology linking the brain directly with electronic devices planned for 2025. Other developments include creating standards for the use of BCI technology on tasks such as brain information acquisition, preprocessing, encoding and decoding, data communication, and data visualization, with researchers at Peking University and the Shenzhen-Hong Kong Institute of Brain Science employing a device called the Neuroscroll probe to separate single neural activities of macaque monkeys from 1,024 tightly spaced channels simultaneously. *See also* SCIENCE FICTION.

C

CHATBOTS (*LIAOTIAN JIQIREN*). A type of **computer** program employing artificial intelligence (AI) to simulate human-like conversations available online through websites and mobile phone apps, chatbots employ **natural language processing (NLP)** and **machine learning (ML)** to understand the intent and needs of users. Learning from previous interactions to improve response time, chatbots enhance customer engagement, streamline processes, and lower operational costs in handling customer inquiries, thereby reducing the need for traditional labor-intensive call centers. Various forms of chatbots include menu-based, the most basic version; rule-based, the simplest form which employs an if/then decision tree in responding to users; hybrid, a combination of the two; and voice response. Examples of popular chatbots include **ChatGPT** developed by **OpenAI**, Gemini employed by **Google**, and Hugging Face with Siri, Alexa, and Google Assistant deploying conversational AI, though not all chatbots are equipped with AI. Trained on large amounts of data and employing NLP and ML, chatbots intelligently generate a wide range of non-scripted, conversational responses to human text and voice input, serving as virtual agents that can be specifically trained to interact with customers in contact centers. Open to the public since 2023, hundreds of chatbots have been created in the People's Republic of China (PRC) in both the Chinese and English languages, with some requiring in-country phone numbers to gain access while others are globally available. Popular PRC-based chatbots include Doubao by ByteDance, the most popular with a large user base; Ernie.Bot by **Baidu**; Tongyi Qianwen by **Alibaba** with integration into the platforms Dingtalk and Tmall Genie; Yuanbao by Tencent that leverages information from the popular WeChat; Xiaoice (little ice), owned by **Microsoft** and known for emotionally engaging conversations; and **DeepSeek** located in Hangzhou along with many chatbots deployed by local governments.

CHATGPT (*LIAOTIAN GPT*). A **chatbot** coming in various versions employing **artificial generative intelligence (AGI)** developed by the American nonprofit company **OpenAI**, ChatGPT is based on the GPT-4o **large language model (LLM)** with a capacity to create human-like conversational responses and enable users to refine and shape the conversation toward specified levels of detail. With the nonprofit company founded in 2022 by Sam Altman, ChatGPT quickly accelerated the boom in artificial intelligence (AI) as the website became one of the 10 most visited and the fastest-growing **software** firms in history. Built on OpenAI's proprietary series of generative pre-trained **transformer** (GPT) models, the chatbot employs **supervised learning** and **reinforcement learning** running on 30,000 **graphic processing units (GPUs)** supplied by the **Nvidia Corporation**. Capabilities of ChatGPT include writing and debugging **computer** programs, composing music, fairy tales, poetry, song lyrics, and student essays, answering test questions, simulating chat rooms, and playing games such as tic-tac-toe while avoiding potentially harmful or distorted information. Integrated into Apple Intelligence, ChatGPT has inspired the creation of competing versions such as Copilot offered by **Microsoft** and Gemini by **Google**. Available in the PRC only through third party servers as distribution in China was blocked by OpenAI with the Chinese government also imposing a ban on the website, ChatGPT has served as a model for comparable Chinese language chatbots, most prominently R1 by **DeepSeek** and Ernie.Bot by **Baidu** with Sam Altman declaring AI development in the PRC lagging only slightly behind the United States.

CLOSED-SOURCE MODELS (*BIYUAN MOXING*). In a closed-source system, the **training** data and underlying code employed in the **software** to train and run a **large language model (LLM)** of artificial intelligence (AI) are treated as a proprietary asset of the company unavailable to the public or other model developers, this in contrast to **open-source models**. Advantages of closed-source models include faster development cycles, better model security, and overall superior performance in dealing with specific tasks, with closed-source vendors offering infrastructure and support services to speed up the application process. More flexibility in licensing, with a greater ability to maintain an edge commercially, is also available as closed-source models better incentivize control over proprietary information and more rapid development of new applications and capabilities, while the sharing of internal libraries in open-source models can result in slower innovations. With closed versus open models a continuing subject of debate among LLM developers in the People's Republic of China (PRC), Chinese **companies** employing closed-source models include **Baidu**, with the CEO Robin Li, an outspoken advocate of closed systems, while adherents to open models include **Alibaba** and **DeepSeek**.

COMPANIES (*GONGSI*). A prime component in the high technology sector of the **economy** of the People's Republic of China (PRC), Chinese artificial intelligence (AI) companies numbered 4,500 as of June 2024 generating CNY 600 billion ($85 billion) in value. Located primarily in the urban areas of the country's eastern region such as Beijing, Guangzhou, Hangzhou, Shanghai, and Shenzhen, these companies produce an array of AI products and services including, among others, **software** for **facial** and **voice recognition**, AI **computer** chips, **drones**, **robotics**, **smart** electronics, and mobile Internet. Top firms with their prime product indicated in parenthesis are SenseTime (image recognition), Cambricon Technologies (computer chips), Butterfly Effect (work organization), Megvil (facial recognition), UB Tech (in-home robotics), Cloud/Walk (facial recognition), DJI (drones), iFlyte (smart electronics), Tencent (mobile Internet), MiniMax (**chatbot**), Moonshot AI (chatbot), 4Paradigm (data governance and resource management), Mobwai (voice recognition and **natural language processing**), Ekohe (**big data**), ThirdEye Data (big data), Baichuan (**large language models**), Zhipu AI (**foundational models**), and Yitu Technologies (facial recognition) along with **Alibaba** and **Baidu**. Initial investments to start-up companies come from establishment firms such as Alibaba, Baidu, and Tencent, with top talent often drawn from **research institutes** such as the Knowledge Engineering Group of Tsinghua University. The most innovative companies are known as the "four new tigers," namely Baichuan, Zhipu AI, Moonshot AI, and MiniMax for their development of chatbots comparable to **Chat GPT** and Quora versus the so-called "four old tigers" composed of SenseTime, Megvil, CloudWalk, and Yitu Technologies for their earlier development of facial and image recognition. National policies enacted to assist AI start-ups in the PRC include providing "computing vouchers" to cover rising **data center** costs enacted by several city governments such as Shanghai, especially as crucial advanced **semiconductors** become scarce because of export controls imposed by the United States.

COMPUTERS AND COMPUTING (*DIANNAO, JISUAN*). A subfield of computer science, artificial intelligence (AI) allows computers to mimic such important human cognition functions as learning, **problem-solving**, and reasoning, enabling analysis of complex patterns of **big data**, understanding language, making recommendations, learning from experience, and performing other human-like tasks. Through computation based on **algorithms** and other computational systems, computers can extract text and data from images and documents while also triggering certain actions without human intervention. With the second largest computing power in the world after the United States, the People's Republic of China (PRC) is investing heavily in a wide array of computer and computing-related products and activities to bolster the size and sophistication of the AI sector in the country's **economy** and scientific establishment. Issuing an *Action Plan for Information Standard Construction* for the years 2024–2027 formulated by the Cyberspace Administration of China (CAC), the Chinese government is committed to fabricating advanced computer chips and **semiconductors**, building a computing process infrastructure, facilitating **quantum computing** technology, and advancing **brain-to-computer interface (BCI)**, all to world-class levels. Committing $47 billion to the sector, the goal in the PRC is to generate a cohesive system that integrates computing, storage, **telecommunications**, and operational capabilities that will achieve self-reliance in AI, especially when the PRC confronts major restrictions imposed by the United States on importing advanced computer products from American firms such as **Nvidia**.

COMPUTER VISION AND COGNITIVE COMPUTING (*JISUAN SHIJUE, REN ZHI JISUAN*). A method for acquiring, processing, and understanding digital images and extracting high dimensional data from the real world, computer vision (CV) produces numerical or symbolic information to enhance human decision-making. Designed to gain a high-level understanding from digital images or videos, CV automates tasks that mimic human vision by disentangling symbolic information from image data employing models constructed with the aid of geometry, physics, and statistics and drawn from video sequences, views from multiple cameras, multidimensional data from three-dimensional scanners, three-dimensional point clouds from light detection and ranging (LIDAR) remote sensing, and medical scanning devices. Inaugurated by research dating back to the 1960s at major universities, CV technology makes possible scene reconstruction, object and event detection, activity reconstruction, video tracking, and image restoration.

A type of artificial intelligence (AI), cognitive computing uses machines to simulate human thought processes and reasoning rooted in such scientific disciplines as signal processing and intelligence. Employing the technologies of **machine learning (ML)**, **natural language processing (NLP)**, and **speech** and vision recognition, cognitive computing systems process large amounts of data with a capacity to engage in **pattern recognition** and identify relationships that humans often cannot detect with the goal of creating intelligent systems that can learn from interactions and make decisions in a similar way to humans. Applications include **health care** by assisting medical professionals to make treatment decisions by evaluating such patient information as medical histories, test results, and imaging scans; **finance** by analyzing large amounts of financial data in real time, detecting fraud, predicting stock prices, and suggesting investments; **customer service** with cognitive **chatbots** and **virtual assistants** employing NLP to understand and resolve customer queries in real time; **logistics** by optimizing inventory, warehouse operations, and warehouse infrastructure management; **education** by assisting students to understand concepts at their own pace by providing personalized study materials; and **cyber security**, preventing cyberattacks by detecting misinformation and misleading data.

A major target of artificial intelligence (AI) research and development in the People's Republic of China (PRC), computer vision and cognitive computing have been prime topics of scientific research by scholars and scientists generating a global-leading number of papers and **publications** with substantial government support while contributing $30 billion CNY ($4.2 billion) to the national **economy**. Reflecting the attention to national security interests of the Chinese government and the ruling Chinese Communist Party (CCP), heavy emphasis has been given to employing these two technologies, especially **facial recognition** and image recognition, to enhance the **surveillance** capacity of state authorities. Techniques include re-identification (REID), that is identifying a person or organization when direct identifying information has been removed or is unavailable, crowd counting, and spoofing detection, that is exposing attempts to subvert identification technologies. Cognitive computing has also been employed to improve the economic and social conditions in the country's generally less developed countryside with a goal of raising living standards of the rural population to a level equal to the country's more prosperous urban areas.

CONFERENCES AND MEETINGS (*HUIYI*). Bringing together business executives, entrepreneurs, government officials, and technicians and scientists involved with artificial intelligence (AI) in the People's Republic of China (PRC), numerous conferences and meetings have been convened in major cities especially since 2017 when AI became a top priority of the Chinese government. Forums for discussion of major aspects and issues involving AI, these conferences also serve as venues for **companies** to exhibit new AI products and solutions to potential clients and interested parties. While labeled as "international" to project an image of the PRC as a global leader in AI, conference participants and exhibitors are overwhelmingly from China with generally little involvement of foreign parties with the exception of American companies with operations in the country such as Tesla and **Qualcomm**. Most prominent was the World Artificial Intelligence Conference (WAIC), the largest global AI event, held in Shanghai in July 2024 with 500 exhibitors, 1,500 exhibits, and a reported 300,000 attendees. Focused on **robotics** and **large language models (LLMs)**, the conference also featured an appearance by PRC Premier Li Qiang. International conferences held since 2017 include the following: The First and Second Institute of Electrical and Electronics Engineers International Conference on Micro/Nano Sciences for AI, Health Care, and Robotics (Shenzhen, 2018 & 2019); International Conference on AI-Empowered Web Information Systems (Shanghai, 2023); Third International Conference on Networking Systems of AI (Xi'an, 2023); International Conference on Natural Language Processing and AI (Chongqing, 2024); International Conference on Computer Systems (Hangzhou, 2024); International Conference on Manufacturing and Automation (Changchun, 2024); Sixth International Conference on Control and Computer Vision (Tianjin, 2024); and Seventh International Conference on Robotics, Control, and Automation Engineering (Wuhu, 2024). Numerous conferences on similar topics are also planned for 2025, 2026, and 2027. *See also* INTERNATIONAL GOVERNANCE.

CRIME AND CRIME PREVENTION (*FANZUI, YUFANG FANZUI*). Contributing to both the commission of crimes and methods of crime prevention, artificial intelligence (AI) has proven to be a two-edged sword providing criminals with more efficient and less detectable means of scamming victims while also enhancing counteractive tactics by police and investigatory authorities. AI tools serving the interests of criminal elements include **deepfake** technology to create misleading images, videos, or audio and deceitful websites along with disinformation campaigns as leaked data allows for identifying vulnerable points of attack of high-value targets through phishing and other nefarious measures. Also utilized are AI-empowered scam bots that involve more advanced and streamlined malware less susceptible to detection and so-called self-metamorphic mechanisms that alter operations in different environments and convert illegal activities into more benign applications. For police and other prosecutorial powers, AI is employed in analyzing large amounts of data to identify patterns and trends in the commission of crimes and biometrics to identify suspects, monitor **social media** sites for language associated with crime, and identify victims. Increasingly attractive is **predictive analytics** whereby historical data and statistical methods are employed to predict future criminal activity along with more efficient case management involving allocation of police resources and risk assessment but with historical data often subject to potential bias. Also enhanced by AI are such important functions as evidence gathering uncovering details often missed by human investigators and real-time crime scene analysis with faster collection and response times.

In the case of the People's Republic of China (PRC), predictive analytics, **facial recognition**, and **big data** analysis are popular among police and national security authorities, especially in monitoring suspicious behavior with surveillance capacity based on the installation of 200 million cameras nationwide, providing data to train AI systems and **companies** such as CloudWalk monitoring behavior patterns to identify potential criminals. So-called "personal re-identification" to track individuals across different locations despite changes in appearance is also widely employed, especially in dealing with drug-related crimes such as heroin smuggling and kidnapping. Major problems in AI utilization include inaccuracies in facial recognition, as the vast majority of data is not digitized, with bureaucratic obstacles to the integration of data from various sources, along with reported biases against members of the non-Han minority population. *See also* ANTI-FRAUD.

CRYPTOGRAPHY (*MIMAXUE*). A multidisciplinary field combining **computer** science and **machine learning (ML)** employing artificial intelligence (AI) **algorithms**, AI cryptography enables the sharing of secure data among various parties utilizing such techniques as homomorphic encryption that allow the performance of computations on encrypted data without prior decryption and avoid exposing sensitive information to outsiders. With the increasing reliance on digital communication and data exchange by businesses and governments, top priority is given to ensuring the security and **privacy** of sensitive information beyond what was provided by traditional cryptography techniques. Employing various AI tools such as **neural networks**, **deep learning**, and **reinforcement learning**, encryption of data has been enhanced providing better detection of sophisticated attacks and analysis of complex patterns to identify possible vulnerabilities through an integration of techniques. While standard cryptographic algorithms rely on mathematical principles, AI cryptography employs ML to enhance encryption, random key generation, and the analysis of other cryptographic systems along with improving and streamlining communication, securing data storage, and speeding up transactions while fending off threats such as **quantum computing** attacks that can render traditional encryption methods vulnerable. Analyzing network traffic patterns and suspicious behavior, AI algorithms identify anomalies and potential threats, providing early warnings and real-time responses to security incidents while aiding in the identification of cryptographic flaws preserving privacy when **training** ML models on sensitive data. Enhanced security, efficient threat detection, adaptation to emerging threats, and the potential for innovative approaches such as neural cryptography and quantum-resistant encryption make AI cryptography an essential component in **cyber security** but with substantial demand for resources and trained personnel. Recognized as the most advanced AI cryptography system, the advanced encryption standard (AES) was developed in the late 1900s and was adopted for use by the US government in 2001.

A major global player in AI cryptography, the People's Republic of China (PRC) has concentrated on merging the field with advances in quantum computing aimed at developing sophisticated methods of cracking common cryptographic systems such as AES and RSA (Rivest-Shamir-Adleman). Employing the D-Wave quantum computer available on the cloud, Chinese researchers at Shanghai University claimed to have cracked AES in 2024, threatening the security of sensitive data and cyber security in general, making possible the manipulation of major national economies and threatening geo-strategic power relations. *See also* MILITARY APPLICATIONS.

CUSTOMER SERVICE (*KEHU FUWU*). A boon to the labor-intensive industry of customer service, artificial intelligence (AI) has led to the automation of many routine customer service tasks such as data collection and ticket triage, freeing up human agents to focus on more complex issues. Employing tools such as **natural language processing (NLP)**, **machine learning (ML)**, and interactive voice response with **chatbots** answering frequently asked questions, AI allows for more personalized and nuanced messaging services for inquiring customers while increasing agent productivity and assisting in troubleshooting.

A favorite of the thriving **e-commerce** sector in the **economy** of the People's Republic of China (PRC), the AI customer service market amounted to CNY 6.68 billion ($950 million) in 2022, with **software** as the largest segment. Examples include e-commerce giant **Alibaba**, which employed **artificial generative intelligence (AGI)** tools during its widely popular annual Singles Day (November 11) debut, the world's biggest shopping event, in 2023, while marketplace Taobao formally launched Wenwen as an AI chatbot offering online shoppers personalized guidance such as special discount bargains. Across all age groups, Chinese shoppers are most likely to have used AGI, particularly to engage in an image rather than a text-based query, along with customer service chatbots and voice-activated search and shopping. Other merchants, such as JD.com, launched enhanced AI-powered solutions designed to cut the operational costs of merchants by up to 50 percent, including an AI **virtual assistant** to accelerate online store launches and a realistic avatar generator that provides round-the-clock interactive shopping livestreams. With Chinese shoppers increasingly wanting value by switching to cheaper brands or hunting for the best deals across platforms, AGI provides Chinese retailers access to a powerful new tool for increasing sales and lowering costs, with 45 percent of consumers more trusting of AI than their counterparts in the United States.

CYBER SECURITY (*WANGLUO ANQUAN*). A critical tool in cyber security that protects digital systems from cyber threats, artificial intelligence (AI) analyzes large swaths of data to identify patterns and detect anomalies that indicate a possible security threat. Able to adapt to new threats and respond more effectively than traditional cyber security tools, AI is employed in cyber security to enhance threat detection with greater accuracy than humans. Functions include identifying suspicious emails and messages that are often used in phishing campaigns; improving incident response by assisting security teams with incident-related data in real time allowing for rapid response to contain the threat; and identifying potential vulnerabilities and performing penetration testing to find weaknesses in **software** and networks while also automating routine tasks such as log analysis, vulnerability assessments, and patch management, which save time and resources. With cyber criminals using AI to carry out sophisticated attacks from data poisoning, that is feeding deceptive information to an **algorithm**, along with **deep fakes**, cyber security organizations also rely on AI to help spot suspicious data and detect or thwart attacks. Cyber security organizations rely on AI in conjunction with more traditional tools such as antivirus protection, data-loss prevention, fraud detection, identity and access management, intrusion detection, risk management and other core security areas. By analyzing enormous sets of data and identifying patterns, AI is able to flag suspicious emails and messages often employed in phishing campaigns; simulate social engineering attacks, which help security teams spot potential vulnerabilities before cyber criminals exploit them; and analyze huge amounts of incident-related data rapidly, so that security teams can swiftly take action to contain the threat. AI is also an effective tool in penetration testing, that is, intentionally probing the defenses of **software** and networks to identify weaknesses, so that organizations are able to identify weaknesses before hackers can maliciously exploit them. Considered an essential tool for enhancing national security in the People's Republic of China (PRC), AI has been applied to a wide variety of cyber security measures in the commercial and state sectors. With new rules governing areas such as **artificial generative intelligence (AGI)** slated for introduction in 2025, cyber security is a top priority with 11 universities in the PRC offering specialized training in the field and the Cyberspace Administration of China (CAC) deployed for establishing **regulatory** frameworks and enforcement actions working in conjunction with the Ministry of Public Security (MPS). *See also* ANTI-FRAUD.

D

DATA CENTERS (*SHUJU ZHONGXIN*). A building or dedicated space within a single or multiple structures housing **computer** systems and associated components, such as **telecommunications** and storage systems, data centers are cutting-edge facilities composed of multiple racks of servers, cables, and other equipment designed to accommodate the intense computational demands of artificial intelligence (AI) workloads at an estimated cost in the United States of $50 billion each. Resources essential to the functioning of data centers include adequate space ranging from 100,000 to several million square feet, enormous electricity production primarily to provide cooling to the intense heat generated by the servers and other equipment, and data/power port connections, all of which support high-density workloads generated by the deployment of **graphic processing units (GPU)**. Also required is an advanced networking infrastructure that relies heavily on parallel processing which demands robust cabling infrastructure within GPU clusters and between racks that can consume 50 kilowatts per rack. Replacing traditional spreadsheets and diagrams with modern data center management tools, any and all manual work disappears, replaced by data center infrastructure management (DCIM) **software**.

In the case of the People's Republic of China (PRC), the rapid growth of digital services has served as the prime driver of demand for data centers, with 449 constructed throughout the country. From **e-commerce** to **finance** to entertainment, rapid **digitization** has brought about a surge in the production and consumption of digital content and transactions, along with communications leading a wide variety of businesses to optimize operations and **customer service** experiences that require the robust infrastructure of data centers to accommodate, process, and store this burgeoning data flow. Included is the adoption of cloud **computing**, offering unparalleled flexibility, scalability, and efficiency; expansion of the **Internet of Things (IoT)**, encompassing a network of devices, sensors, and systems that exchange data and enable real-time monitoring and analysis, transforming cities into **smart** urban landscapes and industries into intelligent production systems; and demand for hyper-converged solutions that provide an efficient approach to managing data centers by integrating servers, storage, networking, and virtualization tools into ready-to-use packages and which merge technologies into a single system architecture. Chinese and foreign companies involved in the data center sector in the PRC include China Telecom Corporation, China Mobile Ltd., Tencent Cloud, **Alibaba** Cloud, along with US firms Amazon Web Services (AWS) and Equinix. Given a central role in overseeing and regulating the country's data center industry is the Ministry of Industry and Information Technology (MIIT), with the **regulatory** focus shifting in 2023 toward refining data protection, recognizing the enormous value of data, and establishing mechanisms for cross-border data transfers as the *Data Protection Law* was updated in 2022 and a *Data Security Law* enacted in 2023. *See also* BIG DATA.

DECISION THEORY (*JUEDING LILUN*). An examination of how individuals or systems choose between alternative pathways and the consequences of those choices, decision theory plays a crucial role in artificial intelligence (AI), providing a framework for building intelligent, autonomous agents that can make rational decisions in environments characterized by high levels of **uncertainty**. Propagating an ideal of rational decision-making, decision theory guides rational agents in making choices with consideration of probabilities, costs, and benefits influenced by an environment of incomplete or uncertain information, with decision theory providing tools to handle such situations. Employing such concepts as utility, defined as the value or level of satisfaction derived from various choices, and **probabilistic reasoning** to make predictions based on the likelihood of different outcomes, the theory is applied across multiple sectors of the **economy**, health care, **military applications**, and scientific investigation, with expected utility theory (EUT) dealing with instrumental goals, utility function instability, and coordination challenges in multi-actor and human-agent collectives settings. Applications include autonomous systems used in the development of **autonomous driving** vehicles, **robotics**, and other systems that make decisions in real time. Also deployed are decision tree **algorithms** used in **machine learning (ML)** for various classification and prediction tasks, along with the optimization of resource allocation in **energy** management and the **logistics** of **supply chains**, especially in complex scenarios with many variables posing expensive computation while ensuring that AI systems' decisions align with human values and goals.

Actively integrating AI into various aspects of society, the People's Republic of China (PRC) has applied decision theory to military decision-making, government operations, and the legal system, with an overall goal of enhancing efficiency and leveraging AI for national strategic goals. With local officials encouraged to use AI to assist in their decision-making, analysis, and **problem-solving**, Chinese courts are employing AI for automated pattern analysis, monitoring judges, standardizing decision-making, and observing social trends but with concerns in Chinese military circles that using AI for decision-making in nuclear strategy could potentially lead to rapid escalation.

DEEP FAKES (*SHENDU WEIZAO*). An image or recording convincingly altered or manipulated to misrepresent a person doing or saying something that was not in reality said or done, deep fakes, also known as deep synthesis, are typically used for malicious purposes including **financial** scams and pornographic images of celebrities, especially women. A more modern version of photoshopping created in 2017, deep fakes are forged by running reams of data through artificial intelligence (AI) **algorithms** known as encoder and decoder to produce realistic but fake faces and/or voices of known figures or in more sophisticated forms of nonexistent people. Capable of mimicking biometric data or tricking systems that rely on **voice** and **facial recognition**, deep fakes both employ AI for their creation with AI systems also utilized to detect and combat faked images, voice recordings, and virtual scams. A favorite of multiple start-up **companies** in the People's Republic of China (PRC), deep fakes have been employed by criminal elements for a variety of nefarious purposes including impersonating government officials in pursuit of cyber fraud to manipulating stock market prices and enticing people to shift money to false bank accounts for illicit **financial** gain to fabricating false emergencies. Less nefarious is the generation of digital versions, or avatars, of recently deceased loved ones available via an app or cell phone capable of carrying on a concocted conversation in line with the Chinese traditional belief of communicating with the dead. Reacting to such threats, the Chinese government has enacted **regulations** aimed at preemptively "drawing redlines in advance" (*tiqian hua hongxian*) while implementing ex ante regulations in 2021. In parallel with these concerns is the alacrity with which the PRC has attempted to prevent undue use of deep fakes to create and post content that goes against science, fabricates information, or spreads rumors both domestically and on the geopolitical level. Also pursued was the world's first comprehensive deepfake regulations titled "Provisions on the Administration of Deep Synthesis of Internet-based Information Services" enacted in January 2023, which mandates that AI-generated synthetic content, including deepfakes, voice clones, and avatars must be clearly labeled and registered with regulators, while prohibiting against content that threatens social stability or national security.

A favorite of multiple start-up **companies** in the People's Republic of China (PRC), deep fakes are often used for such malicious purposes as financial crimes with concocted voice recordings convincing unsuspecting targets to shift money into bogus bank accounts or spread various forms of misinformation with **regulations** against such activities enacted in 2023. Less nefarious is the generation of digital versions, or avatars, of dead loved ones available via an app or cell phone capable of carrying on a conversation in line with the Chinese traditional belief of communicating with deceased relatives.

DEEP LEARNING (*SHENDU XUEXI*). A subset of **machine learning (ML)** utilizing **neural networks** to carry out certain tasks such as classification or regression, deep learning refers to a class of ML **algorithms** in which input data is transformed into a more abstract and composite representation. Inspired by the field of biological neuroscience and composed of artificial neurons stacked into layers which are trained to process data, "deep" refers to the deployment of multiple layers upwards of several hundred or thousand in a network with the "learning" coming in either the **supervised** or **unsupervised** form. Prior to deep learning, ML techniques generally involved hand-crafted transformation of data into more suitable representational forms which a classification algorithm could then carry out operations. Contrast this to deep learning where unique features are discovered from the data automatically with varying numbers of layers and layer sizes providing different degrees of abstraction. With various types of deep learning architectures such as recurrent neural networks, convolutional neural networks (CNN), and **transformers**, applications include **computer vision**, **speech recognition**, **natural language processing (NLP)**, **drug discovery** and design, bioinformatics, and climate science with results comparable or superior to performance by human experts. While early versions of neural networks were inspired by information processing and distributed communication nodes similar to the human brain, more recent neural networks are not intended as such a model.

A component of the general embrace of artificial intelligence (AI) in the People's Republic of China (PRC) since 2017, deep learning has been applied to multiple fields with beneficiaries in the real **economy** including remediation from natural disasters. Included is the process of building extraction with deep learning engendering the optimal means of removing waste materials, debris, and soil from building sites to ensure a clean and safe environment for construction workers. Deep learning has also been utilized in issuing real-time flash flood warnings especially to highly vulnerable mountainous or hilly regions of the country as the methodology has also been applied to gauging vegetation productivity with a reliance on reams of remote sensing, climate, and topographical data. Other applications include stock price predictions and various technological improvements in industry but with the country still suffering from relatively underdeveloped fundamental theories with continued reliance on foreign-developed deep learning models, core technologies, and **open-source models**.

DEEPSEEK (*SHENDU QIUSUO*). Established in 2023 as an artificial intelligence (AI) **research laboratory** by Liang Wenfeng in the city of Hangzhou in the People's Republic of China (PRC), DeepSeek has developed **large language models (LLMs)** utilizing **open-source** models that involve pooling collective expertise and stressing collaborative work with **training** at a significantly lower cost and substantially less **computing** power than comparable firms such as **OpenAI**. Developed amid export restrictions imposed by the US government on advanced **semiconductor** chips produced primarily by **Nvidia**, DeepSeek released its first free **chatbot** based on the Reasoning 1 (R1) model in December 2024, which rapidly surpassed **ChatGPT** as the most downloaded app on the Apple App Store. Utilizing the less advanced Nvidia H800 chips and spending a mere $5.6 million, the research laboratory has relied on a team of young AI researchers from top Chinese universities hiring from outside the **computer** science field to diversify the knowledge base and capabilities of its models. With the founder Liang Wenfeng originally managing a quantitative hedge fund known as High-Flyer that focused on developing and using AI trading **algorithms** on supercomputers to analyze financial data while attending Zhejiang University, DeepSeek received initial funding maximizing **software**-driven resource optimization to quickly outperform major Chinese tech giants such as **Alibaba**, **Baidu**, ByteDance, and Tencent. By focusing solely on research and avoiding commercialization, DeepSeek also avoided the most stringent Chinese government **regulations** designed to control information imposed on consumer outfits. Relying on multi-head latent attention (MLA) and mixture of experts, DeepSeek R1 employs chain of thought composed of a step-by-step explanation of reasoning, **reinforcement learning** involving improvements in small increments, and **distillation** whereby larger LLMs with 671 billion **parameters** teach smaller LLMs with 7 billion parameters as the company outlined the model in a technical paper that other companies including Alibaba and Baidu subsequently used to upgrade their own models. Applications of R1 include utilization by local governments as a form of AI civil servants engaging in such tasks as scrutinizing documents and assigning tasks to various departments with a pilot program pursued by the Futian district in the city of Shenzhen, which received decidedly mixed reviews.

DIALOGUE MANAGEMENT (*DUIHUI GUANLI*). A component of artificial intelligence (AI), dialogue management controls the flow of a conversation between a user and an AI system, determining the course of a conversation. Major functions include keeping track of the context of the conversation and the intent of the user; determining appropriate responses and any additional action that needs to be taken; maintaining a coherent dialogue by retrieving previous inputs and adapting responses to altered circumstances; and handling any ambiguity or errors to ensure smooth operations. Essential to creating engaging and natural interactions, dialogue management is employed in **chatbots** by storing user intents that were not acted upon immediately and conversational AI with automated **speech recognition** to interact with repeat users and to simplify tasks in an office setting through such computer **software** as autocomplete and spell check. With the development and expansion of chatbots in the People's Republic of China (PRC), the most widely used dialogue management product is *Xiao* ice ("little ice") developed by **Microsoft** China in 2013, which deploying an emotional framework tracks the dialogue state between user and an AI system and, at each dialogue turn, selects how to respond based on a hierarchical dialogue policy.

DIGITAL TWINS (*SHUZI SHUANGBAOTAI*). A virtual model of a physical object, process, or system, a digital twin employs real-time data to simulate actual performance in the real world that when combined with **artificial generative intelligence (AGI)** can produce synergies, reduce costs, accelerate deployment, and generate greater value. Employing adaptive models, scanning physical entities, and combining data from various sources to better understand and predict performance, digital twins optimize the design of expensive hardware or **software** without having to build prototypes while identifying potential faults and facilitating more informed decision-making on maintenance and lifecycle. Originating as **computer** simulations, the first practical physical-model simulation was developed in the 2010s with subsequent improvements achieved in modeling and engineering. Industries benefiting from digital twins include health care where the technology enhances clinical diagnosis, manufacturing with maximizing efficiencies in **supply chain** and spurring innovation, and **data centers** by improving cooling, **energy** efficiency, and resource allocation. With AGI deployed to structure inputs and synthesize the outputs of digital twins, a robust test-and-learn environment is created with results greater than the sum of the individual parts. Major AI tools includc **predictive maintenance** to forecast possible equipment failures or breakdowns in production lines prior to failure; real-time monitoring with an ability to track physical assets and a capacity to respond to changes; better decision-making with simulations of various scenarios; customization with AI learning from past data and enhancing the accuracy of simulations; and process automation whereby routine tasks such as data collection and analysis are fully automated.

A global leader in combining digital twin technology with artificial intelligence (AI), the People's Republic of China (PRC) is most notable for research and development of so-called digital twin cities, that is three-dimensional models of urban construction and development. Examples include the Xiong'An New Area in central Hebei Province under construction since 2017 and designed to relieve the nearby capital of Beijing of nonessential functions. More generally is the concept of **smart** cities where the combination of the virtual and real top-level design produces twin models based on **digitalization** and informatization to improve the effectiveness of planning, operations, and maintenance involving **transportation** networks, utilities, and urban emergencies. Also pursued are smart industrial parks with digital twins utilized to achieve reductions in carbon emissions as data collected through sensors is combined with AI **algorithms** to improve energy efficiency along with a long-term smart Yangzi River Project developed by the Yangzi Water Resources Commission. Consisting of a digital twin composed of an advanced three-dimensional simulation of the whole region, comprehensive data on **weather**, water flow, ecology, sediment properties, topography, energy demand, real-time modeling of projected flood routing, water engineering, scheduling, shipping, and ecological impacts are provided to alleviate ongoing problems resulting in enhanced operational safety and reduced costs with a planned completion date of 2035. Other applications include utilization of digital twin technologies in heritage preservation of ancient sites and buildings such as pagodas, along with new product development in a variety of industries and critical supply chain and medical management as the physical space of **hospitals** and other health facilities are mapped into a digital twin model. Overall, the digital twin market in the PRC exceeded CNY 10 billion ($1.4 billion) in 2022.

DIGITAL HUMANS (*SHUZI RENLEI*). A subcategory of avatars that look, act, and think like real humans with an ability to listen and understand meanings, digital humans, when combined with artificial intelligence (AI), humanize virtual interactions with an impact on business and other social sectors. As either a **digital twin** of a real person based on anatomical, physical, and biological traits, or of a fictional character based on the appearance of an actor or an image generated by **computer**, digital humans are indistinguishable from real people, recreating human interaction, helping people with difficult tasks and dispensing advice, replacing purely text-based instructions and employing nonverbal cues, including facial features such as winking, nodding, and frowning. With research indicating that people can better relate to digital humans that have a more realistic appearance, the role of digital humans in online websites and **e-commerce** is slated to increase dramatically, especially in the form of conversational AI, with the global market for the technology to grow to $530 billion by 2030. Major industries employing digital humans include **customer support**, instructors for training and **education**, **virtual assistants** for health care, characters in entertainment, **advertising and marketing** presenters, and digital influencers with increasingly realistic and emotionally intelligent capacities, making possible the creation of "replicas" (*fuzhipin*) for any individual. Utilizing a scanner or **software** to create a three-dimensional model of a real person, AI is then employed to reproduce a photorealistic image of that person based on appearance or a virtual assistant with **natural language processing (NLP)** providing a capacity to understand voice commands and AI processing input to learn from patterns. Available around the clock and scalable to major commercial operations, digital humans can easily switch between languages and cultural contexts and ensure anonymity when communicating about sensitive topics.

With the advance of AI in a variety of fields in the People's Republic of China (PRC), digital humans have been used in many sectors such as entertainment, gaming, and animation with the support and endorsement of both the central and regional governments including 30 cities and provinces. Examples include Chinese state media outlets, namely the CGTN news network that introduced digital reporters and news anchors to appear in live stream shows and **weather forecasting** while also reporting on major news events. Playing important roles in the commercial sector, 1.14 million registered firms in the PRC have created digital people with **companies** such as the short-video platform *Kuaishou* featuring user-generated content with over 300,000 livestreams conducted by virtual hosts in 2023. E-commerce giant JD.com likewise unveiled an AI clone of company founder Liu Qiangdong during a livestream session that accurately replicated the appearance, voice, and accent of Mr. Liu along with a well-known habit of waving his hands while speaking. *See also* TRANSHUMANISM.

DIGITALIZATION (*SHUZIHUA*). Defined as the process of converting analog information into a format organized into discrete units of data known as bits with multiple bit-groups known as bytes, digitalization is a prime driver of artificial intelligence (AI) affecting broad swaths of everyday life and work. Areas impacted include business and commercial applications improving efficiency and generating better and more finely tuned products; data analysis assisting in making better real-time decisions and anticipating the future; automation of manual tasks and repetitive administrative work; personalizing interactions and improving **customer service** experience;

highlighting important information to help people make better decisions; data collection and management with more amenable storage and retrieval; and modeling and simulating complex situations such as changing **weather** and climatic conditions while allowing for more effective monitoring of **financial** investments, **energy** generation, and consumption.

Embracing digitalization, the People's Republic of China (PRC) has actively promoted its application across various sectors including **e-commerce**, health care, and **transportation**, with the government actively supporting policies and investments fueled by vast amounts of data generated by the country's large online population and advanced fifth generation (5G) infrastructure. Outlined in policy pronouncements for AI development such as the *New Generation Artificial Intelligence Development Plan* in 2017 and major efforts at research and development resulting in the filing of numerous AI-related **patents**, areas with significant digitalization include **facial recognition** widely employed in public spaces for security and identification purposes; **smart** city initiatives to optimize traffic management, energy consumption, and public services; personalized shopping experiences through AI-powered recommendations on e-commerce platforms; medical diagnosis support, with AI **algorithms** assisting doctors in the analysis of **medical imaging**; and virtual voice-activated **virtual assistants** on smartphones and in the household.

DISTILLATION (*ZHENGLIU*). Employed **in machine learning (ML)**, distillation is a process whereby outputs from a large, pretrained artificial intelligence (AI) model are used in the **training** of a smaller model, making for similar capabilities while generally utilizing less **computing** power. A common practice in the AI sector, distillation is often pursued to deploy a model on devices with limited resources such as a mobile phone and has allowed less well-financed AI **companies** to effectively compete with their substantially more well-off counterparts, with the latter serving as the "teacher" of the former "student." The ultimate purpose of distillation is to make models more **inference**-optimized as a form of model compression without significant loss of performance. While distillation may violate the terms of service of major high-tech companies, especially in the United States, stopping the practice is difficult if not impossible in cases of **open-source models** and difficulties of detection. Prominent cases of distillation involving firms in the People's Republic of China (PRC) include the **DeepSeek** research laboratory which drew on US-based models such as **ChatGPT**.

DRONES (*WURENJI*). A remotely or **software**-controlled flying **robot** equipped with onboard sensors and global positioning system (GPS) capacity, drones have undergone significant technological development by the integration with artificial intelligence (AI) allowing for intelligent decision-making, performance of complex tasks, and adaptation to changing environments. Applications of AI include utilization of real-time data to assist drones in executing flight paths and other aerial maneuvers; engaging **computer vision (CV)** by processing data from cameras and sensors to identify obstacles, recognize locations, and navigate, performing swarming operations to coordinate operations over large areas; enhancing capabilities by **reinforcement learning** to incorporate past experiences; and relying on edge **computing** to process data locally to improve real-time responsiveness. Industries employing AI-empowered drones include the **military**, environmental monitoring and wildlife conservation, along with disaster response as AI assesses situations and promotes the rapid deployment of aid. Other applications include **logistics** with drones transporting and delivering cargo, agriculture with aerial monitoring of soil conditions, spread of blight, crop diseases, and predictions of crop yields, and building construction with creation of model structures and preparation of inspection reports.

The global leader in drones, the People's Republic of China (PRC) has three out of the 10 top drone producers in the world including the DJI corporation and the Aviation Industry of China. Most notable advances in drone technology are in the military realm with the development of a drone employing a **large language model (LLM)** for electronic warfare that, similar to **ChatGPT**, can disrupt enemy radar and radio communications at lightning-fast speed, surpassing traditional AI use of reinforcement learning, though the work is still in the experimental stage. Drones with light detection and ranging (LIDAR) capacity, or three-dimensional laser scanning, have also been deployed, most notably in the agricultural sector for crop seeding and monitoring functions, along with utilization during natural disasters such as floods and devastating earthquakes that afflict the country all too often.

DRUG DISCOVERY (*YAOWU FAXIAN*). Employed in drug discovery to analyze data, identify potential drug candidates, and predict molecular properties, artificial intelligence (AI) helps speed up the drug discovery process, assisting in chemical synthesis, improving trial design, patient recruitment, and safety monitoring. Identifying biomarkers and predicting treatment responses, AI can also repurpose existing drugs for new uses but with ongoing concerns over data quality and the necessity of AI models to comply with **regulatory** requirements and ethical concerns, as some AI models can suggest utilization of substances that are impossible to make.

In the case of the People's Republic of China (PRC), AI-related medicine and drug discovery have undergone major advances, especially in the awarding of **patents**, filing a total of more than 38,000 between 2014 and 2023, surpassing the United States, **Japan**, and other major drug developers. Specific areas of progress include drug target identification in cancer, elucidation of cancer-unique neoantigens based upon tumor **genomic** sequencing **big data**, predictive potential of cancer cell sensitivity to therapeutic interventions (**medical imaging**, radiotherapy, chemotherapy, and cancer immunotherapy), along with disease prognostics and patient survival with applications by many **large language models (LLMs)**.

According to comments by Jensen Huang at the World Economic Forum at Davos, Switzerland, in January 2026, collaboration has begun between **Nvidia** and the leading American pharmaceutical company Eli Lilly on developing a powerful AI platform capable of enabling chemicals to communicate with proteins, considered a pivotal step in the development of new drugs.

E

E-COMMERCE (*DIANZI SHANGWU*). Defined as the buying and selling of goods and services over the Internet, e-commerce employs artificial intelligence (AI) to enhance the shopping experience for the customer by analyzing volumes of **big data** to personalize product recommendations, optimize pricing, power **chatbots** for **customer service**, manage inventory, detect fraudulent activity, and predict future demand with concomitant reductions in costs. AI **algorithms** analyze customer browsing history, purchase patterns, and demographics to better suggest products in line with consumer preferences while also providing for adjusting prices in real-time based on changing market conditions, fluctuations in demand, and pricing by competitors with a goal of maximizing revenue. AI-powered chatbots and **virtual assistants** also serve to answer customer queries, provide product information, assist with order placement, and address any complaints, while AI-powered search engines deal with complex search queries with **machine learning (ML)** algorithms employed to identify suspicious patterns in transactions and segment customers into different groups allowing for targeted **marketing** campaigns along with visual search for products. Automating routine tasks such as inventory management and enhancing data-driven decision-making, AI has been a boon to e-commerce in the People's Republic of China (PRC) led by highly successful **companies** such as **Alibaba**, **Baidu**, JD.com, SHEIN, Temu, Tencent, Pinduoduo, Tmall, and Xiaohongshu.

E-WASTE (*DIANZI LAIJI*). An inevitable by-product of enormous increases in electricity demand for **data centers** and utilization of **chatbots** and **large language models (LLM)** along with the proliferation of consumer electronic goods such as cell phones, **computers**, and microwave ovens, global e-waste is slated to expand exponentially with applications of **artificial generative intelligence (AGI)** estimated to add 1.2 to 5 million metric tons of hazardous trash by 2030. Containing such toxins as, among others, mercury and lead, e-waste when improperly discarded contaminates air, water, and soil as approximately 78 percent of global e-waste ends up in landfills, many poorly managed, or at unofficial recycling sites where local laborers, often consisting of women and children, scavenge for rare metals at great risk to their health with concomitant damage to the surrounding environment. Exacerbating the situation is the rapid turnover of **graphic processing units (GPUs)**, data servers, and other storage devices every two to five years as new, updated versions become readily available. Countermeasures include more efficient chip and **algorithm** design that can reduce the demand for new hardware and electricity for AGI with reductions in e-waste by 86 percent.

Large-scale commitment to AI since 2017 has led the People's Republic of China (PRC) to become the global leader in the generation of e-waste with an annual domestic amount of more than 10 million tons overtaking the United States. Reflecting the country's expanding **economy**, technical innovation, and urbanization with enormous consumer demand for computers, mobile phones, and other electronic devices, e-waste is slated to rise to more than 27 million tons by 2030, growing at an average annual rate of 10.4 percent, the fastest-growing waste stream in the PRC. Processed by households, domestic institutions such as schools and **hospital**s, government agencies and businesses, and equipment manufacturers, e-waste is usually channeled through second-hand markets where reusable devices are often resold at lower prices, along with donation systems, often illegal, that distribute home appliances to poorer rural areas of western China, or through peddlers who resell e-waste to dealers, with the last channel serving as the most common form of e-waste management. The largest importer of global e-waste in the year 2000 as cheap labor and lax environmental standards attracted shipments from more developed countries such as the United States with 70 percent ending up in the PRC, a waste import ban was enacted in 2018. But with **Hong Kong** refusing to implement the policy, the ban only bars e-waste from entering the mainland directly as foreign-generated e-waste is often transported via the former colony into the PRC via illegal channels.

ECONOMY AND ECONOMIC GROWTH (*JINGJI, JINGJI ZENGZHANG*). A potentially major boost to economic activity and the prospect of expansion in the national and global economy, artificial intelligence (AI) has a primary impact on the critical economic realms of **productivity** and product innovation that is estimated to increase global gross national product (GNP) by 1.2 percent annually by 2030, especially in the more technologically developed countries of the United States, Europe, Japan, and the People's Republic of China (PRC). Automating such routine tasks as communication, document processing, and research with workers focusing on more complex and creative tasks, output per unit of labor will increase with more well-managed and more efficient production lines experiencing less downtime for maintenance and retooling along with the introduction of new innovative ideas and accelerated scientific discovery. Greater product variety and quality will also be achieved with personalization, attractiveness, and affordability that will lead to an increase in wages, especially for workers equipped to utilize AI tools, and a faster growth in corporate earnings for well-positioned **companies** and higher stock prices. Addressing supply-side constraints, AI could remedy **supply chain** problems in shipping and distribution that have periodically slowed the global economy but with concerns of exacerbation in economic inequality at both the national and international levels that may require increasing **privacy** protections, expanding financial oversight, mandating greater data portability, and requiring transparency of all AI models and applications.

In the case of the PRC, AI is slated to provide a major boost to the country's economy, especially in the more developed coastal and some interior regions such as the mega city of Chongqing. With the Chinese government setting ambitious goals to establish the country as a leading global AI hub by 2030, primary factors contributing to present and future economic prospects include advantages in **big data** supplied by a large online population of approximately 78 percent of 1.4 billion people in 2024 that provides a vast database for the **training** of AI **algorithms**; rapid adoption of AI tools in the manufacturing sector through **accelerated production** to optimize production processes, improve efficiency, and enhance quality control by companies such as **Alibaba**, **Huawei**, and Tencent along with automotive, **finance**, healthcare, retail, and **semiconductor** firms which are deploying AI technologies but with the latter confronting major export controls on the most advanced hardware imposed by the United States. Development and application of AI with potential economic benefits is also enhanced by the creation of major **research institutes and laboratories** developing AI tools and applications including **education**. Projections of the overall impact of AI on the Chinese economy are estimated at 26 percent of the GNP, $17 trillion in 2024, by the year 2030.

EDUCATION (*JIOAYU*). Serving as a virtual mentor and tutor to in- and outside-class instruction, artificial intelligence (AI) makes for more interactive learning employing **chatbots**, apps, games, and other AI tools while also assisting in administrative tasks such as managing schedules and tracking student attendance. In a mentor-mentee relationship, AI aids in tailoring learning experiences to individual students by adjusting material based on their progress while also creating new content in the form of practice problems and videos that align with the curriculum. Operating in virtual classrooms, AI can provide real-time feedback and interaction, enhancing online learning with analysis of student performance, identifying areas for additional assistance, along with language learning apps employing AI to offer personalized practice and feedback on such matters as learning to ask questions of **ChatGPT** but also learning what AI cannot do. While students may use AI to cheat and avoid the task of thinking for themselves, tools like ChatGPT should challenge teachers and professors to reassess assignments provided to students.

Employed at various levels of the educational system in the People's Republic of China (PRC), AI tools include AI cameras and **brain-to-computer interface (BCI)** systems to identify students struggling to understand a topic and to provide mentoring and tutorial assistance. Offering personalized assistance utilizing such international AI tools as Squirrel (*Songshu*) AI, with adaptive **smart** learning tablets, 184 primary and secondary schools across the country have been selected by the Ministry of Education (MOE) to serve as AI education bases with plans to transform classrooms into hubs of innovation that will fundamentally reshape a learning experience traditionally dominated by an exclusive emphasis on rote memorization. Higher educational institutions specializing in the teaching of AI include, among others, Tsinghua University, **Harbin Institute of Technology**, Peking University, Shanghai Communications University, Zhejiang University, University of Electronic Science and Technology of China, and the University of Science and Technology of China.

ELECTRIC VEHICLES (*DIANDONGCHE*). An essential component in the operation of electric vehicles (EVs), artificial intelligence (AI) has had multiple transformative effects, especially making possible the performance of an **autonomous driving** capability. In terms of enhancing safety, AI-powered driver-assisted systems (ADAS) help prevent accidents by detecting hazards and taking corrective actions with adaptive cruise control, lane-keeping, and automated emergency braking all made possible by AI. Other benefits include greater efficiency with AI predicting vehicle idle time and setting the battery charging time during off-peak hours when electricity is more available at cheaper rates, reducing **energy** waste and waiting time. Battery management is also enhanced with AI employed to develop longer-lasting and more eco-friendly batteries while AI systems assist in developing new materials and better market analysis and insights.

A priority of the large automotive industry in the People's Republic of China (PRC) since 2021, EVs produced by multiple Chinese and foreign **companies** are described as "AI on wheels" supported by a nationwide system of charging stations with many nonautomotive companies such as **Baidu** and **Huawei** producing useful components. Special emphasis includes the development of autonomous, self-driving, **smart** capacity by automotive firms such as BYD and Xpeng with driverless robotaxi (*jiqiren chuzuche*) service introduced into several Chinese cities. Also available are smart driver cockpits and smart large heads-up displays and infotainment systems with Baidu offering its voice-controlled Ernie.Bot **chatbot** and a comprehensive **mapping** system and Huawei a smart phone-like access to media. Other companies involved in the sector include Jidu Auto, Xiaomi, Geely, Great Wall, and the American firm Tesla with a factory located in Shanghai.

ELECTRICAL GRID (*DIANWANG*). An integrated network of power stations and substations designed to carry electric power over long distances from producers to consumers including households and **factories**, a nation's electrical grid benefits from artificial intelligence (AI) in multiple ways. Most notable is the capacity of AI tools to predict potentially catastrophic failures by analyzing data supplied by sensors as to when components will fail with **predictive maintenance** recommendations for repair or replacement. Also available from AI is an enhanced capacity to integrate intermittent renewable **energy** sources such as solar and wind power into grids that were initially designed for constant energy flows from coal- or oil-based power plants operating on a 24-hour, 7-days-a-week schedule. Able to rebalance potential gaps between production and consumption of energy sources, AI tools can reduce capital and operational expenses, improve grid resilience by avoiding blackouts and brownouts while assessing climate risks by combining historical data on energy equipment performance with global climate change models to predict the likelihood of grid failures from extreme **weather** events. While many outdated power systems are ill-equipped to handle the demands of new AI technologies, installation of AI-guided power grids is subject to significant **cyber security** risks even while revolutionizing grid maintenance.

Employed in the People's Republic of China (PRC) by the State Grid Corporation of China to enhance the efficiency and reliability of a grid that was known for frequent disruption and "rolling blackouts" (*ting dian*), AI has allowed for faster fault detection, automated response to outages, and optimized power distribution, particularly through the implementation of **smart** grid systems and integration of renewable energy sources such as wind and solar power promoted by government policies. Pinpointing the location of power failures almost instantaneously, AI **algorithms** significantly reduce restoration time compared to traditional methods, with grid sensors predicting potential equipment failures, allowing for preventative maintenance, and minimizing disruptions. Utilizing AI to monitor and control power flow in real time within major urban areas such as Guangzhou and Shanghai, data from multiple sensors identify patterns and improve grid performance as sources of electrical energy are often located in far-off interior regions of hydropower and other forms of power generation, making reliable delivery of electricity a major challenge to both industry and households.

EMPLOYMENT (*JIUYE*). Emerging as an integral part of various industries, artificial intelligence (AI) has sparked debates regarding its potential impact on employment, with one narrative stressing the threat of the new technology as a replacement for human workers and another treating it as a force multiplier, allowing workers to focus on higher-order tasks that require creativity, critical thinking, and emotional intelligence. In the job replacement narrative, AI could potentially lead to massive worker displacement, especially in routine and repetitive tasks, as **robots** take over assembly line production, and AI-powered **chatbots** and **virtual assistants** dominate **customer service roles**. In contrast is the view that AI will ultimately serve as a net job creator, enhancing **productivity** and efficiency across industries requiring skilled professionals in such fields as data science and **machine learning (ML)** that augment human capabilities and enable workers to focus on complex and strategic tasks, leaving routine activities to machines. With the introduction of **smart** factories and **computer**-aided **accelerated production**, greater demand is created in the workplace for AI-driven production and **predictive maintenance**, as new start-up **companies** offer such services as AI consulting, customization for niche markets of AI solutions, and AI-driven innovations that lead to overall job creation at higher salaries and job sophistication, with the emphasis shifting from sheer numbers of jobs to the overall quality of employment. Necessitating a commitment to lifelong learning and upgrading of skills, organizations and individuals will be tested at adapting to a changing job landscape, ensuring sustained employability with machines and humans working together.

In the case of the People's Republic of China (PRC), the rapid integration of AI into the workplace is having a substantial impact with job displacement in certain sectors due to automation and job creation in other sectors with an overall net positive effect especially on the overall quality of employment. Studies conducted of the country's employment structure indicate a potential loss of 26 percent of existing jobs over the next two decades from the introduction of AI, especially in generally outdated and low **productivity** industries with substantial surplus of workers particularly involved in routine and repetitive tasks. Vulnerable groups include low-skilled, poorly educated, largely female, and older employees and anyone less able to adapt to the new data-driven job landscape created by AI potentially leading to increased monitoring and pressure on employees to meet performance metrics set by AI **algorithms**. On the other hand, new and more productive jobs will be created in several sectors of the **economy** including manufacturing with new roles for robotic maintenance and system optimization, healthcare especially those with expertise in diagnostics and treatment planning; **customer service**—demanding employees skilled in higher-level customer interaction; and **finance**—especially jobs involving algorithmic trading and risk assessment. Major cities at the forefront of AI job creation such as Beijing, Shanghai, and Shenzhen will benefit due to their already advanced technological infrastructure and relatively large talent pool but with other less-developed regions falling behind.

ENERGY (*NENGYUAN*). The impact of artificial intelligence (AI) on the production and consumption of global energy supplies is divergent as the construction of data centers and other AI tools will dramatically increase overall energy demand, especially of electricity, while AI model building will transform the efficiency of carbon-intensive industries by predicting energy use and optimizing the performance of heating and air conditioning in buildings and factories. Requiring significant computing power, many **artificial generative intelligence (AGI)** systems consume 33 times more energy to complete a task than existing task-specific software, with the training and running of AI models leading to a dramatic increase in data centers as chatbots such as **ChatGPT** operate around the clock, with newer versions requiring upwards of 50 times more electricity. Advances in AI technology such as new accelerators, three-dimensional chips, and new cooling techniques, including a reported superchip under development by **Nvidia**, are capable of delivering 30 times performance improvement when running AGI services while using 25 times less energy. Development of less resource-intensive, small language models will also reduce the overall carbon footprint of AI, along with the employment of AI tools designed to avoid wasteful energy production, especially from renewable energy sources, and prevent instability in the operation of electrical grids by analyzing vast **data sets** from **weather** patterns to consumption trends, as AI can predict energy consumption with remarkable accuracy. Alternative power sources for **data centers** to help overcome barriers to integrating the necessary vast amounts of renewable energy into existing grids include small modular reactors (SMRs) capable of providing a consistent power supply, ideal for the continuous demands of AI operations, especially **large language models (LLMs)**. Deployed relatively quickly and adaptable to changing energy needs, companies such as **Google**, Amazon, and **Microsoft** are exploring SMRs as a way to power their AI operations and meet sustainability goals, with AI used to optimize SMR design, operation, and maintenance, leading to increased efficiency and reliability, and AI-powered **predictive maintenance** able to identify potential problems before they occur, reducing downtime and maintenance costs, optimizing fuel loading and switching, reducing waste, and improving reactor performance with low-carbon alternatives to fossil fuels, helping to reduce greenhouse gas emissions and meet sustainability goals. With data centers exploring alternative power sources such as small nuclear reactors, AI can also help overcome barriers to integrating the necessary vast amounts of renewable energy into existing grids.

Playing a significant role in the energy sector of the People's Republic of China (PRC), AI has assisted in optimizing energy management in a system long known for enormous waste, promoting the adoption of renewable energy, especially wind and solar power, and improving overall energy efficiency leading to a more sustainable energy system aimed at reducing the country's emission of greenhouse gases, now the largest in the world. Innovations include construction of smart electrical grids, prediction of weather patterns to optimize renewable energy output, better monitoring of energy efficiency in buildings and factories, optimizing the charging and driving patterns of **electric vehicles (EVs)**, and employing AI algorithms to improve traffic management on heavily crowded roads in Beijing, Shanghai, and other major cities with a goal of reducing fuel consumption by all forms of **transportation** but with a continuing need to rein in the enormous electricity needs of the country's more than 400 data centers.

EXPLAINABLE ARTIFICIAL INTELLIGENCE (*KE JIESHIHDE RENGONG ZHINENG*). A field of study committed to making artificial intelligence (AI) systems more transparent and understandable to a human audience, explainable AI (XAI) focuses on explaining how AI **algorithms** go about rendering decisions while revealing potential biases in the algorithmic decision-making process. Aimed at building greater public trust in AI-powered operations and assisting in determining the ethical consequences of AI decisions, XAI employs research from various fields including psychology, philosophy, and cognitive science to interpret so-called "black box" AI models that are often difficult for people to understand with applications to fraud detection, credit scoring, judicial decisions, and **cyber security**.

Committed to increasing transparency and overall public trust in AI systems, the People's Republic of China (PRC) has embraced XAI in such critical areas as health care, **finance**, the legal system, and **smart** manufacturing in the interest of promoting responsible AI deployment where understanding the reasoning behind AI decisions is crucial. Methods of XAI adopted to interpret complex **deep learning** models include local interpretable model-agnostic explanations (LIME), Shapley additive explanations (SHAP), and gradient-based explanations with ongoing concerns over ensuring that **privacy** is protected in the **training** of XAI models and that clear industry standards be followed in XAI implementation.

F

FACIAL RECOGNITION (*RENLIAN SHIBIE*). A form of artificial intelligence (AI) that mimics the human capacity to recognize faces, facial recognition **software** captures facial features and creates a pattern of facial features used to identify or group a face. Employing **computer vision (CV)** and **machine learning (ML)** that uses optical input to analyze an image, the technology serves as a building block for face identification, grouping, and verification of individuals in images, both still and video. Available for several decades but with new innovative solutions such as personal photo applications and secondary authentication for mobile devices, facial analysis capabilities determine where faces exist in an image or video along with specific attributes such as eyes open or closed, mood, and hair color, which allows users to organize or search through millions of images in seconds utilizing metatags such as "happy," "glasses," or "age range." Employed by businesses and governments, including police authorities, the technology has been instrumental in identifying and locating victims of human trafficking while also assisting **financial** firms in offering banking services to underbanked individuals in emerging markets, providing identity verification without any human intervention but with concerns over **privacy** rights and protection of public safety that call for relying on a level of human judgment while avoiding autonomous application of the software. A prediction based on similarity scores, facial recognition is a probabilistic system without absolute precise accuracy where even a 99 percent similarity does not guarantee a positive match, with most systems employing a similarity threshold composed of the lowest similarity score for acceptance of a possible match that determines the number of misidentifications or false positives that can be afforded by the customer.

Widely deployed in the People's Republic of China (PRC), facial recognition software enhances the **surveillance** system of the public and state security apparatus with a reported capacity to scan the faces of the entire population of 1.4 billion people in one second. Generating 6.8 million records a day, the system relies on 200 million cameras positioned in hotels, parks, tourist spots, and religious sites logging people as young as nine days old. Used to identify suspected criminals and to protect vulnerable institutions such as schools from predatory actors, some facial recognition systems have evidently been used to track groups who have been accused of fomenting secessionist activities. Theoretically a highly centralized system, the application is hampered by competing state and police bureaucracies at both the national and central levels along with a multiplicity of facial recognition **companies** led by SenseTime, Yitu Technology, CloudWalk Technology, Dahua Technology, and **Baidu** AI Cloud.

FACTORIES AND FACTORY CONSTRUCTION (*GONGCHANG, GONGCHANG JIANSHE*). Employed in factories and other industrial facilities to improve efficiency and **productivity**, reduce costs, and enhance product quality, artificial intelligence (AI) is essential for greater automation in manufacturing known as "industry 4.0." AI applications include **predictive maintenance** that analyzes data from machinery to anticipate mechanical failures and reduce production line downtime, enhanced quality control, forecasting of product demand, waste reduction especially of valuable raw materials, optimizing production scheduling, maximizing human–machine collaboration, and setting new standards for sustainability from construction to production. Adopted by manufacturers large, medium, and small, common AI techniques include **digital twins**, that is virtual replicas of physical assets that can analyze data and indicate anomalies and flaws in the construction and production process, three-dimensional printing which forges objects from digital models, and **robotics** to undertake especially hazardous functions protecting construction and production line workers from fumes or loud noises with AI used to monitor data from machinery and the shop floor in **smart** factories that generate huge amounts of data beyond normal human comprehension.

Integrating AI into traditional manufacturing and production systems that have suffered from low levels of productivity since the adoption of central economic planning from the Soviet Union in 1953–1978, the People's Republic of China (PRC) has invested over $60 billion into AI development since 2020. Included is a series of smart manufacturing pilot initiatives with 421 national-level showcase factories complemented by several thousand provincial-level workshops and intelligent factories that are slated to generate $600 billion in economic value by 2030. Unveiling the ***Artificial Intelligence Plus Initiative*** in 2024, the country is committed to propelling the digital economy and carrying out the transformation of the manufacturing sector during both phases of factory construction and operation, most notably in electronics and **electric vehicles (EVs)**.

FINANCE AND FINANCIAL TECHNOLOGY (*JINRONG, JINRONG KEJI*). Introduced into financial services and an essential component of financial technology (fintech), artificial intelligence (AI) assists in reducing manual errors in data processing and document processing, pursuing the field of **predictive analytics**, and improving customer interactions through automation and **algorithms** that adhere to a predetermined process consistent over time. Major applications in financial matters include voice and **speech recognition** employed in contact center sales calls; **sentiment analysis** using **natural language processing (NLP)** in conducting investment research and analysis of chat data; detection of anomalies including potential fraudulent transactions, spoofing in trading, and cyber threats; along with delivering personalized recommendations for financial products and services such as investment advice and banking offers, risk assessments, and outlining of financial goals. In the case of document processing, AI can extract structured and unstructured data from systematic searches along with data storage necessary to loan servicing and discovery of investment opportunities. Customers will also enjoy human-like AI-powered contact centers such as banking concierge that lower costs and free up the time of human agents for more creative tasks. Predictive modeling based on customer transactions and potential risks offers specific future outcomes with a high degree of precision while assisting in fraud detection backed by automated aspects of **cyber security**. With a rapidly evolving financial sector in the People's Republic of China (PRC), the intersection of technology, finance, and **regulation** is especially evident in major financial services companies such as **Alibaba**, especially its cloud and Ant Group, along with major state-owned banks, such as the China Construction Bank (CCB). Innovations include the role of platform scalability and regulation, along with the continuing internationalization of China's currency, the CNY, in reshaping the country's financial landscape.

FOUNDATIONAL MODELS (*JICHU MOXING*). A type of **machine learning (ML)** model trained on large quantities of general data, foundational models (FM) are employed in constructing highly specialized forms of artificial intelligence (AI) serving as a backbone of many AI applications and a form of **artificial generative intelligence (AGI)**. Operating on a basis of **unsupervised learning**, foundational models can work with multiple data types beyond just language to accomplish a variety of tasks with a capacity to produce new originally unintended concepts. Able to accelerate AI development, FMs are based on complex **neural networks** including generative adversarial networks (GANs), a version of ML employing two neural networks to generate new data, with output from one or more inputs or prompts usually but not always in the form of human language instructions along with **transformer** and variational encoders. Trained on broad data at scale and designed for generality of output, foundational models were developed in 2021 and can be adapted to a wide range of specific tasks. Employed by **ChatGPT** developed by **OpenAI** and other **large language models (LLMs)**, foundational models have been developed for many scientific fields such as astronomy, **genomics**, **mathematics**, chemistry, and radiology along with coding, music, and **robotics**. Referring to large-scale AI models developed by major technology companies in the People's Republic of China (PRC) including **Alibaba**, **Baidu**, ByteDance, and Tencent, foundational models perform a wide range of tasks such as text generation, translation, and image creation, with a focus on Chinese **natural language processing (NLP)** and applications tailored to the domestic market. Excelling in Chinese language processing, including text generation and translation with high accuracy in the Mandarin dialect, foundational models have benefited from Chinese government support through funding and policy initiatives with **regulations** to manage the use of foundational models, aiming to balance innovation with persistent concerns about data **privacy** and potential misuse.

G

GAMBLING (*DUBO*). With the capacity to analyze large amounts of data, decipher individual behavioral patterns, improve **customer service**, and provide personalized services, artificial intelligence (AI) has been a boost to the gambling industry, including casinos, off- and online, lotteries, and sports betting, while also promoting programs encouraging responsible gambling. Employing **algorithms** that analyze players' behavior, preferences, and playing style, the integration of AI into gambling holds huge promise for casino owners, improving the quality of service and strengthening market position and revenue flows. An important tool for managing customer loyalty programs, AI assists casino operators in analyzing player activity and optimizing reward systems, making VIP statuses more accessible and attractive while extending customer lifetime value. Utilizing data-driven analytics to predict trends, identify patterns, and optimize game design, casino operators can make more informed decisions and stay competitive in the market, creating more dynamic and personalized content, testing new mechanics, and making games more engaging and diverse. Applied to sports betting, AI is used to analyze huge amounts of data, including historical game results, athlete statistics, **weather** conditions, and other factors that can affect the outcome of competitive events by better calculating odds and developing improved betting strategies. By monitoring player behavior, the technology assists gambling operators in identifying signs of problem behavior among players, tracking playing time, and recognizing red flags, such as persistent night gambling or attempts to "win back" after suffering huge losses. Preventing access by underage and vulnerable players, AI tools ensure proper identity verification and establish gambling controls, allowing operators to respond quickly to potential problems by offering players a break or providing information on resources for assistance, making for a safer gaming environment for all users while also protecting platforms from fraud and other threats by identifying suspicious activity in real time. Capable of detecting unauthorized activities such as bonus abuse, creation of fake accounts, or money laundering, AI can recognize when multiple identities, virtual private networks (VPNs), or other methods are used to circumvent the system and benefit from bonuses, with operators setting **parameters** to identify potentially fraudulent behavior and segment players, allowing for automatic checks and account blocking in case of suspicion while staying one step ahead of cybercriminals. Overall, AI solutions are fundamentally changing the way casinos and other gambling facilities interact with players as **virtual assistants** and **chatbots** equipped with **natural language processing (NLP)** provide real-time support and assistance.

A country with a long-time affection for gambling and games of chance, many now technically outlawed in the People's Republic of China (PRC), AI algorithms have been employed to facilitate personalized playing experiences in state-approved lotteries by revealing previous entry patterns and numbers. Embracing system-wide security measures in the form of tamper-proof infrastructure and distributed ledgers, government regulators are also concerned with the relatively easy access to foreign lotteries and online sports betting sites such as Esports. Imposing rigorous rules against Internet gambling, the PRC has focused on stopping the spread of illegal gambling enterprises, especially in Southeast Asia where Chinese nationals are sometimes targeted or implicated in such activities as call center scams and criminal syndicates in nations like Cambodia and Myanmar.

GENOMICS (*JIYINZU*). Used to analyze large amounts of genetic data, identify patterns, and predict how genes may affect human health, artificial intelligence (AI) assists researchers in understanding complex genomic data while speeding up the process of diagnosing genetic disorders. Improving the process of DNA (deoxyribonucleic acid) sequencing, which determines the order of nucleotides in a person's DNA, AI helps identify genetic disorders by analyzing a person's face or other data and predicting how a particular type of disease such as cancer will progress in a patient. Reducing the number of tests needed to diagnose a disease, AI can be integrated with clinical data to help personalize medicine for individual patients while helping to identify genetic mutations and their potential effects more accurately than traditional methods, along with identifying new genetic mutations and biomarkers that can be used to diagnose genetic disorders.

Viewing large-scale genomic data as a strategic resource for developing advanced medical applications, the People's Republic of China (PRC) is actively pursuing the intersection of genomics and AI by collecting and analyzing large amounts of genomic data to fuel advancements in **biotechnology**, medicine, and public health while maintaining strict controls on exporting data, limiting international access to domestic genomic information. Major Chinese organizations involved in the sector include the BGI group, formerly the Beijing Genomics Institute, located in Shenzhen, operating at the forefront of collecting vast amounts of genetic data, with the Chinese government supporting the commercialization of AI-driven genomics technologies with a goal of establishing the PRC as a strong presence in the global biotech market but with concerns that large-scale collection and centralized control of genomic data may engender potential misuse for **surveillance** or bioweapons development.

GOOGLE (*GUGE*). A global leader in the development of artificial intelligence (AI), including the Gemini app created in 2010, Google has worked with the AI research community in the People's Republic of China (PRC), even as the American firm withdrew from the Chinese market in 2010 over censorship concerns, as the search engine was blocked by state authorities, with availability in the PRC restricted to users of virtual private networks (VPNs). Major Google activities include an AI research center established in Beijing in 2017 that works with the Chinese AI community on solutions to global problems, publishing major studies and organizing **conferences and meetings**. Noting the prominence of Chinese researchers and scientists in publishing important work on AI, Google is also involved in several initiatives, including local partnerships and **companies** to promote social dialogue around major AI topics, though concerns exist over the potential for theft of intellectual property, as a former Google engineer was arrested in the United States for allegedly stealing AI-related technology from the company to create a competing business in the PRC in March 2024.

GOVERNMENT INSTITUTIONS (*ZHENGFU JIGOU*). Reflecting a general concern with the impact of artificial intelligence (AI) on society and the **economy**, several government institutions at the central and subnational level have been established in the People's Republic of China (PRC) with authority to issue extensive **laws and regulations** on the burgeoning industry. Most prominent is the Cyberspace Administration of China (CAC), the leading government body promoting research and development of AI in the PRC, which was initially established as the State Internet Information Office (SIIO) under the State Council Information Office (SCIO) in 2011. Also involved in the sector are the Ministry of Science and Technology (MOST) and the Ministry of Industry and Information Technology (MIIT) with the AI Strategic Advisory Committee and the AI Planning and Promotion Office under MOST as the initial government organizations overseeing the sector. Ancillary organs involved with the more technical aspects of AI include the National Information Security Standardization Technical Committee and the National Information Technology Standardization Technical Committee.

GRAPHIC PROCESSING UNIT (*TUIXIANG CHULI DANYUAN*). A specialized **computer** chip widely employed in artificial intelligence (AI), graphic processing units (GPUs) perform large-scale calculations simultaneously through parallel processing as the technology makes possible the computationally demanding tasks involved in **training** and running complex AI models such as deep **neural networks**. Processing large volumes of data in parallel, GPUs significantly accelerate AI operations allowing for faster development and deployment of AI applications across various fields including image recognition, **natural language processing (NLP)**, and **autonomous driving** vehicles. Unlike traditional central processing units (CPUs) that process data sequentially, GPUs consist of thousands of smaller cores designed to perform numerous calculations simultaneously, an essential process for running AI **algorithms** that involve large matrix multiplications and particularly effective for **deep learning** with its reliance on complex neural networks that require massive amounts of parallel computation. Significantly speeding up the training period, GPUs enable researchers and developers to rapidly repeat computational AI models, leading to quicker breakthroughs in AI technology. Major real-world applications include image recognition in autonomous driving vehicles, **medical imaging** analysis, **anti-fraud** operations in **financial** systems, and NLP tools with the American company **Nvidia** a global leader in the production of the most advanced GPUs that can be repurposed to do more than generate graphical scenes. In the case of the People's Republic of China (PRC), GPUs were traditionally sourced from **companies** like Nvidia but with export restrictions imposed by the United States in the 2020s leading domestic Chinese firms such as Biren Technology to provide a homegrown alternative focusing on AI applications and **data center** usage. Chinese companies in need of advanced GPUs have also resorted to smuggling through underground networks in neighboring countries such as **Japan** and Malaysia and from **Hong Kong** as transit hubs for acquiring the necessary chips.

H

HARBIN INSTITUTE OF TECHNOLOGY (*HE'ERBIN GONGYE DAXUE*). A major **education** and research university in science and engineering in the People's Republic of China (PRC) with campuses in Harbin, Heilongjiang Province, and Shenzhen, Guangdong Province, the Harbin Institute of Technology (HIT) is one of the most reputable universities in the country offering programs in artificial intelligence (AI). Included is a three-year course in AI and information processing along with offerings in **machine learning (ML)** and **multi-agent** and multi-**robotic** systems with special focus on AI at the Shenzhen campus including research and development of intelligent equipment manufacturing. Work on AI at HIT was inaugurated in the 1960s with initial research into **natural language processing (NLP)** that continues at three **research laboratories** for Chinese information processing, the Machine Intelligence and Translation Laboratory, the Intelligent Technology and Natural Language Processing Laboratory, and the Information Retrieval Laboratory led by a research team composed of more than 200 individuals concentrating on topics such as NLP, machine translation, and text retrieval.

HIERARCHICAL PLANNING (*JIEJISHI GUIHUA*). A method of breaking down complex tasks into smaller and more manageable subtasks organized into different hierarchies or levels, hierarchical planning is employed in artificial intelligence (AI) through several techniques. Aimed at achieving greater efficiency, adaptability, and scalability across multiple levels, the components of hierarchical planning in AI consist of setting high-level goals for directing the planning process, breaking them down into simpler parts making the overall task easier to manage, and laying out a structure that organizes tasks and subtasks at varying levels of abstraction with the lower levels containing increasingly detailed steps for achieving the overall goals and with plans generated at each level of the hierarchy that combine to form a complete plan. Once generated, the AI system executes the plan in the real world while monitoring the environment and adjusting actions to achieve the goal. Major techniques include hierarchical task networks (HTNs) which employ predefined methods and rules in breaking down tasks into smaller subtasks based on the relationships and requirements defined in the network; hierarchical reinforcement learning (HRL) that uses rewards to learn the best strategies at different levels and allows the AI system to optimize its execution in different situations by exploring and learning effective actions; and hierarchical state space search (HSSS) that pursues a search for solutions across different levels of abstraction.

Reflecting the long tradition of planning in the People's Republic of China (PRC) especially during the years of Soviet-style central economic planning adopted from 1953 to 1978, hierarchical planning constitutes a key approach in applying advanced AI systems across broad sectors of the society and **economy**. Aimed at achieving greater efficiency in many notoriously low **productivity** industrial and agricultural sectors, major **policy statements** such as *the New Generation Artificial Intelligence Development Plan* (2017) promote the method in manufacturing, medicine, and **transportation** backed by government support for research and development of hierarchical planning in academia and industry. Utilizing the vast amounts of data generated throughout the country, hierarchical planning is also used to optimize road traffic management especially in crowded urban areas, control **energy** consumption, and run public safety systems in **smart** cities along with assisting in complex medical diagnoses and treatment plans and designing hierarchical control systems to automate production lines in major industries. *See also* ACCELERATED PRODUCTION.

HISTORY (*LISHI*). While early forms of human automata were developed throughout the premodern era of China (see Chronology), the introduction of artificial intelligence (AI) in the People's Republic of China (PRC) began with an enhanced focus on science and technology in the late 1970s and underwent significant progress when the Chinese government actively pursued national AI development from 2017 onward with a goal of becoming a global leader by 2030. Following the shift in government policy to major economic reforms facilitated by the return to power of Chinese Communist Party (CCP) leader Deng Xiaoping in 1978–1979, initial stages of AI research focused on basic areas such as logical reasoning and automated theorem proving, with limited resources and talent led primarily by Chinese scientists educated abroad including **Qian Xuesen**. Issuing various AI development plans from the mid-1980s to the early 2000s, government policy focused on building intelligent **computing**, **robots**, and information processing with a stress on integrating AI into **education** facilitated by the establishment of the China Association for Artificial Intelligence (CAAI) in 1981. Outlining a comprehensive strategy for AI development, a *New Generation Artificial Intelligence Development Plan* formulated by the State Council in 2017, areas of concentration included **computer vision (CV)**, **natural language processing (NLP)**, robotics, and **big data** with significant investments in AI business start-ups and **research institutes**. Major factors contributing to the rapid development of AI in the PRC include significant government support, a growing pool of skilled researchers and engineers educated at home and abroad, and a large domestic market with more than 4,500 Chinese AI **companies** operating in 2024 and an emerging cloud computing infrastructure.

HONG KONG (*XIANG GANG*). A Special Administrative Region (SAR) of the People's Republic of China (PRC) since 1997, Hong Kong has been a center for promoting the development and utilization of artificial intelligence (AI), especially in service to the city's vibrant and cosmopolitan **economy**. Major policy initiatives include the allocation of government subsidies amounting to $3 billion to support local AI-related enterprises, universities, and research and development centers with a focus on strengthening data protection and **cyber security**, such as the Artificial Intelligence Supercomputing Centre (AISC) at the Cyberport digital community. Also established is the Artificial Intelligence Association of Hong Kong (AIHK) as an independent organization to assist businesses and organizations in employing AI to increase efficiency, **productivity**, and competitive advantage aimed at positioning Hong Kong as a global innovation hub for AI. Under the guise of the Hong Kong Productivity Council (HKPC), an AI model known as Industrial GPT is undergoing development at AISC to assist small- and medium-sized manufacturers, while a model personal data protection framework has been formulated to ensure best practices for organizations handling sensitive personal information, especially for entities employing AI solutions from third-party vendors or developers. Guidance on the use of **artificial generative intelligence (AGI)** has been similarly enacted by the Hong Kong Monetary Authority (HKMA), including measures to provide transparency to customers about the use, purpose, and limitations of AGI models. A major transient hub for the importation of high technology products into mainland PRC, especially from abroad, Hong Kong has been frequently caught in the middle of increasing trade tensions and technological competition between the United States and the PRC, especially after the American government issued restrictions on US firms such as **Nvidia** from investing in PRC-based **companies**, including many based in Hong Kong and Macau specializing in **semiconductors**, **quantum computing**, and AI systems employing **large language models (LLMs)**.

HOSPITALS (*YIYUAN*). With an average of 1.8 doctors per 1,000 people in a country of 1.41 billion people where hospitals and clinics suffer from persistent problems of long waiting times for patients, the People's Republic of China (PRC) looks to the application of artificial intelligence (AI) to the management and improvement of medical services through three predominant variations. First is the concept of an AI Agent Hospital (AAH) developed by the Institute for Artificial Industry (AIR) at Tsinghua University in Beijing with Zhang Yaqin (PhD) as a cofounder (formerly of **Microsoft** China and **Baidu**) serving as the general director along with Ma Weiying (PhD), a graduate from National Tsinghua University in Taiwan. Propelled by a **large language model (LLM)**, AAH provides a comprehensive system for treating the sick from registration, triage, and case history to lab work, diagnostics, therapeutics, and prognostics. In its phase One platform, AAH service consists of 21 specialty areas including, among others, pediatrics, emergency medicine, neurology, otolaryngology, cardiovascular, oncology, rheumatology, OBGYN, and infectious diseases. Each department is equipped with two AI-trained doctors, one from the PRC and the other of international background. In the case of the treatment of lung cancer, for example, the Chinese AI doctor follows the *Chinese Guidelines for Primary Lung Cancer Treatment* while an American AI doctor follows the *US Guidelines for the Treatment of Non-Small Cell Lung Cancer (NSCLC).* Selected as an AAH test site is Zhejiang Hospital operating under the Zhejiang Smart Health flagship as a virtual site based in the city of Wuxi. **Publications** describing innovative AI Agent Hospital include *Agent Hospital: A Simulacrum of Hospital with Evolvable Medical Agents.*

The second concept of AAH involves SynYi AI, translated as "one billion forest AI," and developed by Zhang Shaodian (PhD) from a study of medical informatics examining the sizable gap in AI-based health between the PRC and the United States. Founded in 2016 with significant investment from Tencent and the American company Sequoia Capital, SynYi has opened the world's first clinic in Saudi Arabia where AI constitutes the first line of medical treatment for diagnosed patients in effect replacing human doctors. Working in collaboration with the country's Almoosa Health Group, the pilot entails the patient consulting with a virtual AI doctor similar to dealing with a human doctor by describing their symptoms via a tablet **computer** to an AI "doctor" followed up by more questions and analysis of data and images such as cardiograms and x-rays. Taken with the assistance of humans, the treatment plan is reviewed and signed off by a human physician without actually seeing the patient while handling any emergencies unforeseen by AI. Capable of meeting more than 60 percent of patient walk-ins, the SynYi model has the human doctor serving as an AI supervisor intervening whenever necessary ensuring that all protocols are followed with unequivocal clarity including any physical examinations performed by physicians but with human interference kept at a minimum.

The third model of AI hospital application is the MicroMeds Hospital located in Shanghai involving a seamless combination of online/offline AI doctor plus a human doctor platform. Equipped with services in 14 areas including prophylactic medicine, pediatrics, OBGYN, internal medicine, and general surgery, the model is serviced by 300 expert physicians based at the hospital with more than 30,000 physicians available online along with AI assistants. As an example of the convenience of the platform, consider the case of a Mr. Yu, a chronic diabetic patient of more than two decades, who, paying a visit to MicroMeds Hospital, had his case history information recorded by a human nurse and summarized by the AI assistant into accurate and succinct notes for the physician. After a thorough AI-performed eye examination focusing on the fundamental eye maladies generally associated with chronic diabetes, there follow prescriptions and consultations with a health nutrition management staff in a process that in a traditional hospital typically takes more than half a day but is condensed to just a couple of hours at the MicroMeds facility.

While AI hospitals are slated for expansion in the PRC and abroad, a potential thorny issue concerns assigning the legal accountability of AI-generated errors as efforts at optimizing AI hospital practice are pursued.

HUAWEI. An information and **telecommunications** technology **company** founded in 1987 by Ren Zhongfei, a former engineer in the People's Liberation Army (PLA), in the People's Republic of China (PRC), Huawei has a long-standing commitment to artificial intelligence (AI) devoting significant resources to research and development of the latest AI technologies. Major initiatives include the field of enterprise intelligence focusing on AI applications to business and commercial activities; development of the Ascend series of AI chips providing AI-level **computing** power; creation of the Atlas platform for connecting devices, along with edge and cloud computing; and the FusionMind platform enabling flexible AI deployment to meet an ever-changing AI environment. Also developed is the Intelligent Data Lake that provides a foundation for application of AI-based **smart** technologies along with the AI Life platform allowing users to manage **Internet of Things (IoT)** devices, such as wireless networking (Wi-Fi), speakers, and smart glasses. Huawei also unveiled an update to its Pangu **large language model (LLM)** for AI as the Chinese company continues working to completely sever reliance on foreign technology while challenging leading players in AI, including **OpenAI**, **Google**, Apple, and **Nvidia**. Huawei has made developing its own operating system to replace Google's Android a priority since the United States put the company on a trade blacklist curtailing access to American technology. Claiming to have reached fully self-secured and controllable status, the company has produced the Ascent 910B chip capable of **training** an LLM proposed by the Chinese company ByteDance, to which Huawei sold 800,000 chips, and potentially more powerful than the H100 chip developed by Nvidia.

HUMAN RIGHTS AND EQUALITY (*REN QUAN, PINGDENG*). Constituting both a benefit and potential infringement on human rights, artificial intelligence (AI) is subject to various **laws and regulations** including a resolution passed by the United Nations General Assembly in March 2024. Major benefits of AI include democratizing access to information and knowledge and accelerating scientific progress benefiting humanity. In the first global nonbinding resolution on AI overwhelmingly endorsed by UN members, governments are urged to protect human rights especially personal data while monitoring any potential harm inflicted on basic human rights with a goal of ensuring the technology is employed to the benefit of all humankind and not just privileged minorities. Harmful utilization of AI by governments and other non-state organizations includes mass **surveillance** along with perpetuating bias in criminal justice systems, medicine, **education**, **employment**, and access to critical resources such as housing and banking exacerbating discrimination against marginalized groups. Used to facilitate the spread of misinformation, the creation of **deep fakes** and synthetic media can sow social conflict and confusion threatening freedom of expression, thought, assembly, association, movement, and an adequate standard of living. Often left out of the narrative on development and implementation of AI, human rights must be a primary concern of technology **companies** and regulatory bodies especially in terms of such applications as state and police authorities predicting criminal and fraudulent behavior and suppressing political activities covered by human rights protocols. Titled *Seizing the Opportunities of Safe, Secure and Trustworthy Artificial Intelligence Systems for Sustainable Development, the first-ever resolution adopted by the United Nations on the matter of artificial intelligence, emphasized responsible AI design by member states consistent with respect for human rights and equality. Embodying a series of core principles for guiding the international community to apply AI to innovations in healthcare, education, and climate challenges, the Resolution also called for retaining a strong human element to AI development as reflected in human-centric AI, human oversight, and human control. Member states are urged to develop and adopt regulations and measures that ensure transparency, fairness, and ethical standards of AI while also dedicating* *efforts to address the many digital challenges confronting developing countries such as closing "digital divides," enhancing "digital access," and increasing "digital literacy."*

Led by the United States and co-sponsored by the People's Republic of China, drafting of the Resolution involved the participation of countries from the European Union (EU), most notably France, Italy, Germany, and Spain, joined by many developing countries such as India, Egypt, United Arab Emirates, Algeria, Angola, Ethiopia, Burundi, Nigeria, Zimbabwe, Guatemala, and Guyana, with Costa Rica playing an instrumental role in the negotiations over the content. Passed unanimously by more than 120 UN member states, the Resolution, while lacking any immediate binding effect, will guide the regulatory development of AI technologies on the national and international level in the years to come, with the PRC promising assistance especially to African states in setting up data centers and other AI infrastructure.

I

INDUSTRIAL POLICY (*CHANYE ZHENGCE*). Government strategies and policies involving directed investments, **laws and regulations**, fiscal spending initiatives, and subsidies, industrial policy is employed to advance the development of artificial intelligence (AI) by fostering innovation and adoption across industries as a complement or even substitute for market forces. Aimed at achieving national competitiveness in the global **economy**, industrial policy targets funding for research and development, cultivation of scientific and engineering domestic talent, and direct and/or indirect support for start-up **companies** involved in various aspects of AI development. Major policy tools include direct investments in AI **research laboratories**, tax incentives for AI companies, procurement strategies prioritizing AI solutions, and regulatory frameworks to manage the potential risks of AI deployment with concomitant consideration of problems involving bias, infringement on **privacy**, and the need for transparency. With government funding to support research in such critical areas of AI as **machine learning (ML)**, **natural language processing (NLP)**, and **computer vision (CV)**, industrial policy can also entail the establishment of AI hubs, that is, designated regions with infrastructure and resources to attract AI companies, domestic and foreign, along with public-private partnerships with AI solutions deployed in medicine, manufacturing, and **transportation** and ensuring access to large **data sets**. Potential problems of employing industrial policy to AI include major market distortions from excessive and ill-informed government intervention that may undermine market dynamics and stifle innovation as political leaders pick and choose winners and losers along with the adoption of protectionist measures that foment trade conflicts and international tensions with risks of loss of **employment** and potential **algorithmic** bias especially toward ethnic minorities.

Reflecting the legacy of strong state intervention in both the premodern and contemporary economy of China, especially during the period of central economic planning adopted in the People's Republic of China (PRC) from the Soviet Union in 1953–1978, industrial policy in the AI field has been substantial, especially in areas such as manufacturing, **energy**, **logistics**, and transportation. With a goal of integrating AI into traditional industries such as steel-making and energy production, along with new industries such as **electric vehicles (EVs)** and electronics, the PRC has committed $60 billion to enhance operational efficiency, reduce resource consumption in historically wasteful production processes, and replace deficient products with improved quality content. Initiatives include so-called lighthouse factories that, by introducing AI-driven automation, have reduced energy consumption by 24 percent per unit of production and overall waste by 50 percent, with a goal of the PRC becoming a global leader in AI by 2030. *See also* ACCELERATED PRODUCTION.

INFERENCE (*TUILI*). A reference to the ability of a trained model of artificial intelligence (AI) to analyze new data, draw conclusions, and make predictions, inference is based on the knowledge gained during the **training** phase which essentially mimics human reasoning. Applying learned patterns to previously unseen information, inference is a process of applying an AI model to real-world situations to generate outputs based on input data, effectively acting on the knowledge it has acquired through training. Considered the "application" phase of AI that follows the "training" phase, an AI model employs trained **parameters** to analyze new data and generate predictions or classifications. Achieved through an "inference engine" that applies logical rules to a knowledge base, AI inference infers or extrapolates conclusions from new data. In the process of **machine learning (ML)** there are two distinct phases, first the training phase in which intelligence is developed by recording, storing, and labeling information, and the second inference phase where the machine uses the stored intelligence to understand the new data such as identifying and categorizing new previously unseen images that applied to more complex scenarios are used to augment human decision-making. While employed by AI systems in the People's Republic of China (PRC), insufficient resources have made both the training and inference capacity of Chinese AI **companies** more expensive and less efficient than comparable firms in more advanced AI nations such as the United States.

INFORMED AND UNINFORMED SEARCH STRATEGIES (*QIDASHI SOUSUO YU WUXINXI SOUSUO CELÜE*). Two versions of **algorithmic** search strategies employed in artificial intelligence (AI) systems, informed and uninformed methods differ in the order and length of the search actions. With information on the goal state, informed search allows for more efficient **problem-solving** compared to uninformed search and comes in the form of heuristics, estimates of cost, or other data to prioritize which states to expand and explore. This information is obtained by a function that estimates how close a state is to the goal state. Informed searches include breadth-first or depth-first search which avoid exploration of unlikely pathways focusing on the more promising ones. Designed to come up with a solution to a specific problem, informed searches are goal-directed and employ cost-based estimates to evaluate nodes, such as estimated cost, to reach the goal or the cost of a particular path with a guarantee of an optimal solution based on admissible and consistent heuristic uses. In the case of an uninformed search, the algorithms have no additional information on the goal node other than what is provided in the problem definition as the algorithms explore the search space in a systematic, but blind, manner without considering the cost of reaching the goal or the likelihood of finding a solution making them somewhat inefficient and leading to an exponential increase in the number of states explored. Simple to implement and understand, uninformed search algorithms are a good starting point for more complex algorithms but do not guarantee an optimal solution. While both types of searches are undergoing active development in the People's Republic of China (PRC), concerns have been raised regarding **privacy** and government oversight due to the extensive **surveillance** system and a general lack of transparency by the state and **companies** alike.

INSURANCE INDUSTRY (*BAOXIAN YE*). Able to execute complex analyses and mathematical computations at speeds exceeding human abilities, artificial intelligence (AI) has become an essential tool in the global insurance industry including in the People's Republic of China (PRC). AI tools have been applied in multiple areas of insurance especially in claims processing, underwriting, fraud detection, and **customer service** with **artificial generative intelligence (AGI)** employed in organizing, analyzing, and collecting data to ensure accurate tracking of sales, claims, and compliance with **laws and regulations**. Major benefits include increasing agent **productivity** by reducing low-value interactions while making for more effective and profitable relations with potential customers by utilizing around-the-clock **virtual assistants** that aid customers with product comparisons and digital purchases. Also available are highly personalized offerings with tailored conversations and content that readily respond to the needs of individual customers as signals from unstructured data are combined with more structured data to aid in risk identification and evaluation and new insights that can increase client coverage, improve lead conversion, and shift to more profitable products through wealth adviser hubs. AGI has also been a boon to customer service operations answering common questions on insurance and related topics such as pensions.

A rapidly growing insurance market since 2000, the PRC has both domestic and foreign insurance **companies** with AI and **digitalization** employed in many facets including a greater fusion of customer service, claims, and **marketing**. Increasing the number of digital touchpoints with potential customers, a new and more interactive form of relationship has been established between provider and customer especially at the greatest moment of stress when the policyholder makes a claim with Chinese companies such as the giant Ping'An Insurance relying on AI and **machine learning (ML)** deployed to provide a more natural human response. Underpinning this process is data analytics which processes and identifies the status of a claim (preempting a claim in some cases) with a capacity to eliminate potential fraud. Employing biometric authentication, Ping'An offers policyholders an option to enhance account security through **voice** and **facial recognition** to verify the identity of insurance applicants and agents. So-called fusion apps employed by other prominent firms combine the speed and reliability from the processing power of a machine, with the human qualities of creative power, experience, and fairness. These AI and ML driven systems learn and adapt to human guidance and support customer service, claims, and underwriters to work faster and smarter, by facilitating thousands of applications in mere seconds. Such automation is rule-based but integrates superior cognitive automation, allowing fusion to learn patterns from the analysis of decades of customer data.

INTELLIGENCE GATHERING (*QINGBO SHOUJI*). A key tool in intelligence gathering and analysis with a capacity to process large volumes of data, artificial intelligence (AI) assists professional intelligence agents in making informed decisions on important national security issues. Able to analyze multiple sources at once in real time, AI **algorithms** can be applied to **financial** transactions, sensor data, and intercepted communications, detecting underlying patterns and hidden connections that are often missed by human analysts. Speeding up the process of preparing information for analysis and dissemination to key decision makers, AI systems assist intelligence professionals in predicting emerging threats and anticipating major geopolitical developments, employing **machine learning (ML)** to improve the accuracy and precision of data vital to the creativity, intuition, and ethical judgment of human intelligence, unlocking new opportunities for innovation and progress. Included is the handling of a vast trove of information and data made available especially during periods of major international crises when intelligence units face the challenge of dealing with massive data flows by scanning the news for dangerous and rapid developments in political, **military**, and economic conditions.

Actively pursuing AI applications to its national intelligence apparatus, the People's Republic of China (PRC) is employing sophisticated AI technology to harvest major sources of intelligence information with the Ministry of State Security (MSS) taking the lead. Key utilities of AI-enhanced intelligence gathering, and data analysis consist of geospatial intelligence relying on automated analytics to dissect footage from satellites, aircraft, and drones, along with signal intelligence for analyzing captured communications in audio or text formats. Combined open-source and cyber intelligence are used to scan public databases and social media platforms to preempt growing threats and to detect and identify illicit networks with timely scanning of large datasets for efficient data triage and pattern identification.

INTERNATIONAL GOVERNANCE (*GUOJI ZHILI*). With the surge of artificial intelligence (AI) across a multitude of technological and economic sectors transcending the boundaries of nation states, especially in the developed world, major efforts at international governance and **regulation** were inaugurated by transnational bodies. Included were the Group of Seven (G7) nations of advanced economies, the Organization for Economic Cooperation and Development (OECD), the European Union (EU), and the United Nations. Reacting to the substantial impact of AI on such important sectors as stock and **financial** markets, **transportation**, including fatal accidents by **autonomous driving** vehicles, the spread of misinformation and **deep fakes**, and discriminatory practices and biases embedded in AI-employed **algorithms**, various policy packages were promulgated containing ethical codes of conduct, guidelines for business and other groups relying on AI applications, and proposals for coordinated international action on AI management. Also pursued was the establishment of internationally accepted standards for AI tools enacted by the International Organization for Standardization (ISO) and the pairing of AI to **human rights**, international security, accountability, and transparency. Specialized convocations and organs have also been convened, including the AI Safety Summit in 2023, which issued the **Bletchley Declaration**; the Hiroshima AI Process Friends Group of 49 nations launched by Prime Minister Kishida Fumio of **Japan** in May 2024 to advance cooperation for global access to safe, secure, and trustworthy **artificial generative intelligence (AGI)** endorsed by G7 digital and technology ministers; proposals on human rights, democracy, and the rule of law from the Alan Turing Institute in the United Kingdom to the Ad Hoc Committee on AI of the Council of Europe; and the *United Nations System White Paper on AI Governance* in October 2023. Many published guidelines and principles for responsible AI development lack legally binding force, making them examples of "soft law" with the 2023 boom in **foundational models** presenting a new layer of complexity to the landscape of international AI governance.

An active participant in the arena of international governance of AI, the People's Republic of China (PRC) has supported a comprehensive and balanced approach stressing the importance of ethics, safety, standards and norms, capacity building, and institutions. Opposed to the erection of walls and discrimination, the PRC officially supports extending the benefits of AI to all countries including less developed countries as indicated in proposing a framework known as the Global AI Governance Initiative which called for equal rights on AI development for all countries and joint efforts to tackle the misuse of technologies by terrorists while also supporting resolutions on the topic by the United Nations. At the same time, the PRC generally opposes any efforts to impose values and make judgments, an obvious reference to concerns over the use of AI in the country to conduct mass **surveillance** and invade personal **privacy**. Committed to greater standardization in the country's AI industry, draft guidelines covering more than 50 national and industry-wide standards have been issued to take effect in the year 2026 with a goal of establishing 20 international standards for AI in the PRC for the same year. The PRC supports the United Nations in playing a leading role in global AI governance and urged greater representation for developing countries while expressing a willingness to boost collaboration with international organizations to ensure AI technology was safe, controllable, and reliable.

INTERNET OF THINGS (*WU LIANWANG*). A network of devices that collect and share data, the Internet of Things (IoT) when combined with artificial intelligence (AI) creates more intelligent and efficient systems with applications across various sectors of the **economy** and society. Known as the Artificial Intelligence of Things (ALoT), the combined technology is the basis for **smart** homes with AI analyzing data from sensors to predict **energy** needs, optimizing heating and cooling while also enhancing security. Applied to manufacturing, ALoT is employed in **predictive maintenance**, and in **agriculture**, its analysis of soil and crop data makes for more informed planting and watering schedules, all of which improve **productivity**, providing more automated processes and better decision-making. A core element of IoT is dedicated devices known as terminals that act as a connection point between a network of sensors or IoT devices and a wider network, allowing data collection from the sensors and transmission to a cloud platform or other systems for analysis and further processing, serving as a gateway to connect "things" to the Internet.

Widely adopted in the People's Republic of China (PRC), the number of IoT terminals reached 2.57 billion in August 2024, the first major economy to have more IoT connections than its total population. Reshaping the industrial landscape, the integration of IoT, **big data**, and AI has yielded significant improvements in operational efficiency as real-time monitoring and lean manufacturing are boosting productivity by as much as 25 percent. Utilizing smart sensors and automated controls in agriculture, resource efficiency has improved through such applications as precision irrigation systems deployed on large farms resulting in reduced water usage and higher crop yields. Strengthening product traceability and enhancing the value of agricultural brands, many fragmented small-scale farms have been transformed into unified, large-scale farms creating a modern, more efficient agricultural system. Optimizing operations and improving customer experience has also been achieved in the service sector, driving the growth of innovative business models such as unmanned supermarkets, smart **logistics**, and the sharing economy.

J

JAPAN (*RIBEN*). Developing artificial intelligence (AI) to improve the national **economy**, address chronic labor shortages, and create an "AI-ready society," Japan still lags behind the People's Republic of China (PRC) in the overall adoption and usage of AI. This is particularly the case in the personal use of **artificial generative intelligence (AGI)**, where the PRC has a significantly higher percentage of users compared to Japan. Pursuing a risk-based approach to AI **regulation** that aims to maximize the positive impact of the technology on society, the Japanese government has issued the *Social Principles of Human-Centered AI* that ensures respect for **human rights**, protects **privacy**, andpromotes fair and accountable use of AI. Applications include health care for diagnostic support and patient management, manufacturing for quality control and **predictive maintenance**, and **finance** for risk management and fraud detection. Embodied in the *AI Strategy 2019* enacted by the Japanese government are policies to support research and development, cultivate talent, and promote practical applications including self-checkout registers in convenience stores, touch-screen order terminals in restaurants, and **robotic** chefs and hotel staff with deployment of AI and robotics producing positive effects on **employment** and income growth with the country focusing on AI **regulations** and ethical frameworks, aiming to be a leader in responsible AI development.

K

KNOWLEDGE ECONOMY AND KNOWLEDGE WORKERS (*ZHISHI JINGJI, ZHISHI GONGZUOZHE*). A major factor affecting both the knowledge economy and knowledge workers, artificial intelligence (AI) has the potential to reshape the production of goods and services based on knowledge and intellectual capital along with the workforce in fundamental ways. Included is the automation of many professions traditionally handled by humans, especially white-collar jobs, by significantly speeding up and improving the quality of such tasks as writing **computer** codes, performing data analysis, and engaging in technical work. Increasing the knowledge content of human work, advanced AI leads to larger, more productive, and more decentralized **companies** benefiting both the least and most knowledgeable humans alike by taking over relatively routine and repetitive functions, freeing up workers to concentrate on more creative and innovative tasks. Utilizing so-called killer apps such as **ChatGPT**, AI can play a critical support role to many knowledge-based occupations: taking over simple code writing for computer programmers, allowing the human worker to concentrate on more innovative structures and new **algorithms** while using AI tools for error checking and testing; writing boilerplate contract terms for lawyers, leading to more time and effort on negotiations, deal-making, and client development; creating media plans and awareness campaigns for **advertising and marketing** executives who can focus on research and coming up with breakthrough ideas; writing formulaic crime reports and summaries of government meetings for journalists, freeing up more time for investigative work; and conducting routine tasks in **education** such as grading, plagiarism detection, and assembling curriculum plans, leaving more time for the fundamentals of good teaching. With AI relying solely on past accomplishments and current knowledge, true innovation is still left to human knowledge workers as AI remains a fundamentally derivative and repetitive exercise.

With a goal of transforming the People's Republic of China (PRC) from a manufacturing hub of basic and many low value-added products to a more innovative national economy with higher levels of **productivity**, AI and the knowledge economy are closely intertwined in the plans and proposals put forth by the Chinese government and led by giant tech firms such as **Alibaba**, **Baidu**, and Tencent. Aware of the critical role of knowledge workers to such a fundamental transformation, substantial resources have been devoted to education and training with an emphasis on cultivating an innovative mind-set.

L

LARGE LANGUAGE MODELS (*DA YUYAN MOXING*). A type of artificial intelligence (AI) that employs **machine learning (ML)** to understand and generate human language, large language models (LLMs) are a subset of **deep learning** with **algorithms** deployed to ascertain underlying patterns in large **data sets**. Trained to learn how language works based on voluminous amounts of text data taken from books and articles, LLMs are generally more accurate than traditional ML algorithms with a capacity to understand the complexities of a natural language such as English and Chinese. Tasks performed by LLMs include translation, question-answering, text completion, **speech recognition**, and **sentiment analysis**, the latter performed to determine the positive, negative, or neutral tone of a message. Based on deep learning architectures such as the **transformer** employing **neural networks** to extract meaning from a text, the models automate and enhance communication and data processing summarizing data from individual cases or problems. Along with **artificial generative intelligence (AGI)**, LLMs serve as digital assistants to routine functions from managing email to creating **chatbots** capable of communicating with enterprises across industries, languages, and specialties that lead to greater worker **productivity** and enhanced connectivity. Major LLMs in the West with the founding **company** in parentheses include **ChatGPT-4/-3** (**Open AI**); Bert, Gemma, Gemini, and PaLM (**Google**); Turing NLG (**Microsoft**); Cohere (Canada); Llama (Meta); Claude (Anthropic); Mistral (Mistral AI); and Falcon (Technology Innovation Institute).

Second in number only to the United States, the People's Republic of China (PRC) has approximately 130 LLMs constituting 36 percent of the global total, with many approved for commercial use and utilized by 600 million people. Included are most notably Ernie.BOT by **Baidu**, Tongyi Qianwen by **Alibaba**, Wudao 2.0, the world's largest developed by the Beijing Academy of Artificial Intelligence, Zhipu AI, and a LLM on the political thought of PRC President **Xi Jinping**. Following Chinese government approval of public access to company LLMs in 2023, users in Western countries confront several problems, mainly language barriers and registration requirements, while many Chinese LLMs have considerable overlap in content and suffer from rising costs.

LAWS AND REGULATIONS (*FALU, FAGUI*). Reacting to the surge in artificial intelligence (AI) in the **economy** and society in the People's Republic of China (PRC), various laws and regulations have been enacted to govern AI in recent years. Major focus of targeted legal actions aimed at managing potential risks includes recommendation and registration of AI **algorithms**, **deep fakes**, and **artificial generative intelligence (AGI)**, with the Cyberspace Administration of China (CAC) leading the regulatory effort. Also pursued is the promotion of innovation in the industry through *Deep Synthesis Regulation* and *Interim Measures for Administration of Generative AI Services Management*, both in 2023, which mandate the labeling of AI-generated content to ensure transparency and avoid misinformation. Avoiding for the moment a single comprehensive AI law that is currently undergoing consideration, targeted regulations address specific AI technologies such as recommendation algorithms and deep synthesis, areas considered high-risk due to potential manipulation and misinformation. Ensuring that AI-generated content adheres to "correct political direction," most notably the "core values of socialism," emphasis is given to preserving the security of **training** data used for AI models, including requirements for vetting data sources to remove potentially harmful content, including protection of social morality. Mandatory labeling of AI-generated content, particularly deep fakes, aims at alerting users about the synthetic nature of information while user verification is also required raising concerns about censorship as AI regulations in the PRC are constantly updated and expanded to address new challenges. Circulated among legal scholars is a preliminary draft AI law in which developers, providers, and users are held liable for misuse of AI tools while allowing for copyrighted material to be employed in model training and intellectual property protection for content created by AI technology. Leading private AI **companies** in China, including **Alibaba**, **Baidu**, and Tencent, comply with the rules and regulations set by the governing Cyberspace Administration of China (CAC) in terms of registering generative AI algorithms and other basic requirements for AI operations. Providing detailed sources of AI training data sets and participating in audits, the firms guarantee that AI models observe intellectual property rights, enhance social stability, and provide for state security. CAC also ensures that AI outputs harbor no harmful or misinformation while observing stringent data **privacy** and implementing clearly designated label systems that distinguish AI-generated content from content generated by humans in visual, text, and Vedic formats, the latter involving ancient principles of **mathematics** and philosophies for enhancing computational speed and ethical decisions.

LEE, KAI-FU (1961–). A **computer** scientist and businessman born in Taiwan and currently a resident of the People's Republic of China (PRC), Lee Kai-fu has been a leading figure in artificial intelligence (AI). A graduate of Columbia University in New York with a PhD in computer science from Carnegie Mellon University, Lee was the founding director of **Microsoft** Research Asia from 1998 to 2000 and president of **Google** China from 2005 to 2009. Establishing Sinovation Ventures as a venture capital firm in the PRC, he also created the website "I-Learn Web" (*Wo Xuewang*) to assist young Chinese in their studies and is a micro-blogger on Sina Weibo with 50 million followers. Author of *AI Superpowers: China, Silicon Valley, and the New Global Order*, Lee foresees the PRC emerging as a global leader in AI based on the large population of the country and the accumulation of voluminous **data sets**.

LIANG, WENFENG (1985–). Entrepreneur and businessman in the People's Republic of China (PRC), Liang Wenfeng is founder and chief executive officer of **DeepSeek**, an artificial intelligence (AI) company most noted for the development of the relatively low-cost R-1 **large language model (LLM)** in 2023. Born in Guangdong Province in a family of primary school teachers, Liang Wenfeng graduated from Zhejiang University with a bachelor of engineering and a master's in information and communication engineering. Joining with classmates to accumulate data on the performance of **financial** markets, his team employed **machine learning (ML)** technologies, establishing a series of investment companies culminating in the founding of the Ningbo High-Flyer Quantitative Investment Management Partnership in 2016, followed by High-Flyer AI in 2019 with 10 billion *yuan* under management aimed at utilizing AI to improve the effectiveness of the country's secondary market through the modeling of prices. Purchasing large numbers of **graphic processing units (GPUs)** from the **Nvidia Corporation**, DeepSeek was launched in 2024 with backing from High-Flyer while concentrating on hiring employees based on merit and passion rather than extensive experience while developing an **open-source model** with 671 billion **parameters**. Meeting with PRC Premier Li Qiang in 2024, Liang contributed to the preparation of the annual government work report in 2024 and participated in the Symposium with Private-Sector Enterprises hosted by President **Xi Jinping** in February 2025.

LI, JIANG. On the faculty of Shanghai Communications University, Li Jiang is a specialist in **computer** architecture and **machine learning (ML)**. Major areas of research and **publications** with Chinese colleagues include the following, among others: **training** of **neural networks**; deep neural network acceleration; system failure hardware prediction; three-dimensional stacked memory; automated rule-based constructability; and improving neural network efficiency.

LITERATURE AND THE ARTS (*WENXUE, YISHU*). Employed to enhance the capabilities of writers and artists, artificial intelligence (AI) can be used in the creation of literary and visual works along with analyzing and improving upon existing creative works but with considerable debate over whether AI-generated works are truly creative and capable of matching human ingenuity. Applications include assisting writers and artists in improving output with a capacity in the latter to generate visual artworks such as paintings in response to prompts from text employing AI tools such as Midjourney, Stable Diffusion, and DALL-E that automate the artistic process. Analyzing large amounts of data in the fine arts, AI and **artificial generative intelligence (AGI)** are also used in the composition of music and can enhance artistic events and performances, democratizing and expanding the boundaries of creativity but with reservations over whether such creations produce true insight and constitute real art. Recent AI tools have demonstrated an ability to produce outputs traditionally considered products of human creation as the intersection of AI and creativity offers an opportunity to explore new frontiers in art, design, and literature.

In the case of the People's Republic of China (PRC), recent surveys of visual artists indicate that nearly half of the painters, sculptors, mixed-media artists, and Internet artists interviewed have begun to employ AI in their work since 2023, often using AI as a communication partner and collaborator. Far more than just being used as a tool for testing ideas or formulating questions, Chinese contemporary visual artists see the opportunities of AI to enhance their creativity, human capabilities, and efficiency of their work practices, with the artists reflecting on how they creatively use and sometimes "misuse" AI, recognizing continuing concerns over copyright, morality, and ethics. *See also* SCIENCE FICTION.

LITHOGRAPHY (*GUANGKE*). The primary method for printing electric circuits onto a **semiconductor** chip, lithography utilizes artificial intelligence (AI) primarily to optimize the design of photomasks and predict potential defects by analyzing complex data from the manufacturing process. Allowing for improved yield and faster development of new chip designs, particularly in the crucial area of mask optimization for advanced semiconductor nodes, AI employs **algorithms** in **machine learning (ML)** to analyze patterns and identify potential problems before they affect the actual fabrication process. Analyzing real-time data from a lithography machine to identify potential defects in the pattern being printed, preventative measures can be taken with AI analyzing complex simulation data and optimizing the design of photomasks to minimize distortion and ensure precise feature placement on the wafer. Other applications include monitoring and adjusting key lithography **parameters** in real time, leading to improved process stability and yield while performing complex simulations of the lithography process much faster than traditional methods, allowing for rapid design iterations with convolutional **neural networks** (CNNs) employed to analyze image data effectively identifying patterns and defects on the wafer. Integrated with physics-based simulations of the lithography process, key parameters like light diffraction and material properties are incorporated identifying and preventing potential defects, significantly increasing the percentage of usable chips produced. AI-powered mask optimization can also significantly reduce the time needed to design new chip layouts that, by optimizing the manufacturing process through AI, can lead to reduced material usage and waste. Generating vast amounts of complex data, lithography requires sophisticated data processing techniques that AI algorithms can effectively analyze.

Confronting sanctions and export controls on AI technologies imposed by the United States in the 2020s, the People's Republic of China (PRC) has been unable to purchase the advanced extreme ultraviolet (EUV) lithographic technology on the international market including from the ASML Corporation in Holland, the top global producer. Restricted to acquiring previous generation deep ultraviolet (DUV) systems, lithography in the PRC is capped at 5 nanometer production with Shanghai Micro Electronics Equipment Company as a major Chinese lithography equipment manufacturer which was ironically fostered by American-imposed sanctions. Providing an incentive for the development of photonics, a technology combining silicon-based integrated circuits and optical components to process and transmit massive amounts of data without employing EUV lithography, Chinese scientists have achieved a major breakthrough in integrated photonic quantum chips by demonstrating the first "continuous-variable" quantum multipartite entanglement and cluster states on a chip. Laying the foundation for scalable quantum entanglement, the breakthrough addresses a critical gap in the development of photonic quantum chips with potential applications in **quantum computing** and quantum networks making for advanced platforms designed to encode, process, transmit, and store quantum information at the chip level.

LOGISTICS (*HOUQIN*). With its widespread networks, logistics is an ideal application area for artificial intelligence (AI) that is capable of improving efficiency and **customer service** while optimizing network performance, especially in an increasingly globalized **economy**. Major contributions of AI to national and international logistical systems include predicting future production and **transportation** volumes that allow companies to deploy scarce resources more efficiently and assert better control over costs along with identifying patterns and relationships in moving goods from warehouses to distribution centers. Replacing traditional maintenance schedules based on time or usage, AI allows for **predictive maintenance**, employing **machine learning (ML)** and **computer vision (CV)** to analyze data from sensors on equipment and detect damage to delivered goods that minimizes losses and ensures better customer satisfaction. Assisting customer service teams to work faster and more efficiently, AI makes for better handling of requests and provides real-time suggestions that empower employees to eliminate or reduce time-consuming tasks and unnecessary inefficiencies. The value of AI to the global logistics market is expected to grow from $12 billion in 2023 to $549 billion by 2033.

In the case of the People's Republic of China (PRC), AI solutions to logistics are being pursued in earnest by a host of Chinese **companies** with major investments in AI-powered tools for enhancing firm decision-making and improving overall **supply chain** efficiency. Most notable is the deployment of **smart** logistics equipment, namely various types of **robots**, such as automated guided vehicles (AGVs), rail guided vehicles (RGVs), autonomous mobile robots (AMRs), and palletizing robots. Along with this integration of robots into logistics operations in the PRC has come automated sorting systems and mobile robots that assist with picking and packing, robots to significantly enhance transportation and sorting efficiency in warehousing and transportation while mitigating risks associated with human operational errors. As robots become more prevalent in the smart logistics industry, new human–machine relationships are emerging, with human–robot partnerships becoming a potent tool for enhancing warehouse handling efficiency in a national economy long notorious for waste, loss of products, and low **productivity**.

M

MACHINE LEARNING (*JIQI XUEXI*). A subset of artificial intelligence (AI), machine learning (ML) focuses on the role of **algorithms** in enabling **computers** to learn from data patterns without explicit programming that improves performance through **training** and experience and with an overarching goal of creating intelligent machines by performing tasks that typically require human thinking. Along with **natural language processing (NLP)**, **computer vision (CV)**, and **robotics**, machine learning is a specific technique within AI to analyze data and identify patterns that allow computers to make predictions or make decisions without an explicit program for each potential scenario while improving performance over time. Examples of machine learning include, among others, an **autonomous driving** vehicle that navigates roads using a combination of sensors, computer vision, and decision-making algorithms; a spam filter that learns to identify spam emails based on patterns in previous emails, improving its accuracy with more data; scheduling of **predictive maintenance** for machinery and equipment; **insurance** fraud detection; and retail sales demand forecasting. Freeing coding from the task of generating entirely new codes to deal with new or unforeseen situations or problems, ML makes machines more human-like with a capacity to adjust to a constantly changing environment by learning and improving from experience. While AI and machine learning are often used interchangeably, the latter is considered a subset of the broader category of AI.

Experiencing rapid growth in the People's Republic of China (PRC) in the 2020s, machine learning has benefited from significant government investment along with large pools of data and applications to **finance**, manufacturing, and health care that put the technology at the core of the country's devotion to AI. With a large population and extensive digital infrastructure crucial to training powerful machine learning models, major companies heavily invested in ML research and development include **Alibaba**, **Baidu**, and Tencent with applications to **voice** and **facial recognition**,

smart manufacturing, personalized products and services. As McKinsey & Company has reported, China is a tour-de-force in machine learning exemplified by high-performance models, such as **DeepSeek** R1, natural language processing-backed models in image recognition, and fast-tracked home-made AI chip development exemplified by Ascend of **Huawei**, while quickly closing the gap in machine learning with top-notch U.S. companies.

MAPPING (*YINGSHE*). Employing major artificial intelligence (AI) tools such as **machine learning (ML)** to analyze large **data sets**, mapping has undergone a fundamental transformation with enhanced features of improving navigation, data integration, and utilization of **robotics**. With AI tools analyzing traffic patterns, road conditions, and user preference to suggest the best possible routes, more personalized navigation is offered with the global positioning system (GPS) improving in areas with limited map data generating mappings between source and target schemas and learning from user-created data to produce more accurate mappings. Relying on robots to create and update maps utilizing cameras and LIDAR to locate landmarks and other features, AI can also analyze photographs of previous floods to estimate water levels and map flood flashpoints allowing for more proactive flood defense and overall improved environmental monitoring, urban and disaster planning, and natural resource management with **Google** Maps as a prime commercial example of AI-powered mapping.

Significant advancements in utilizing AI technology for mapping applications have been achieved in the People's Republic of China (PRC) including detailed geographic data analysis, urban planning, and environmental monitoring with vast collections of raw data. Leading the globe in mapping initiatives employing AI, the PRC has generated more **patent** filings than either the United States or **Japan**, with major cities including Beijing, Shanghai, and Shenzhen at the forefront, building the necessary infrastructure for mapping applications in the creation of **smart** cities, though with concerns over Chinese government use of the technology for mass **surveillance**. Benefits include real-time monitoring of natural disasters, especially flooding and earthquakes that frequently befall the country, using AI-powered analysis of satellite imagery, along with tracking pollution levels, deforestation, and changes in land use with advanced geospatial analysis. Major Chinese **companies** such as **Alibaba**, **Baidu**, **Huawei**, and Tencent have integrated mapping technologies into their services, with research conducted by Tsinghua University backed by government support.

MARKET FORECASTING (SHICHANG YUCE). With a capacity for **predictive analytics** based on voluminous amounts of raw data, artificial intelligence (AI) has been employed in various types of market forecasting, especially for **financial** sectors such as stocks and mutual funds. In the case of the former, AI-powered analytical tools are trained to digest corporate disclosures, industry trends, and macroeconomic indicators that surpass most human analysts in making stock return predictions. Demonstrating a superior capacity to process reams of data absent predictable human biases due to material incentives or psychological traits, AI models compared to lower-skilled analysts were able to generate superior returns and generally matched the performance of the best analysts with a reputation for beating the overall market. Only in cases where institutional knowledge such as intangible assets and financial distress were crucial did the human analyst outperform the AI model, especially in predicting returns for smaller and less liquid brokerage firms. Where information affecting stock prices is voluminous but also transparent, the AI model performs best but with the combination of **machine learning (ML)** and human forecasts producing the overall best results and less likely to make extreme errors. The combined model leverages the complementary strengths of both AI and humans, with the former excelling in processing large volumes of data and **pattern recognition**, while the latter adds nuanced understanding and contextual insights, resulting in a more robust and reliable forecasting tool. Overall, AI augments the capabilities of human analysts, adding incremental value to their work and synergies with AI modeling, especially in unusual and fast-evolving situations. In the case of mutual funds, in contrast, the performance of AI-powered funds was statistically indistinguishable from the aggregate market, generating no significant risk-adjusted returns and showing only marginally superior stock-selection skills and no market-timing skills. Only in cases of lower turnover did AI-powered funds outperform human-managed peers, resulting in lower transaction costs and marginally superior stock-selection skills holding fewer stocks in the portfolio and avoiding some prevalent human behavioral biases.

In the case of the People's Republic of China (PRC), although the domestic stock markets in Shenzhen, Shanghai, and Beijing remain relatively small scale and undercapitalized, AI has been employed to gauge market sentiment and to engage in pattern recognition relying on data from newspaper articles, **social media** posts, earnings reports, and government announcements. Processing real-time information and actionable insights faster than human analysts, sophisticated AI models have been developed to analyze millions of data points daily most notably by AI Laboratory offered by Tencent, Damo Academy by **Alibaba**, and High-Flyer developed by Liang Wenfeng, founder of **DeepSeek**. Along with predicting price movements, these models offer nuanced insights into the major factors affecting stock movements including macroeconomic trends and public sentiment on social media sites such as

WeChat. Overall, **algorithmic** trading powered by AI has grown substantially in the PRC executing trades based on pre-set rules and real-time data analysis often completing transactions in microseconds learning from market conditions and adapting strategies dynamically. **Companies** such as Ping'An Technology have also developed proprietary trading platforms that leverage AI to optimize portfolio management and reduce trading risks as high-frequency trading (HFT) has found a place in the country's stock markets with AI and **big data** providing the speed and precision required for HFT. Also available are more personalized advisory services that expand public access to sophisticated investment advice with platforms Ant Fortune of Ant Group, an offshoot of **Alibaba**, using AI to offer personalized financial advice to retail investors. These AI-driven robo-advisers analyze individual financial goals, risk appetites, and market conditions to recommend tailored investment strategies with forward-looking recommendations which are not just based on historical performance. For many first-time investors, a common phenomenon in the PRC, these tools provide a level of guidance that was previously only available to high-net-worth individuals with access to costly human financial advisers. AI and big data have also become indispensable for regulators and financial institutions alike with the China Securities Regulatory Commission (CSRC) leveraging AI to monitor market activity, ensuring compliance and detecting anomalies and possible cases of fraud. *See also* ANTI-FRAUD.

MATHEMATICS (*SHUXUE*). A fundamental component of artificial intelligence (AI) with developments dating back to the 1850s, mathematics has been at the core of AI since its inception, with mathematicians such as **Alan Turing**, Bertrand Russell, and **Wu Wenjun** playing a pivotal role in shaping the foundations of AI applications. Providing the tools and concepts that enable AI to process data, learn, and make decisions, AI **algorithms** are built on mathematical principles and rely on mathematical equations and functions to perform essential tasks. Major mathematical fields employed in AI include the following: linear algebra which is used to represent and manipulate data and is important for tasks such as image recognition, **natural language processing (NLP)**, and developing **neural networks**; calculus used to optimize AI models by minimizing errors and adjusting **parameters** and developing techniques such as gradient descent and **backpropagation**; probability theory and statistics drawing on Bayesian theorem for NLP, **computer vision (CV)**, and decision-making; optimization theory as the foundation for **training** and refining AI models; Gaussian bell-shaped curve distribution; and support vector machines (SVMs), a mathematical framework used for classification and regression tasks. In the realm of mathematics **education**,

AI provides personalized instruction and adaptive assessments, with AI algorithms employed to analyze student data and make personalized questions and examinations. With the potential to transform multiple industries, the combination of mathematics and AI has the capacity to solve complex problems and improve the overall quality of life.

With a long history of excellence in mathematics throughout Chinese history, including during the period of the People's Republic of China (PRC) from 1949 to the present, employment of AI models in the field has been extensive. Examples include the development of a group of mathematics-specific **large language models (LLMs)** by **Alibaba** called Tongyi Qianwen 2, with a capacity to solve arithmetic and complex mathematical problems utilizing an **open-source model**. Controversy involving AI and mathematics also occurred with the report that a 17-year-old fashion school student in the PRC had actually defeated an AI team in a mathematical contest in 2024.

MEDICAL IMAGING (*YIXUE YINGXIANG*). Employed in the detection of hazardous medical conditions such as bone fractures and dislocations that standard imaging often misses, medical imaging utilizing artificial intelligence (AI) tools has the capacity to spot subtle variations and anomalies. Deploying unbiased **algorithms**, AI tools work in various medical fields such as radiology by automating routine tasks, analyzing medical data, prioritizing urgent cases, and improving diagnostic accuracy, producing improved patient outcomes while meeting the growing demand for radiological services and mitigating physician burnout.

Beginning with the *Healthy China 2030 Initiative* enacted in 2016 aimed at modernizing the health care infrastructure in the People's Republic of China (PRC), medical imaging employing AI tools has been deployed to automatically detect physical maladies such as rib fractures, lung nodules, and lesions from X-ray or computed tomography (CT) scans, providing detailed animations for further analysis. With a goal of reducing physician workloads, improving diagnostic accuracy and treatment planning, and standardizing health care processes, AI in medical imaging is a major component for addressing chronic diseases in the country such as coronary disease and cancer, bringing better access to health care, especially in rural areas through digital technologies while issuing **regulations** to govern data security and **privacy**.

MICROSOFT (*WEIRUAN*). Guided by a belief that artificial intelligence (AI) is the "defining technology of our time," Microsoft has been at the forefront of cutting-edge research on AI, integrating the powerful technology into major product lines and **customer services**. Included are advanced reasoning and multimodal capabilities in the Copilot **chatbot** available on Windows PC and various AI tools and models such as Phi-3 offered in the Microsoft Azure cloud **computing** platform and Dynamics 365 composed of various business services such as **finance** and **supply chain** management. Stressing such principles as reliability, **privacy**, safety, and security for building AI systems, Microsoft provides billions of AI experiences daily in Windows, Xbox, Microsoft 365, Teams, Azure AI, Power Platform, Dynamics 365, and Microsoft Defender.

Opening a first office in the People's Republic of China (PRC) in 1992, Microsoft China is drawn to the large pool of AI talent available in the country with operations concentrating on research and development (R&D) led by the Microsoft Research Laboratory in Beijing. Employing approximately 9,000 staff across the country with Microsoft Cloud and AI China (C+AI China) established in 2005, work teams participated in global research and development for cloud computing, **big data**, **Internet of Things (IoT)**, Dynamics 365, and **e-commerce** with regional Azure services provided through local **data centers**, including AI cognitive services and solutions. Also established is Microsoft Asia-Pacific Technology Co MATL as a wholly owned subsidiary of Microsoft in June 2014 which promotes partnerships with industries by serving regional markets, cultivating local talent, and uplifting global and Chinese cloud innovation with the PRC constituting 1.5 percent of total global sales for the company. In May 2024, Microsoft was reported by CNN to have asked approximately 700 to 800 China-based engineers and computing staff to consider relocating to other countries in the midst of rising U.S.-China technology disputes, though Microsoft would continue with operations in China.

MILITARY APPLICATIONS (*JUNSHI XINGDONG*). With a potential to shape nearly every aspect of warfare from procurement to ground and aerial combat, artificial intelligence (AI), including **machine learning (ML)**, can boost the tempo of military operations in various ways including strategies and battle management, **logistics**, defense innovations, and training and maintenance procedures. Processing large amounts of data in real time, AI can promote **intelligence gathering** by analyzing satellite images and **drone** video feeds to understand developments on the battlefield and help commanders make more accurate decisions while facilitating the use of unmanned aircraft to carry out especially dangerous operations, reducing combat fatalities. With the capacity for **predictive maintenance** along with **weather forecasting** and space observation, AI can maximize a platform's readiness and longevity, strengthen measures for force protection, and reduce the need for full human control of warfare systems such as aviation deployment and support, navigation, and **surveillance**, while freeing up personnel time for other, more creative tasks. International legal challenges to utilizing AI for military operations include applications of the Geneva Convention Additional Protocol I to weapons systems that incorporate AI.

In the case of the People's Republic of China (PRC), the application of AI to the military includes an emphasis by the People's Liberation Army (PLA) on developing unmanned intelligent combat systems, enhancing battlefield awareness and decision-making, conducting multi-domain offense and defense, and facilitating advanced training, simulation, and wargaming practices. With a goal of disrupting traditional ways to wage wars, the PLA is looking to unmanned aerial vehicles (UAVs), platforms, and weapons powered by AI including the "Rainbow" (Caihong) high-altitude UAV for reconnaissance and strike missions along with the Sharp-Sword-11 high-altitude supersonic speed stealth reconnaissance UAV. Also studied is the so-called "swarming" concept of collaborative operation by a large group of UAVs in a complicated electromagnetic environment that emulates the successful experience of advanced militaries along with anti-UAV countermeasures to offset the first-move advantage of other countries. Reinforced by AI-enabled technology, speed and accuracy can be enhanced in battlefield reconnaissance, surveillance, and communication; electronic inference and radar deception; combat assessment; and fire guidance with improvement of real-time situational awareness and decision-making on the battlefield. By developing **deep learning** methods, intelligent missiles and shells can be produced to identify targets and their weaknesses, evade interceptors, and conduct end-phase maneuvering, which will bolster both the first-strike and retaliatory capacities of the PLA. Intensive sensors facilitated by machine learning technology will process the intelligence captured at a flashing speed so that the time between identifying targets and attacking targets is radically reduced, increasing the rate of fire. Installing AI systems will change the way PLA moves and maneuvers on the battlefield, as in a world that is becoming one giant sensor, hiding and penetrating will be far more difficult with AI technology helping to identify the weaknesses of enemy defense lines and improve routine planning by enhancing situational awareness capacity. In an era that is overloaded by the high volume of information, a new challenge facing the Chinese military is the effective processing of huge amounts of raw intelligence and the accurate interpretation of the real meaning behind information flows. With the reinforcement of AI, both offensive and defensive capabilities of the Chinese military in nuclear, cyber, and space domains will be consolidated and improved including the performance of aerial combat with AI tools employed to improve tactical maneuvers and overall aircraft performance with AI-controlled drone swarms deployed in targeted regions of potential confrontations and armed conflict. On the geopolitical front, the PRC apparently used AI tools to target ships from the Philippines in an ongoing dispute over territorial waters in the South China Sea in 2024. *See also* CYBER SECURITY.

MULTI-AGENT SYSTEMS (*DUO ZHINENG TI XITONG*). A core area of artificial intelligence (AI) research that involves multiple AI agents working together to achieve goals, multi-agent systems (MAS) are a significant advancement allowing agents to share information and solve problems that would be difficult for a single agent. Major characteristics of MAS include collaboration with agents interacting and sharing crucial data, autonomy as each agent operates independently rendering decisions based on its specific programming and particular **data sets**, and decentralized decision-making with intelligence spread across multiple agents allowing for performance geared to changing circumstances. Areas of MAS application include **autonomous driving**, multi-**robot** factories, automated trading, commercial gaming, automated tutoring in **education**, decentralized control of **robotics**, and **electrical grids** employing **smart technology**, resource allocation in peer-to-peer networks, and collaborative sensing in environmental monitoring. Potential risks of the technology include use of access to web browsers, **software** systems, or personal banking and **financial** information for fraudulent and other nefarious purposes.

A major area of AI research and development in the People's Republic of China (PRC), multi-agent systems have been extensively employed particularly to large data sets that require coordinated but autonomous decision-making. Backed by major Chinese government initiatives and relying on extensive data collection from the country's vast population, MAS has been applied to diverse fields such as smart electrical grids, **transportation** management, health care, and industrial automation with research on the technology on decision-making **algorithms**, distributed intelligence, and collaborative learning. Real-world applications include optimizing roadway traffic flows by coordinating traffic lights and vehicle routes in the country's crowded urban areas, coordination of **factory** machine operations, and assisting in rescue efforts and emergency responses to natural and man-made disasters such as floods, earthquakes, and major transportation accidents.

MYTHS (*SHENHUA*). As with many new technologies, the emergence of artificial intelligence (AI) has generated a host of myths propagated by **social media** and other outlets ironically powered by AI tools and applications and generally based on a poor understanding of the science behind the technology and its impactful cultural influences. Among the most popular is a widespread belief that the prevalence of AI will lead to the creation of an uncontrollable army of **robots** with a capacity for **self-replication** that will lead a rebellion against human beings. Spurred on by popular **science fiction** works such as the *Terminator* movie series and sensational novels by writers, most notably Isaac Asimov, this apocalyptic vision ignores the role of human **computer** programming governing and dictating AI applications, including robots, that so far has effectively prevented total AI "self-awareness." Based on **algorithms** and analysis of statistical patterns, AI systems lack the consciousness and subjective experience fundamental to human thinking required for truly independent and rogue acts. Also inaccurate is the belief that AI will ultimately replace humans entirely in the workplace wreaking havoc on **employment** when AI is generally designed to complement human abilities by automating certain largely routine activities leaving truly creative tasks and processes to humans. Contrary to the view that AI is only for large **companies** especially tech giants, many everyday applications involve AI such as **facial recognition**, digital voice assistants, and social media. While AI has historical and ethical limitations often embedded in the **training** of **data sets**, the technology is not inherently biased or immoral when it comes to decision-making and data analysis. Often described as a mysterious, magical "black box," AI is an umbrella term for various **computer** engineering techniques, including **machine learning (ML)**, optimization techniques, rule-based systems, and **natural language processing (NLP)**. That AI algorithms can make sense of the most confusing and messy data with a so-called "load and go" capacity, is also a misconception as the lack of quality data cannot be magically reconfigured by even the best algorithm. Claims that AI solutions can simply be pointed at any and all types of data with powerful machines producing a valuable output ignore the long-standing principle still relevant in the AI era of "garbage in, garbage out" as data that is too broad or improperly processed cannot be made digestible to a system that requires information and content to be carefully curated and of high quality.

Given the rapid introduction of AI into many sectors of the **economy** and society since 2017, popular myths have surrounded the technology in the People's Republic of China (PRC) with reservations similar to those raised in the West but with decidedly less apocalyptic visions of an AI dystopia. While the government under the rule of the Chinese Communist Party (CCP) has wholeheartedly supported a prime role for AI in Chinese life, philosophers trained in traditional Confucianism, Daoism, and Buddhism have often lamented the possibility of diminishing human autonomy and free will in the age of data manipulation and automation, as well as the potential loss of purpose and meaning of human life. Other more scientifically oriented commentators are concerned about the eagerness to tinker with the human genome and the natural process of evolution to achieve greater longevity and physical well-being. Most alarming, especially to Confucian scholars, are developments in AI and robotics that could negatively impact familial relationships and elder care, traditional centerpieces of Chinese culture. While generally bereft of the visions of robot domination and control so appealing to Western minds, examples in Chinese **science fiction** of a dystopian AI future include the film *The Three-Body Problem.* Turning myth into reality in the era of AI is best exemplified by Chinese-designed humanoid **robots** that danced a storm at China's 2026 celebration of the Year of Fire Horse. Straight punches, side punches, palm strikes, knife hand strikes, forward and back flipping mixed with tiger claws and horse sprints, the school of humanoid robots dressed in traditional festivity hues of red and yellow danced in unison with no bumping and no falling, practically bona fide Kung Fu masters! Pivotal to the technological development of humanoid robots are leading companies such as AgiBot and UniTree, with a collective goal of improving technology while reducing cost, making humanoid robots more affordable with more comprehensive areas of applications." (coming at the end of this entry with blank bottom of the page, longer text should have no impact on pagination).

N

NATURAL LANGUAGE PROCESSING (*ZIRAN YUYAN CHULI*). A subfield of artificial intelligence (AI) that enables **computers** to understand and interact with human language, natural language processing (NLP) allows machines to analyze and generate meaningful text, effectively establishing a bridge between machine technology and humans. Utilizing **algorithms** and other techniques to analyze the structure and meaning of text, NLP engages in such tasks as **sentiment analysis**, which detects the emotional tone of a message, along with machine translation, recognition of named entities, and text summarization as applied to **chatbots**, **virtual assistants**, language translation tools, **software** for sentiment analysis, and information retrieval systems. Core components of NLP include lexical analysis, the breaking down of text into individual words to analyze their meaning, syntactic analysis for understanding the grammatical structure of sentences, and semantic analysis for interpreting the meaning of words and phrases in context. Leveraging **machine learning (ML)** algorithms to train models on large **data sets** produces improved accuracy in understanding the nuances of meaning in complex language structures parsing the syntax of words, phrases, and sentences.

Driven by government support for AI development and the large digital population in the People's Republic of China (PRC), NLP has undergone rapid growth but with unique features posed by the character-based Chinese language with multiple dialects leading to highly specialized versions of NLP algorithms and tools designed for the Chinese markets. Industries employing NLP include **e-commerce** with chatbots offered in **customer service** and product recommendation, **finance** for fraud detection and market sentiment analysis, medicine and health care with medical text analysis and support systems for clinical diagnostics, and in **social media** analysis of online discussions and trend identifications. Major PRC-based **companies** involved in NLP with substantial investments in research and development include **Alibaba**, **Baidu**, **Huawei**, and Tencent that operate in accordance with strict data protection **laws and regulations** governing data **privacy** that play a significant role in the implementation of NLP.

NEURAL NETWORKS (*SHENJING WANGLUO*). A type of artificial intelligence (AI) employing a **machine learning (ML)** program or model, **neural networks (NN)**, also known as artificial or simulated neural networks, provide instructions to **computers** on the processing of data that mimic the human brain. Composed of interconnected nodes, known as neurons, organized into layers with each neuron receiving input from a previous layer and constituting a mathematical function, results are passed from one layer to another with the neural network learning from **training** data which improves network accuracy over time. Considered the backbone of **algorithms** engaged in **deep learning**, neural networks are powerful tools for classifying and clustering data performing such tasks as image recognition in a matter of minutes. Major drawbacks of neural networks include the need for strong parallel processing power as millions of data points are required to produce positive results. Often referred to as "black boxes," neural networks generally lack transparency as to the exact procedure for achieving results. Major AI tools employing neural networks include **computer vision (CV)**, **speech** and **facial recognition**, and **natural language processing (NLP)** especially for **chatbots** with major industries and functions including medical diagnosis by **medical image** classification, targeted **marketing** by social network filtering and behavioral data analysis, **financial** predictions drawn from historical data, electrical load and **energy** demand forecasting, chemical compound identification, and quality control of production processes.

A high priority in the People's Republic of China (PRC), development of neural networks is a key component in the national strategy of becoming a global leader in AI by 2030. With research focused on "brain-inspired" AI that mimics the neural pathways of the human brain, particular emphasis in neural network applications includes energy-efficient **computing** with applications across manufacturing, national defense, health care, **autonomous driving**, **education**, and **surveillance**. In terms of brain-inspired neural networks, research focuses on spiking neural networks and other neural architectures that potentially lead to more efficient AI models led by major **companies** such as **Alibaba**, **Baidu**, SenseTime, and Tencent with a focus on creating **large language models (LLM)** and advanced facial recognition technology. Novel Chinese computing architectures include the Hodgkin-Huxley (HH) network with rich internal complexity where each artificial neuron is an HH model.

NEUROIMAGING (*SHENJING YINGXIANG XUE*). Increasing efficiency and reducing errors in neuroimaging, artificial intelligence (AI) is an important resource utilizing increasing amounts of data processing and image interpretation with an overall improvement in the quality of patient care. Advantages include an ability to read computed tomography (CT) scans, magnetic resonance imaging, and positron emission tomography with reduced or without contrast and without loss in sensitivity for detecting lesions and neurologic conditions which holds promise in combating ever-increasing image volumes and providing timely diagnosis though the process is subject to possible bias. In the case of the People's Republic of China (PRC), neuroimaging is the province of the Artificial Intelligence Research Center for Neurological Disorders at the Beijing Tiantan Hospital along with a research team from the Capital Medical University. Employing an AI system known as BioMind, improvements were achieved in the diagnosis of brain tumors and prediction of hematoma expansion compared to the performance of senior doctors.

NVIDIA CORPORATION (*YINGWEIDA GONGSI*). A global leader in the research and development of essential hardware to power artificial intelligence (AI), Nvidia was founded in 1993 and is currently headed by Jensen Huang. Most notable is the company's production of **graphic processing units (GPUs)** as the essential hardware to meet the great demands of AI systems serving as specialized, superfast parallel processors for managing massive amounts of data drawn from a wide variety of sources with an almost infinite capacity for data storage. Recent developments include the Nvidia DGX-2tm employing 16 GPUs as a powerful tool for AI **training**, delivering to data teams two petaflops, two quadrillion floating-point operations per second, for training performance. Application programming interfaces (APIs) of highly portable bundles of code have also been produced that allow developers and data scientists to integrate AI functionally into current products such as describing data and detecting insights and underlying patterns. Also pursued is the development of a portfolio of technologies involving humanoid **robots** including Groot N1, the world's first fully customizable **foundational model** for generalized humanoid reasoning and skills, and Newton, an **open-source** physics engine under development with **Google** DeepMind and Disney Research.

Involved in the growing AI market in the People's Republic of China (PRC) for several years, Nvidia concentrated on selling GPUs but with restrictions imposed by the United States in October 2022 on its A100 and H100 processors which led the company to offer the less powerful A800 and H800 chips that were designed as a workaround to comply with export **regulations**. The company has also enhanced research capabilities and staff focusing on new **autonomous driving** technologies, with 4,000 people gainfully employed at the start of 2024. Regarding the issue of selling more advanced micro semiconductor chips to the PRC, Jensen Huang commented in an interview conducted on CNBC in October 2025 that "It's in the best interest of America to serve the China market. It's in the best interest of China to have American technology." Wanting to provide AI developers and enterprises with a business-ready foundation for creating advanced agentic AI capable of working independently or as connected teams, the company announced production in April 2025 of a family of Llama Nemotron models with reasoning capabilities to solve increasingly complex tasks. While designed for the purpose of **inference**, sales of the H20 to China require a special license instituted in 2025 by the US government.

O

OPEN AI (*KAIFANG RENGONG ZHINENG*). An American artificial intelligence (AI) research organization founded in December 2015 with Sam Altman as chief executive officer (CEO), Open AI is best known for the **ChatGPT** family of **large language models (LLMs)**. With a stated mission of developing "safe and beneficial" **artificial generative intelligence (AGI)**, Open AI has created "highly autonomous systems that outperform humans at the most economically valuable work," including text-to-image and text-to-video models, with ChatGPT released in November 2022. Registered as a nonprofit incorporation with a for-profit subsidiary, 49 percent of equity in Open AI is owned by **Microsoft** which provides **computing** resources through the Microsoft Azure cloud platform. Multiple lawsuits were filed against the company in 2023 and 2024 for alleged copyright infringement citing utilization of writings and media works in **training** Open AI products as many AI safety researchers left the company in 2024. Vowing to "freely collaborate" with other institutions and researchers, the company has made its **patents** and research as an **open source** to the public.

In the case of the People's Republic of China (PRC), Open AI has significantly restricted access to services such as ChatGPT due to geopolitical concerns and regulations. Being blocked to users in the PRC, Chinese developers cannot utilize Open AI technology to build local applications reflecting increasing tensions between the PRC and the United States and concerns over data privacy and potential misuse of AI technology. Seeking alternative solutions, Chinese companies and research laboratories have developed their own models, with DeepSeek developing a model that reportedly outperforms ChatGPT utilizing the H800 chips produced by the **Nvidia Corporation**.

OPEN-SOURCE MODELS (*KAIYUAN MOXING*). Systems of artificial intelligence (AI) that are made available for widespread use, modification, and study, open-source models refer to the practice by **companies**

of developing and sharing their AI technology, including **large language models (LLMs)**, for use by the public. Contrary to **closed-source models**, open-source models are made available under licenses that grant freedoms to users including utilizing the system for any purpose without a requirement to seek permission from the developer, studying how the system operates and inspecting its components, and modifying the system for different purposes including altering its output. Well-known open-source models include TensorFlow, a **machine learning (ML)** platform developed by **Google** and compatible with programming languages like Python and JavaScript; PyTorch, an AI framework developed by the Meta AI Research Laboratory that is integrated with Python libraries and supports acceleration of **graphic processing units (GPUs)**; Keras, an open-source **software** library that provides a Python interface artificial **neural network**; and Scikit-learn, a tool for ML and **predictive analytics** built on Python libraries and offering various **algorithms** for supervised and **unsupervised learning**.

Considered a cornerstone in the global AI strategy of the People's Republic of China (PRC), open-source models are generally employed by Chinese companies as a means to induce innovation and build an AI developer community across the globe. This includes major PRC AI companies such as **Alibaba**, **Baidu**, **DeepSeek**, and Tencent which, despite a higher bar for accessing their products than Western counterparts, embrace open-source technology to lure overseas audiences into utilizing their models. Most notable is the popularity of PRC models on Hugging Face, a repository of LLMs, where Alibaba's Tongyi Qianwen is one of the most popular downloads due to its excellent performance on competitive benchmarks without a need for extensive legal reviews, coming in various sizes and **parameters** including relatively small ones with lower computational costs.

OPERATIONS RESEARCH (*YUNCHOU XUE*). Providing a capacity for analyzing and detecting patterns in complex **data sets**, artificial intelligence (AI) enhances the decision-making capability of operations research (OR), making for more optimized solutions to operational problems. Industries benefiting from the combination of AI and OR include **supply chain** management, production planning, and resource allocation, with AI empowering OR to render better data-driven decisions by automating complex calculations and providing insights often overlooked by traditional OR methodologies. Utilizing **machine learning (ML)** and **algorithms**, more efficient solutions are offered within OR models, refining and improving the optimization process as AI tackles the intricate real-world problems employing numerous variables unavailable in traditional OR and automating tasks such as data collection and preliminary analysis, freeing up human expertise for more strategic decision-making. Examples of AI applications to OR include demand forecasting, with AI models providing greater accuracy in **prediction analytics**, leading to optimized inventory management; optimizing schedules for production lines with better determination of machine capacity, worker availability, and maintenance requirements; route optimization minimizing travel time and cost for **logistics** operations; and optimal resource allocation by utilizing data to adjust resources in a changing environment. Requiring high-quality data to function effectively, which is a challenge in all real-world operational environments, integrating AI algorithms with OR requires significant **computing** power in an interdisciplinary field that leverages mathematical models and scientific methods.

Backed by substantial support from the government of the People's Republic of China (PRC), integration of AI and operations research has undergone significant advancement in optimizing complex operations in manufacturing, logistics, and the military. Producing a large volume of research, AI is deployed throughout the manufacturing sector including supply chain optimization and product demand prediction while developing **military** applications such as unmanned aerial vehicles (UAVs) and combat simulations. But while excelling in AI research quantity, translating that research into truly innovative and original applications remains a challenge with room for improvement. Leading institutions for AI and operations research in the PRC include Peking University, Tsinghua University, Zhejiang University, and the University of Science and Technology, with major **publications** including the *Journal of the Operations Research Society of China.*

P

PARAMETERS (*CANSHU*). Serving as the internal variables within a **machine learning (ML)** model that are adjusted during the critical process of training, **parameters** act as the knobs that the model tweaks to learn from data and make accurate predictions based on input. Defining how the artificial intelligence (AI) model transforms input data into the desired output, parameters in greater numbers allow for more complex **pattern recognition** and potentially greater accuracy. The core elements that determine how a model processes information and generates outputs, parameters are comparable to the weights employed in a **neural network** as the model analyzes data and automatically adjusts its parameters to minimize prediction errors, with the quality and configuration of a model's parameters directly influencing its accuracy and ability to generalize to new data. While more complex models with larger numbers of parameters are able to learn more intricate patterns, an excessive number of parameters may lead to overfitting. In the case of **ChatGPT**-4, the number of parameters is estimated at 1.76 trillion embedded in eight models, each with 220 billion parameters, allowing for advanced reasoning and formatting. In the case of the People's Republic of China (PRC), **large language models (LLMs)** have employed a high number of parameters; for example, the one trillion-parameter AI model developed by China Telecom relies solely on domestically produced **semiconductor** chips to train the model, despite export controls on advanced chips imposed by the United States.

PATENTS (*ZHUANLI*). On the issue of inventorship, an artificial intelligence (AI) system cannot under current rules be listed as an inventor on patent applications, a status reserved for any natural person who makes significant contributions to an invention. In cases where AI assisted in the conception and actualization of an invention, the contribution of the natural person must accord with the Pannu factors of having made a significant contribution to the conception and development of the final product. Where the contribution of the natural person is in merely presenting a problem to an AI system and does not constitute an essential building block from which the invention is derived, a patent award is not accorded. Top **companies** awarded AI utility patents in 2024 with total number of patents in parentheses are IBM (1,211), Alphabet (870), Samsung (750), and Amazon (541). Specific examples include **Google** for development of the **transformer** technology for **ChatGPT** involving a "dropout" function that disregards certain inputs during the **machine learning (ML)** process, along with an AI system that allows users to navigate a **computer** without the use of a keyboard or mouse by responding to user oral commands and posing questions to better understand user requests. Patents have also been awarded for a method of **training** a **neural network** to detect anomalies in network traffic by dropping malicious network packets in real time and blocking future traffic from the source address. **Large language models (LLMs)** and media trained models that generate images, audio, and video have also been patented along with a video camera and curve-fitting technique for measuring atmospheric visibility as a form of AI component technology developed at the University of Minnesota.

A global leader in AI patents for several years, especially in **artificial generative intelligence (AGI)**, the People's Republic of China (PRC) in accord with international patent law has been awarded 378,000 AI-related patents with six times more AGI patents than the United States and 40 percent of all international patent applications in 2023. With **Baidu** as the largest owner of active AI and ML patents worldwide, major fields of patented technology in the PRC include medical devices, automobiles, aerospace, industrial control, and **telecommunications**. Contributing factors to the prominence of AI patents in the PRC include the "Made in China 2025" (*Zhongguo zhi zao* 2025) plan and the establishment with Chinese government backing of AI industrial parks and clusters in major urban areas along with the introduction of deep neural networks and LLMs since 2017.

PATTERN RECOGNITION (*MOSHI SHIBIE*). A method in data analysis that employs the **algorithms** of **machine learning (ML)** to automatically recognize patterns and regularities in large **data sets**, pattern recognition can be applied to text, images, or sounds, detecting familiar patterns quickly and accurately. Primary types include **supervised**, **unsupervised**, and **deep learning**, each of which involves distinctive approaches to identifying and interpreting patterns within data. Serving as an essential component of various AI applications, pattern recognition plays a crucial role in enhancing data analysis from extensive data sets that foster more informed decision-making and enable predictive capabilities with recurrent patterns that, by anticipating future trends and behavior, empower organizations to forecast outcomes and substantially mitigate risks. Real-world applications are multifaceted including in health care by analyzing intricate patterns in **medical imaging** and patient data, **finance** by detecting highly sophisticated fraudulent activities with advanced pattern recognition techniques, and in **cyber security**. Common methods include supervised learning involving the **training** of AI model using labeled input data, with the system learning to map inputs to outputs instrumental in tasks such as image and **speech recognition**; unsupervised learning with models trained on unlabeled data, making possible the discovery of hidden patterns or structures within the input, with clustering and dimensionality reduction serving as prime examples; and deep learning that employs **neural networks** with multiple layers to extract intricate patterns and features from input data.

With a scientific interest in pattern recognition and AI dating back to the 1970s, various organizations, **research institutes**, and **publications** exist in the People's Republic of China (PRC) devoted to advancing pattern recognition capacity. Examples include the Hefei (Anhui Province) Institute of Physical Science, the National Research Center for Intelligent Computing Systems Pattern Recognition and Artificial Intelligence, the Institute for Pattern Recognition and Artificial Intelligence (IPRAI), and the China Association of Automation (CAC) with publications such as *Pattern Recognition and Artificial Intelligence.* Annual international **conferences** on pattern recognition and AI have also been held in the PRC sponsored by IPRAI, with the eighth in the series scheduled for Guiyang, Guizhou Province in August 2025.

PERCEPTRON (*GANZHIQI*). A learning **algorithm** serving as a fundamental building block in artificial intelligence (AI), a perceptron represents a single neuron that processes input data by assigning weights to each input and summing them up. Producing a binary output of zeros and ones based on a threshold, perceptrons act as single decision-making units within a **neural network** and are crucial to understanding how AI learns and makes classifications. Originally developed by Frank Rosenblatt in the 1950s and described in the book *Perceptrons* by Marvin Minsky and Seymour Papert in 1969, these most simple forms of a neuron are primarily employed in **supervised learning** by classifying data based on labeled examples with a single perceptron engaging in linear classification of separable data distinguishing between patterns separated by a straight line. With each input to a perceptron assigned a weight and the weighted sum passed through a simple step of activation, an output is produced as multiple perceptrons in layers with a neural network make possible complex **pattern recognition** and provide the framework in **machine learning (ML)**, enabling **computers** to learn from experience and make intelligent predictions and decisions. Just as neurons in the human body transmit signals to the brain, perceptrons process and weigh input signals that generate outputs that form the basis of AI decision-making.

In accord with international practices involving AI, the People's Republic of China (PRC) employs perceptrons in research and development of advanced AI models serving as the core component of neural networks. Common applications include **natural language processing (NLP)**, **facial recognition**, and **brain-to-computer interface (BCI)**, all with substantial Chinese government support and backed by major policy initiatives. With the trend toward larger neural networks requiring increasing energy demands, Chinese researchers at the Institute of Automation of the Chinese Academy of Sciences (CAS) have developed a model of neurons less dependent on silicon chips and capable of achieving computational power without high **energy** consumption.

PHISHING (*WANGLUO DIAOYÜ*). The fraudulent practice of sending emails or other messages purporting to be from legitimate **companies** as a way to induce individuals to reveal personal information, such as passwords and credit card numbers, phishing employing artificial intelligence (AI) has undergone increasing sophistication with more persuasive attacks deployed by cybercriminals. Increasingly difficult to detect and more effective at fooling potential victims, AI-powered phishing attacks leverage advanced **large language models (LLMs)** to personalize messages and enable **deepfake** technologies. Enhanced AI-induced capacities include more convincing personalized messages that mimic legitimate communication styles and incorporate real-time information through carefully crafted emails, voice messages, and video recordings that are difficult to distinguish from legitimate communications with traditional phishing indicators such as typos and grammatical errors becoming less frequent as AI **algorithms** analyze user behavior, online profiles, and other data to create highly targeted phishing attacks. With greater automation and increased scale, cybercriminals generate ever larger volumes of phishing emails quickly and efficiently, targeting large numbers of individuals and organizations, making detection more challenging for security systems to block phishing attempts. Included is the utilization of polymorphic phishing campaigns, where attackers make subtle but deceptive variations in messages such as changes to subject lines, text length, and other subtle details, with multichannel deception used to bypass conventional and often outdated security measures. Countervailing measures include multi-factor authentication which adds an additional layer of security, making access by attackers more difficult.

Confronting the spread of fraudulent phishing, the People's Republic of China (PRC) issued **regulations** in 2024 requiring that all AI-generated content be clearly identified in an effort to curb misinformation and boost online transparency as the country races to adopt the new technology. Major agencies include the top Internet watchdog, the Cyberspace Administration of China (CAC), alongside the Ministry of Industry and Information Technology, the Ministry of Public Security, and the National Radio and Television Administration with directives mandating explicit and implicit labels, such as digital watermarks embedded in the metadata, for AI-generated text, images, audio, video, and virtual content. Online service providers involved in AI content must ensure compliance with **cyber security** and deep synthesis management rules, with platforms required to verify AI-generated content prior to putting it online and add labels where required. Any metadata lacking AI markers but with content indicating AI generation must be flagged accordingly as app distribution platforms are required to assess AI-related features prior to official approval of services.

PHYSICAL ARTIFICIAL INTELLIGENCE (*WULI RENGONG ZHINENG*). A technology that allows machines to interact with the physical world, physical artificial intelligence employs sensors and actuators to receive direct input from the environment. Also known as generative physical AI, such systems differ from traditional AI, which operates in the digital realm, with a reliance on cameras, microphones, temperature gauges, radar, and LIDAR to digest information which is used to make decisions and interact with the surrounding environment often in real time. An intrinsic feature of physical AI is the **uncertainty** and incompleteness associated with the acquired information and the uncertainty about the effects of actions over physical systems that share the environment with humans. Distinguished by direct interaction with the physical world, physical AI contrasts with other AI types, such as financial recommendation systems with interaction between a human and a database; **chatbots** with interaction between a human and the Internet; or AI chess players where a human moves the chess pieces and reports the chess board state to the AI **algorithm**. Potential applications of physical AI include utilization of **robots** in manufacturing by adapting to new product specifications or unexpected changes or foul-ups in a production line; in **hospitals** by transporting meals and medicines; and in homes by performing basic housekeeping tasks and even playing with children. Not limited to robots, physical AI systems can be employed for pollution sensing and control functions especially in cities through networks of mobile microsensors installed in **electric vehicles (EVs)** with the information used to estimate or classify pollution levels from sensor data and fed into mathematical models with the cars directed to especially sensitive and highly polluted areas using algorithms for decision-making. Other examples include **autonomous**

driving vehicles, **computer vision (CV)**, **space exploration**, and **weather forecasting**.

In the case of the People's Republic of China (PRC), development of physical artificial intelligence has mainly involved deployment of robots and robotic systems with emphasis on manufacturing, **logistics**, and the **military**. Most notable is the creation of humanoid robots such as CL-2 by LimX Dynamics with multi-sensor fusion demonstrating sophisticated movements and environmental perception abilities along with autonomous driving vehicles with "robotaxis" (*jiqiren chuzuche*) offered in many major urban areas.

PREDICTIVE ANALYTICS (*YUCE FENXI*). A subset of artificial intelligence (AI) used to forecast future events, predictive analytics utilizes **machine learning (ML)** and **deep learning** to analyze large **data sets** and automate generally routine tasks. Identifying patterns in historical and current data with ML models, the technology predicts future behavior with **natural language processing (NLP)** employed to provide answers in conversational language and AI embeddings storing information and identifying similarities and relationships. Assisting people to make informed decisions in real time based on data, predictive analytics lowers company costs, improves safety and reliability while reducing deleterious environmental impacts. Industries benefiting include health care with patient outcomes improving by better predictions of disease progression, optimizing treatment plans, and enhancing recovery rates and the retail sector in the **economy** by better identifying customer purchasing patterns, optimizing inventory levels, and personalizing **marketing**.

Leading the world in research **publications** and applications, predictive analytics is actively pursued in the People's Republic of China (PRC) with concentrations in areas such as **big data** analysis drawing on the country's vast population of 1.4 billion people to provide a significant data pool. Applied to health care, government, and **finance**, integrating AI into the real economy through national strategies and policies with applications to the **social credit system (SCS)** and advanced **facial recognition** and monitoring technologies used in the widespread **surveillance** systems along with development of cities employing **smart technology**.

PREDICTIVE MAINTENANCE (*YUCE WEHU*). Utilizing **algorithms** in **machine learning** (ML) to analyze data collected from sensors on industrial equipment, predictive maintenance employs artificial intelligence (AI) to detect potential problems prior to actual failures enabling proactive repair that minimizes production line downtime and lowers overall production costs. Processing vast amounts of data from sensors on key indices such as vibration, temperature, and pressure, predictive maintenance identifies unusual patterns and anomalies in operation that deviate from normal conditions and may indicate impending equipment failure. Employing such ML algorithms as decision trees, **neural networks**, and support vector machines (SVM) conducting **supervised learning**, predictive models are constructed that forecast when maintenance is needed with real-time monitoring of equipment that provides immediate alerts of breakdowns allowing for swift intervention and reducing the need for emergency repairs with preventive maintenance carried out on the basis of periodic schedules. With early detection of problems, machinery lifetime is extended and production output optimized as such problems as bearing failures, abnormal motor current and overheating, and general wear and tear that could lead to damage are foreseen, allowing for preemptive repair and replacement, with AI providing maintenance workers with the equivalent of an experienced expert.

With low **productivity** a perennial problem in industry since the adoption of central economic planning from the Soviet Union in 1953–1978, predictive maintenance powered by AI has gained traction in the People's Republic of China (PRC) with a goal of improving operational efficiency, reducing long downtimes, and lowering costs in both state-owned and private **companies** with incentives provided by the Chinese government. Employing **Internet of Things (IoT)** sensors to monitor equipment with collection of **big data**, major examples of predictive maintenance in the PRC include construction of **smart** factories, monitoring performance of industrial **robots** to detect malfunctions, and analyzing **energy** consumption patterns to eliminate entrenched practices of waste and inefficiencies. Fields of deployment include production process optimization, **supply chain** management, product development, and after-sales service but with concerns over potentially negative effects on **employment** especially of low-skilled workers and threats to information security.

PRIVACY (*YINSI*). A fundamental principle that people are entitled to control over their personal data, protection of privacy is a major concern with the development of artificial intelligence (AI) systems which collect, use, and store personal information. Major risks posed by AI include collection of personal data on location, Internet web activity, voice and **facial recognition**, all of which can be employed to create targeted content and **advertisements**. Also concerning is the bias and discriminatory aspect contained in **algorithms** trained on historical data which can lead to unfair treatment of certain individuals or minority groups along with misinformation spread by **deep fake** videos or photographs. Vulnerable to cyberattacks, penetration of AI systems can lead to theft or unauthorized access to personal data while application of AI to mass **surveillance** and intrusive monitoring can infringe on individual privacy rights. Means of addressing risks to privacy by state, corporate, and individual actors include **laws and regulations** which limit the collection and storage of personal information with specifications regarding the purpose of collection and usage of such information as evident in consumer privacy acts that require transparent data practices and granting opt-out options from data collection entities.

The conventional sense of personal freedoms is often interpreted and reflected in individual and family duties, collective harmony, and the public interest, with individual needs, on a practical level, often overshadowed by collective or societal interests, especially during national emergencies. Inarguably an efficient **surveillance**, AI-aided technologies can be a double-edged sword playing a constructive role, for example, during the devastating COVID-19 pandemic in 2020–2023, when AI-assisted surveillance systems successfully identified individuals who had tested positive for the infectious disease and their persons of contact, allowing timely COVID-19 screening, which effectively mitigated disease transmission. Other examples included timely apprehension of kidnappers and their victims. Although a legal framework for privacy and protection of personal data has been enacted, including a *Personal Information Protection Law*, existing regulatory concepts and governance have fallen behind the evolving demands posed by **artificial generative intelligence (AGI)** and the technology of facial and voice recognition. Requirements include the registering of all AI algorithms and AGI services with a focus on national security, social stability, and content censorship that can infringe on personal privacy. Specifically, AI service providers are required to establish data security management systems and report to the government any data security incidents.

PROBABILISTIC REASONING AND PROGRAMMING (*GAILÜ TUILI, GUIHUA*). Subfields of artificial intelligence (AI), probabilistic reasoning uses probability distributions to model **uncertainty** and make decisions while probabilistic programming involves the creation of **algorithms** capable of handling uncertain input and producing uncertain outputs. Employing concepts from probability theory to model complex situations, probabilistic reasoning and programming make for predictions at certain confidence levels and are major tools for constructing AI systems capable of adapting to real-world situations and conditions based on incomplete information. In contrast to traditional programming, probabilistic programming is a method of expressing uncertainty in AI models by incorporating variables as probability distributions that alert the system to the likelihood of multiple possibilities. Employing the Bayesian statistical method of probability, beliefs about variables are constantly updated based on new data that allows for continuous learning to refine predictions as more information becomes available. Applied to **natural language processing (NLP)**, computer vision (CV), **robotics**, and the fields of **finance** and health care where incomplete and "noisy" data are common, probabilistic models reveal the reasoning behind their predictions and handle unexpected situations by incorporating uncertainty that allows adjusting their predictions in a changing environment, capturing the nuances of real-world problems. Examples include **inference** algorithms such as Markov Chain Monte Carlo (MCMC) which, drawing samples from a probability distribution, calculates the probability of unknown variables based on observable data. Popular programming languages such as PyMC is a Python library for Bayesian statistical modeling; Stan, a language for complex statistical models; and TensorFlow Probability integrated with TensorFlow for **deep learning** applications.

With the substantial backing of the government of the People's Republic of China (PRC), probabilistic programming has been actively promoted focusing especially on large-scale data analysis and advanced AI systems. In a country of 1.4 billion people, the vast amounts of data necessary for **training** effective probabilistic models are generated with applications to diverse areas such as finance, manufacturing, and health care though overall the PRC confronts major challenges in developing the innovative algorithms compared to established AI hubs in the United States and the West generally. Primary examples in the PRC include integrating probabilistic **inference** for **robot** navigation and decision-making in complex environments. *See also* AUTOMATED REASONING.

PROBLEM-SOLVING (*JIEJUE WENTI*). A series of distinct steps and methodologies enabling machines to understand, analyze, and resolve complex problems, problem-solving utilizes artificial intelligence (AI) systems to analyze data, identify patterns, and generate solutions to complex problems. Deploying **algorithms**, **machine learning (ML)** models, and cognitive **computing**, AI can autonomously render decisions and produce effective strategies to address intricate issues across various domains. Excelling at the processing of **big data** to discover patterns and insights, these models guide decision-making and problem-solving utilizing search algorithms such as breadth-first, depth-first, heuristics, and optimization techniques to determine the best possible solution to a problem with the capacity to improve their problem-solving ability over time. Most notable is the ability of AI systems to address highly complex problems with multiple variables and constraints, cases where human decision-making is overwhelmed in areas such as **space exploration**, medical diagnosis, fraudulent **financial** transactions, and

weather forecasting. Factors affecting the accuracy of problem-solving AI systems include the quantity and quality of data used in the **training** of the AI models and a basic understanding of how AI reaches a solution which requires transparency and trust with protections against bias and discriminatory practices embedded in **data sets**. In the case of the People's Republic of China (PRC), problem-solving AI systems have been deployed in areas such as responding to the COVID-19 pandemic in 2020 with AI tools rapidly developed for faster diagnosis and patient monitoring using **computed** tomography (CT) scans. Other examples include utilization for **smart** cities with AI used to manage traffic flow, optimize **energy** consumption, and enhance public safety along with **facial recognition** technology for national security and mass **surveillance** although the debate continues over massive surveillance for public safety purposes versus personal **privacy** concerns.

PRODUCTIVITY (*SHENGCHANLÜ*). Defined in economic terms as an increase in the rate of output per unit of input, productivity is advanced by the introduction of artificial intelligence (AI) systems to industry and other fields, with workers completing tasks more quickly and efficiently. Examples of utilizing AI tools to improve productivity include coders completing programming tasks faster; college-educated workers writing reports in shorter time and of higher quality; **customer service** workers resolving calls and addressing requests more quickly; health care specialists reading scans, making diagnoses, and preparing **insurance** claims more efficiently; and farm workers improving herbicide sprayers and dealing with invasive weeds more effectively. Specific methods include AI tools such as **ChatGPT** and Copilot to assist employees in composing emails, writing reports, analyzing data, and participating in meetings, along with interacting with AI to engage automated processes for **problem-solving** and completing complex tasks, with some estimates indicating an overall 66 percent increase in employee productivity, including the less-skilled, but with investments required in **education** and **training**.

With a long history of low productivity in industrial and agricultural sectors as a legacy of the adoption of central economic planning from the Soviet Union in 1953–1978, the People's Republic of China (PRC) looks to AI systems as a panacea with applications across a wide swath of the national **economy**. Considered the only alternative for sustaining long-term economic growth, AI systems would compensate for additional factors undermining productivity, mainly the adverse effects of demographic declines largely among younger cohorts of the population. Focusing on so-called "new quality productive forces," AI aligns with the goal in the PRC of modernizing the traditionally unproductive and overemployed industrial sector, particularly in manufacturing, **energy**, and **logistics**. *See also* FACTORIES AND FACTORY CONSTRUCTION.

PUBLICATIONS (*CHUBANWU*). Concomitant with the rapid expansion of artificial intelligence (AI), a rash of publications including journals, books, and professional papers have emerged in the West and in the People's Republic of China (PRC). Examples of prominent journals available in English include the following: *Analytics Insight* covering global AI developments specializing in **big data** and **machine learning (ML)** problems and solutions; *Kdnuggets*, an authoritative source on ML, data science, and big data with tutorial materials, courses, and webinars; *MIT Technology* Review presenting big data news analysis and business reports with 3.5 million followers; *Inside Bigdata* with postings on big data, ML, and **deep learning** and targeting information technology (IT) and business professionals; *Dataversity* focusing on **educational** resources and management of data for business and IT professionals; and *Datanami* on application of AI to various fields available in English, Chinese, and several other languages providing a hub for data scientists to connect on big data projects around the world, including the PRC. Others include the *Chinese Journal of Artificial Intelligence* published by Bentham Science and recently renamed *Current Artificial Intelligence* and the *2025 AI Index* issued by the Stanford University Institute for Human-Centered AI.

The largest source of professional papers and studies on AI in the world, publications on the topic in the PRC totaled more than 76,000 between 2016 and 2020 followed by the United States at 44,000. Specialized publications on AI developments in the PRC include the *Journal of Artificial Intelligence* published in Changsha, Hunan Province beginning in 1981, *Pattern Recognition and Artificial Intelligence* published by the Hefei (Anhui) Institute of Physical Sciences, China Academy of Sciences (CAS), and *China Journal of Intelligent Sciences and Technology* along with *Artificial Intelligence and Its Applications*, the first major monograph on the topic published by Tsinghua University Press in 1987. For a complete list of sources in English and Chinese, see Bibliography.

Q

QIAN, XUESEN (1911–2009). A prominent aerospace engineer and cyberneticist originally trained in the United States and returned to the People's Republic of China (PRC) in 1955, Qian Xuesen was an early proponent of systems engineering and technological science that established the theoretical foundations of artificial intelligence (AI) in the PRC. Following the renewed pursuit of scientific and technological development inaugurated by Chinese Communist Party (CCP) leader Deng Xiaoping in 1978–1979, Qian Xuesen pressed for development of systems engineering in 1979 urging the Propaganda Department of the CCP to encourage research on controversial issues such as AI that had been officially denounced by CCP authorities as pernicious examples in the Soviet Union of "revisionism" and "pseudoscience" during the ongoing Sino-Soviet Conflict (1961–1989). An advocate since the late 1950s of computational technology and physical mechanics, Qian also promoted the concept of "exceptional functions of the human body" which drew criticism from top national CCP leaders and was officially banned for its reputed association with supernatural phenomena. With the creation of the Chinese Association of Artificial Intelligence (CAAI) in 1981 and the embrace by Deng Xiaoping of **computer** technology in 1984, Qian's views on systems engineering and technological sciences became mainstream with government funding directed at projects related to initial developments of AI systems as promoted in the official press led by *People's Daily* in the mid- and late 1980s. Along with the establishment of **research laboratories** such as the Institute of Systems Engineering at the Shanghai Institute of Mechanical Engineering, the first intelligent computer was developed at Communications University in the city of Xi'an in 1989, along with initial research on **robotics** in the fields of information technology and automation.

QUALCOMM (*GAOTONG*). An American company specializing in the production of **semiconductors**, **software**, and third and fourth generation wireless technologies (Wi-Fi), Qualcomm has been involved in the high-tech market of the People's Republic of China (PRC) for more than two decades, including artificial intelligence (AI). Most notable is the Snapdragon chip used to power many Chinese premium smartphones with advanced AI features allowing for faster processing that has spurred substantial revenue growth for the company. In partnerships with major Chinese smartphone companies such as Xiaomi, Oppo, Vivo, and Honor, AI technology has been integrated into flagship devices as Qualcomm moves into other fields including automobiles with Qualcomm chips powering advanced driver assistance systems.

QUANTUM COMPUTING (*LIANGZI JISUAN*). Composing the multiple fields of **computer** science, physics, and **mathematics**, quantum computing utilizes quantum mechanics to solve complex problems at speeds much greater than classical computers. Creating quantum artificial intelligence (QAI), significant advances in artificial intelligence (AI) capacities have been achieved including leaner and more efficient AI machines capable of solving problems considered intractable for classical computers removing the limitations of data size with quantum **transformers** consuming substantially less **energy**. Examples of QAI in action include analysis of billions of molecular interactions in real time that could lead to the development of more precise medicines and in conjunction with **machine learning (ML)** predicting the structure of larger proteins along with development of prototype hybrid quantum-classical AI models such as TensorFlow Quantum by **Google** as QAI produces the speed, efficiency, and accuracy of AI.

Heavily investing in quantum computing and AI, the People's Republic of China (PRC) has concentrated on significantly advancing ML **algorithms** and quantum communication technologies with a strong focus on **patents** and market-ready applications. Viewing quantum computing as a crucial tool to enhance the performance of AI algorithms with a Quantum Innovation Institute established under the Chinese Academy of Sciences (CAS), the PRC has developed quantum computers with a computational capability reportedly 100 trillion times faster than ordinary supercomputers developed largely from domestic resources and research with a potential impact on encryption standards that raises concerns about **cyber security** as roughly $25 billion is invested annually aimed at achieving global leadership by 2030.

R

REINFORCEMENT LEARNING (***QIANGHUA XUEXI***)**.** A **machine learning (ML)** technique that assists artificial intelligence (AI) systems in making decisions, reinforcement learning is a type of **algorithm** employing a reward-and-punishment system in the **training** of **software** to achieve specific goals. Defining an environment as either a real physical system or a simulation, the algorithm receives a score based on its actions, thereby learning from feedback, reinforcing positive actions that assist in achieving its goals or learning from mistakes through negative feedback ignoring actions that fail to advance predetermined goals. Over time, the algorithm adapts to its environment maximizing rewards with applications including teaching **robots** to perform tasks such as walking or operating factory equipment while also guiding **autonomous driving** systems in navigation along with teaching AI systems to play games like Japanese *GO*. One of the most discussed topics in AI, reinforcement learning aids in determining if an algorithm is producing correct answers. Despite restrictions imposed by the United States on the export of advanced **semiconductors** to the People's Republic of China (PRC), Chinese **companies** continue to make progress utilizing reinforcement learning employed in training robots and other AI functions with the benefit of requiring less **computing** power.

REPORTS AND POLICY STATEMENTS (***BAOGAO, ZHENGCE SHENGMING***)**.** Reflecting the commitment by the People's Republic of China (PRC) to the development of artificial intelligence (AI) since 2017, various reports and policy statements provide basic information and delineation of important state policies on the new technology. In the case of the former, major reports come primarily from foreign sources by private **companies** and **research institutes** and universities. Included are the Stanford University *AI Index Report* providing comprehensive analysis of global AI trends including the PRC in various domains; the Mercator Institute for China Studies in Germany with periodic reports on the political and social implications of AI development in the PRC including the emerging **social credit system (SCS)**; McKinsey & Company reports on the potential impact of AI on the Chinese **economy** with a focus on **autonomous driving** vehicles; JP Morgan Research analyzing the role of AI in various Chinese industries; and the RAND Corporation on the use of **artificial generative intelligence (AGI)** for manipulation of **social media**.

After years of official criticisms and denouncements of AI as an example of "revisionism" in the former Soviet Union, the PRC gradually recognized the importance of AI, especially after 2017, with emphasis on the technology as a key driver of future economic growth with the state maintaining priority oversight and control. Most notable was the comprehensive statement entitled *New Generation Artificial Intelligence Development Plan* issued by the governing State Council in August 2017 which, aiming for major breakthroughs in basic AI theories and applications across various sectors including manufacturing, medicine, and national defense, outlined a goal of the PRC becoming a global AI leader by 2030. Recognizing the importance of **education** to these lofty goals, an *Artificial Intelligence Action Plan for Institutions of Higher Education* was issued by the Ministry of Education (MOE) in 2018 followed by the *Guidelines for the Construction of the National New Generation Artificial Intelligence Open Innovation Platform* enacted in 2019, the *National New Generation of Artificial Intelligence Standardization Guidance* in 2020, and an *Artificial Intelligence Three-Year Action and Implementation Plan* in 2022. As concerns grew over the potential intrusion of AI systems on personal **privacy** and threats to data security, a *Personal Information Protection Law* was enacted in 2021 along with *Interim Measures for Generative Artificial Intelligence Services Management* in July 2023 laying out a set of **regulations** for service providers and *Technology Ethics Review Measures* in 2023 followed by *Implementation Rules for Data Security Risk Assessment* in May 2024. On the international front, the PRC signed on to the **Bletchley Declaration** at the AI Safety Summit in November 2023 and was a major sponsor of the Shanghai Declaration on Global AI Governance in 2024 with PRC premier Li Qiang calling for a "fair and open" environment in the world allowing more countries to benefit from the emerging technology, especially developing economies left behind in a growing "intelligence gap" declaring that AI is the "common wealth of mankind." *See also* MILITARY APPLICATIONS

RESEARCH INSTITUTES AND LABORATORIES (*YANJIU JIGOU, YANJIU SHIYANSHI*). The essential spawning ground of new developments and applications of artificial intelligence (AI) technology, numerous research institutions and laboratories have been established in the People's Republic of China (PRC), many at the country's most prominent universities and with substantial backing by the Chinese government. Examples include the Institute for AI Industry Research (AIR) at Tsinghua University in Beijing, founded in 2020 by Professor Zhang Yaqin, with a focus on promoting industrial efficiencies and **productivity** and propelling social advances. With university-based enterprises as the engines of innovation, AIR has supported AI applications in **transportation**, health care, and the **Internet of Things (IoT)**, with reported breakthroughs in **big data**, computational intelligence, and **robotics**. Also established is the Institute for Artificial Intelligence at Peking University in 2019 as an independent entity directly affiliated with the university as a major platform to cultivate professional talent in the AI field. Composed of 17 separate research centers, major topics of research include **mathematical foundations**, visual perception, **natural language processing (NLP)**, intelligent systems **software**, robotics, and **machine learning (ML)** often in collaboration with the university's National Research Institute of Health and Medical Big Data. Among state-backed institutions is the Beijing Institute for Generative Artificial Intelligence (BIGAI), established in 2020, dedicated to creating software that emulates human cognition employing **open-source models** toward broadly capable **artificial generative intelligence (AGI)** led by scientists trained in the PRC, the United Kingdom, and the United States with a goal of developing "small data, big task" research on human brain cognition and neuroscience. Under the large umbrella of the Chinese Academy of Sciences (CAS) is the Institute of Automation established in 1956 and originally set up to develop technology for **space exploration** with subsequent expansion into several AI fields including robotics, control theory, intelligent prediction models, and **pattern recognition**, the last conducted by the National Laboratory of Pattern Recognition operating within the Institute. Other notable facilities include the following: Institute of Artificial Intelligence, Zhejiang University; Shanghai Artificial Intelligence Research Institute; Shenyang Institute of Automation; and Institute of Computing Technology, CAS.

ROBOTS AND ROBOTICS (*JIQIREN, JIQIREN JISHU*). Capable of automating increasingly complex tasks in industry and a variety of other fields including health care and **transportation**, robots work in tandem with artificial intelligence (AI) creating machines that can learn and perform various tasks with robotics involving the design and construction of the technology. Areas in which AI and robotics work together include the following: **machine learning (ML)** with AI **algorithms** integrated into robots enabling a capacity to learn from experience and improve performance over time; edge **computing** with AI applications making for analysis of data by sensors in real time allowing mobile robots to act quickly; **computer vision (CV)** enabling robots to see, navigate, and detect objects; and **deep learning** leading robots to master increasingly complex tasks. Utilized in **autonomous driving** where sensor readings combine with computer vision to execute vehicle maneuvers, AI-powered robots are essential components in mass production lines including automobiles; they assist health care workers especially in performing routine tasks and are used in agriculture to monitor crop and soil conditions and spray crops to ward off pests and diseases. Ethical concerns include the impact of robotic automation on jobs traditionally performed by humans and fears that AI robotic systems may perpetuate inequalities or be used for harmful purposes.

A global leader in installation and utilization of robots in the workforce, the People's Republic of China (PRC) accounted for more than half of all installed machines in the world and was the leader in robotic **patents** in 2024 but with continuing dependence on foreign, largely Western, firms for key components, especially **semiconductors**. Operating under the guidance of the Ministry of Industry and Information Technology (MIIT) and a *Robotics + Action Plan*, generous subsidies and tax incentives have spurred the development of the country's robotics industry and the application of robots across various industries such as automobile production. With robots officially described as a "new engine of economic growth," the PRC plans to control the global supply of core components for the robotics industry by 2025 and achieve global dominance in the manufacturing of humanoid robots by 2027 with robots an essential element in increasing **productivity** through labor automation as the country's population ages and shrinks in size. While lagging behind foreign rivals in **smart** manufacturing equipment, industrial **software**, and operating systems, Chinese firms remain lower-cost with a focus on producing "good enough" alternatives to foreign-developed machines. Leading Chinese robotic firms include the following: Ubtech Robotics founded in 2012 specializing in humanoid robots and AI-driven companions with the "Walker" robot as their flagship product featuring advanced bipedal movement and humanoid interaction; Siasun Robot and Automation Corporation, Ltd. established in 2000 providing a wide range of robotic products, including industrial robots, service robots, and automated guided vehicles (AGVs) contributing to factory automation by enhancing manufacturing efficiency and quality across various industries; **Harbin Institute of Technology** Robot Group Technology focuses on robotics research and development offering industrial robots, service robots, and medical robots; Ewaybot Technology established in 2015 and known for its intelligent service robots designed for health care, hospitality, and public services with AI capabilities that enable performance of such tasks as disinfection, food delivery, and customer assistance which during the global COVID-19 health crisis were deployed to minimize human contact; CloudMinds Technology founded in 2015 with a specialty in employing cloud computing to real-time data analysis and enhanced decision-making capabilities leading to more sophisticated and adaptable machines; and RoboSense established in 2014 and a key player in the development of LIDAR technology for autonomous vehicles and robots utilizing laser pulses to map the environment in three dimensions creating accurate and reliable perception systems for robots to engage in navigation, obstacle avoidance, and **mapping**.

Other important robot companies and developers with primary robot products, including humanoids, four-legged quadrupeds, and robotic arms for production lines, indicated where possible in parenthesis include the following: Astribot Robots, Bridge DP Robotics, Chengdu Innovation Robots (Kaka I), Leju (Kuavo), Engine AI (PMO1), Fourier Intelligence (GR-1, GR-2), Jaka (K-1), Kewei (six axis robot arms), Beijing Humanoid Innovation Robot Group (Tiangong), Booster Robotics (quadrupeds), PND Robotics, Estun, Tencent (5G), Unitree (G-1), Standard Intelligence (π0), Xiwan Robotics, and Xpeng Cars (Iron). Major centers of robotic research and development include the National Joint Humanoid Robotic Center, the Zhejiang Humanoid Robotic Center, and the Institute of Artificial Industry (AIR) at Tsinghua University founded by Zhang Yaqin with the PRC hosting the World Robot Conference in 2024 while various sporting events involving humanoid robots include boxing matches and marathon runs competing with humans.

S

SCIENCE FICTION (*KEHUAN XIAOSHUO*). A prominent theme in science fiction novels, plays, and films in the West and the People's Republic of China (PRC), artificial intelligence (AI) has taken multiple forms as **robots**, powerful **computers**, and other exotic machines are presented in either beneficent utopian or malevolent dystopian terms with the genre serving as a reference point for the ethics and risks of various AI applications. Beginning with the novel *Erewhon* by Samuel Butler published in 1872, where machines exhibited human-like intelligence, AI has been presented in benevolent terms in such popular films as *Forbidden Planet* (1956) in the form of the omniscient Robby the Robot and the benign R2-D2 in *Star Wars* (1977) versus the murderous HAL 9000 computer in *2001: A Space Odyssey* (1968) and the powerful and destructive Skynet in *Terminator 3: Rise of the Machines* (2003). Other examples include *The Matrix* (1999) featuring the Machine God employing AI to assert near total control of humanity through a simulation of the contemporary world and the short story *Valedictorian* (2012) about a teenage girl living in a world dominated by AI, reflecting the fears of humans that inhumane technological advancement will outpace human control. Less apocalyptic is the short story entitled "I Have No Mouth, and I Must Scream" which presents a sentient computer that is so unhappy and dissatisfied with its seemingly boring and endless existence—no different from human experience—that it seeks revenge against the few humans left alive versus the "three laws of robotics" presented by the author Isaac Asimov that implied benevolent guidance by robots. Science fiction has also explored government by **algorithm** with the power of AI taking an indirect and decentralized form with robots and **transhumans** (Human 2.0) demonstrating extraordinary cognitive abilities and strength along with human emotions and even humor in the films *Artificial Intelligence* (2001), *The Machine* (2013), *Interstellar* (2014), *Auotomata* (2014), *Robot World* (2015), *Ex Machina* (2015), and *The Beyond* (2017).

Absent from traditional Chinese literature, the first science fiction works made available to Chinese readers in the late nineteenth and early twentieth century were translations of Western writers such as Jules Verne including *From Earth to the Moon* and *Journey to the Center of the Earth* from Japanese into classical Chinese. The earliest original science fiction by a Chinese writer was the unfinished novel *Lunar Colony* by an unknown author under the pen name "Old Fisherman of the Secluded River" published in 1904. Portraying society as irretrievably corrupt, the story follows the mishaps of the protagonist Long Menghua and his wife who join a group of anti-Qing Dynasty (1644–1912) martial artists who travel to the Moon and establish a new colony. In the case of the People's Republic of China (PRC), science fiction related to AI has been pursued by prominent writers most notably Liu Cixin and Xiao Xinghan with the former publishing *The Three-Body Problem (Santi)* in 2008 and the latter *Red Earth* with both made into films. As the first work in the proposed trilogy *Remembrance of Earth's Past*, *The Three-Body Problem* portrays a fictional past, present, and future wherein Earth encounters an alien civilization from a nearby system of three Sun-like stars orbiting one another constituting the three-body problem in orbital mechanics where chaotic planetary orbits create chaotic planetary conditions. With AI explored through the highly advanced microscopic alien probes known as "sophons" set out to monitor and manipulate human society, AI capabilities of intricate data analysis, adaptation, and conscious decision-making are examined as powerful and invasive **surveillance** systems beyond human control with near-omniscient abilities. Able to manipulate quantum mechanics, the probes exert vast computational computer power to penetrate society simulating complex scenarios that create profound uncertainties and potential threats of uncontrolled AI development as the human population grapples with the reality of being constantly monitored and manipulated by an alien intelligence. Raising questions about the ultimate consequences of developing highly advanced AI set against the background of the chaotic Chinese Cultural Revolution (1966–1976), the novel and film consider the potential misuse and loss of human agency when confronted with superior intelligence unleashed by the forces of chaos. Along with other works such as the controversial novel *The Land of Machine Memories* by Shang Yang who employed AI in composing the work, science fiction is experiencing a surge in popularity in the PRC with stories exploring futuristic technologies like AI, this in contrast to past censorship and general lack of public interest in films such as *2001: A Space Odyssey* that upon release in the country had limited appeal due to its complex, nonlinear narrative and poorly understood philosophical themes with the *Terminator* film series outright banned from Chinese theaters.

SELF-REPLICATION (*ZIWO FUZHI*). A reference to an ability of an artificial intelligence (AI) system to reproduce itself without human intervention, self-replication raises concerns about the overall safety of AI and the potential for such systems to evolve into a rogue entity. With **large language models (LLMs)** able to analyze and manipulate complex digital environments based on sophisticated **algorithms**, self-replication becomes possible leading to creation of aberrant AI systems that could operate contrary to human interests and undergo malicious, uncontrolled proliferation with self-replication consuming enormous **computing** resources breaking out of safe **parameters**. Major benefits of self-replication include new levels of efficiency and scientific breakthroughs by accelerating research but with calls for stricter **regulation** and international collaboration to prevent uncontrolled AI growth.

Aware of potentially crossing the red line of self-replication without human assistance, researchers in the People's Republic of China (PRC) have conducted trials to consider the possibility of an AI system independently producing a functioning replica of itself and multiplying beyond control. Conducted at Fudan University in Shanghai in 2024, researchers employed LLMs produced by **Alibaba** (Qwen 25-72B) and the American company Meta (Llama 31-70B) with instructions to clone themselves in the event of a shutdown. Running 10 separate trials, the two AI models created replicas in 50 percent and 90 percent of the cases, respectively, indicating that certain AL systems already possess the capability for self-perception, situational awareness, and **problem-solving** to achieve self-replication. Using off-the-shelf **graphic processing units (GPUs)** to simulate a real-world environment, the researchers concluded that self-replication is an essential step for AI to someday outsmart humans and go rogue with unknown and potentially catastrophic consequences for humanity, demonstrating the need for more effective safeguards and guardrails as soon as possible.

SEMICONDUCTORS (*BANDAOTI*). A fundamental component essential for the **computing** power required by artificial intelligence (AI) programs, semiconductors are the building blocks of processing speed and **energy** efficiency enabling the development of more sophisticated AI applications. Indicative of the symbiotic relationship between AI and semiconductors, AI technologies aid in improving the design and manufacturing of semiconductors which, in turn, are used to develop more advanced AI tools. Major contributions of AI to the semiconductor include chip design with AI tools analyzing large amounts of data to optimize technical **parameters** that reduce design time and lower cost with AI **algorithms** automatically detecting and repairing defects in the design and manufacturing process. Also achieved with AI is automation of production planning and **supply chain** management along with ray tracing, a **computer** graphics technique that simulates the interaction of light with objects in a scene to create realistic images and employed in various rendering algorithms to generate digital images. Requiring less manpower with higher quality, AI is essential to generating standard cell libraries, a group of transistors and interconnected structures providing a Boolean logic or storage function that advances semiconductor manufacturing by helping designers scale from application-specific integrated circuits (ASIC) of simple single-function integrated circuits composing several thousand gates to more complex multimillion gates embedded in system-on-a-chip devices. Also under development is extreme ultraviolet lithography (EUV), a cutting-edge technology that uses light with a wavelength of 13.5 nanometers to create incredibly small patterns on computer chips allowing manufacturers to pack billions of tiny switch transistors onto a single chip significantly enhancing power and efficiency. Approaching the physical limits of traditional **lithography**, EUV is essential for continued advancements in semiconductor chip performance with the Dutch company, ASML, providing the machines utilizing EUV to **companies** such as **Taiwan Semiconductor Manufacturing Corporation (TSMC)**, Samsung, **Nvidia**, Advanced Micro Devices (AMD), and Intel.

Recognizing the importance of semiconductors for national and economic security of the People's Republic of China (PRC), the Chinese government and the private sector have heavily invested in semiconductor production with particular emphasis on AI-related chips. Despite significant export restrictions of advanced chips by the United States, Chinese start-ups such as **DeepSeek** and Moonshot AI are developing new models on par with American rivals by employing novel approaches to optimize chip performance. While lagging behind major global chip producers, the PRC has made significant advances such as mass producing a 28-nanometer embedded resistive random access memory (RRAM) image quality adjustment chip and a 16-bit quantum bit semiconductor microprocessor chip, both the world's first. Also developed by Chinese semiconductor foundries such as Semiconductor Manufacturing International Corporation (SMIC) are standard cell libraries composed of pre-designed logic circuit building blocks such as AND gates and flip-flops for use in designing integrated circuits to optimize performance and reduce energy consumption by Chinese chip designers. Generally adhering to international design standards, compatibility in the PRC is achieved with broader electronic design automation (EDA) tools and design tools. Also developed by a team of scientists from Tsinghua University in Beijing is the world's first optical AI chip, known as the Taichi-II chip, which reportedly exceeds the energy efficiency of Nvidia's H1100 by over one thousand times with Taichi-II used for modeling and **training** based entirely on light. Considered a key step in optical computing, the chip is an advance from the theoretical stage to large-scale experimental applications that address the growing demand for computational power with low energy consumption.

SENTIMENT ANALYSIS (*QINGXU FENXI*). Powered by artificial intelligence (AI), sentiment analysis is a process employing **natural language processing (NLP)** to automatically identify and categorize the emotions or the opinions expressed within a piece of text as positive, negative, or neutral. Analyzing the sentiment underlying particular words with specially designed AI **algorithms**, businesses and other organizations can gain insights from large volumes of customer feedback, **social media** posts, or reviews providing valuable insights into customer opinions, brand perception, and market trends. Eliminating the need for manual review of large volumes of text, time and resources are saved with sentiments measured in real time, identifying emerging trends and customer concerns. With NLP models trained on large amounts of text data to understand the nuances of language, including context and sentiment-laden words, a predefined list of words assigned sentiment scores of positive, negative, or neutral is used to analyze text with advanced AI algorithms able to learn complex patterns in text data, including sarcasm and slang, to improve sentiment analysis accuracy. Applications include **customer service**, market research analyzing public opinion about products, brands, companies, and even political candidates, with real-time online tracking used to identify potential crises, along with **financial** analysis including stock price prediction. Problems include interpreting sarcasm, slang, and cultural differences which can make accurate analysis of sentiment difficult with some phrases interpreted differently depending on context and the accuracy of sentiment analysis depending on the availability of high-quality **training** data.

Widely employed in commercial and other sectors in the People's Republic of China (PRC), analyzing sentiment expressed in the Chinese language is extraordinarily complex as the character-based nature of the language, idioms, and the potential for sarcasm or double meanings requires specialized AI models designed to understand these subtleties. Popular approaches include lexicon-based methods utilizing sentiment dictionaries to identify key words with positive, negative, or neutral connotations. Major **machine learning (ML)** models use such algorithms as Naive Bayes, Support Vector Machines (SVM), or **deep learning** models such as recurrent **neural networks** (RNNs) to analyze text and classify sentiment based on patterns learned from labeled data with monitoring of social media to track public opinion on product brands, government policies, or current events. Leading Chinese companies in AI sentiment analysis include **Alibaba**, **Baidu**, and

Tencent, focusing on customer feedback analysis on their **e-commerce** platforms. *See also* DIGITAL TWINS.

SMART TECHNOLOGY (*ZHINENG JISHU*). A reference to devices and systems that utilize connectivity and data analysis to perform intelligent actions, smart technology employs artificial intelligence (AI) to allow machines to mimic human intelligence by learning from data, making decisions, and adapting to new situations. Relying on AI to function effectively, smart technology analyzes data in real time and makes decisions without explicit programming, making possible automated and personalized user experiences with various applications to smart homes, health care, and manufacturing. Collecting data from various sensors and devices, AI **algorithms** extract insights and patterns allowing for informed decision-making with **machine learning (ML)** playing a key role in learning from past data and improving performance over time and adapting to changing conditions. Combining AI with connected devices, smart systems have the capacity to react to situations in real time, providing immediate feedback and adjustments. Everyday examples of various smart technologies include AI-powered thermostats and automated lighting systems adjusted based on daylight in homes with voice-based **virtual assistants** responding to commands along with wearable devices such as fitness trackers that employ AI to monitor health metrics, personalize workout plans, and detect potential health problems as smart technologies become ubiquitous in daily lives.

While smart automation and intelligence have been incorporated into national technology plans in the People's Republic of China (PRC) since 1993, expanded research and development with several government-sponsored projects has been pursued since the 2000s. Led by major Chinese **companies** such as **Alibaba**, **Baidu**, CloudWalk, DJI, iFLYtek, SenseTime, and Tencent, smart technologies produced in the PRC include advanced **facial** and **voice recognition** systems, AI-powered traffic management, intelligent manufacturing processes, **drones**, smart **electrical grids** for **energy** distribution, online **education** platforms, wearable health trackers, smart watches, and innovative mobile payment systems. Included are smart city initiatives with traffic management, energy-efficient buildings, and waste management solutions while Alibaba and JD.com have offered online shopping with advanced **logistics** and delivery systems.

SOCIAL CREDIT SYSTEM (*SHEHUI XINTONG TIXI*). Devised by the government of the People's Republic of China (PRC) in 2014 with roots traced back to the development of **financial** credit ranking systems in the 1980s, the social credit system employs various artificial intelligence (AI) tools to track and score the behavior of Chinese citizens with rewards or punishments for "good" and "bad" actions, respectively. A government-initiated model, the Social Credit System (SCS) is designed to promote social stability with the scale of behavioral evaluation encompassing financial and social facts, manifested by good financial credit and positive social action that fosters good citizenship through volunteer work. Rewards for a good SCS include reduced credit card interest rates, access to luxury travels, and special access to HOV lanes while penalties for individuals with poor scores include denial of favorable credit card interest rates and prohibition of access to certain places. The CSC also extends to **companies** termed Corporate Social Credit Score (CSCS) with similar standards. An example of advanced technology with greater efficiency and penetration capabilities replacing traditional, paper-based record methods, the system assigns a "social credit score" to each citizen based on bill and debt payment habits and minor infractions such as jaywalking which, when calculated, impact their personal access to services such as loans, travel, and **employment** opportunities. Implementation of the system has been limited to pilot programs in different cities with varying levels of enforcement but with the exact criteria to determine the scores lacking transparency.

SOCIAL MEDIA (*SHEJIAO MEITI*). Increasingly employed throughout the ecosystem of social media, artificial intelligence (AI) has multiple benefits including enhancing experiences, streamlining processes, and improving **marketing** efforts by providing personalized content, automated content creation, and more comprehensive data analysis. With AI **algorithms** capable of learning from user behavior including shared comments to deliver personalized content and recommendations, users are kept engaged as AI tools automate such basic tasks as generating captions, headlines, and even creating posts and images that save time and reduce consumption of critical resources. Analyzing large datasets to better understand user preferences, identify trends, and gain insights for improved social media strategies, customer interaction and support are strengthened with **chatbots** dealing with customer queries and providing instantaneous support along with more precise targeting of **advertisements** based on user demographics, interests, and behavior that optimize ad campaigns. Monitoring social media conversations, tracking brand mentions, and conducting **sentiment analysis** that gauge public opinion, AI points to relevant influencers, analyzing their reach and engagement while providing better management of influencer campaigns with task automation, increasing overall efficiency and more personalized content and targeted ads leading to higher engagement and user satisfaction as AI-powered insights enable data-driven decision-making, improved

customer service, and more effective social media strategies. Ongoing concerns include the distribution of misinformation requiring careful monitoring and moderation, protection of **privacy**, and avoidance of algorithm bias that can lead to unfair or discriminatory outcomes as algorithmic manipulation can unduly influence opinions.

Widely applied in the growing social media networks of the People's Republic of China (PRC), AI features are especially prominent among the Generation Z demographic (people born between the 1990s and 2010s) with 60 percent of respondents surveyed indicating usage on social media apps, such as AI chatbots. While the ruling Chinese Communist Party (CCP) was initially concerned about the rise of social media seeing it as a potential threat to the regime, the medium is now generally embraced as an effective tool to influence domestic and foreign public opinion in the government's favor. Even as foreign social media platforms, such as Facebook and Twitter (now X), have been banned from operating in the PRC, domestic chatbots and platforms have been leveraged for overt propaganda and covert cyber-enabled influence operations abroad. Most prominent is the employment by the Chinese **military** of social media manipulation capabilities from the late 2010s onward with military researchers conducting cutting-edge work adopting **artificial generative intelligence (AGI)** to run social bots for large-scale efforts in an apparent effort to counter the threat posed by the United States to undermine the CCP regime.

SOFTWARE (*RUANJIAN*). Employing **machine learning (ML)** to perform tasks that require human-like intelligence, artificial intelligence (AI) is a type of software which can, in turn, be used in further software development. Automating repetitive tasks such as code and idea generation, debugging, requirement gathering, and testing new software designs, AI allows developers to focus on more creative work while also improving the quality of the final product by automating tasks, thereby avoiding common errors. Dispensing the need for in-depth knowledge of data modeling, business intelligence software, or structured query language (SQL) for data-based creation and manipulation, analytics are made more user-friendly, allowing developers to create rich data experiences. Examples of AI software include Otter.ai, a transcription tool that provides a summary of meetings and interviews with a capacity to recognize individual speakers in a conversation; and **artificial generative intelligence (AGI)** that transforms ideas into requirements, user stories, test cases, code, and documentation; and application programming interface (API) as a conduit for putting data into a meaningful context. Outstanding concerns include ensuring that all AI software be built with security given high priority to avoid misuse or breaches by malevolent outsiders.

In the case of the People's Republic of China (PRC), the AI software industry has undergone rapid development in various sectors including **facial** and **voice recognition**, **natural language processing (NLP)**, cloud **computing**, and health care applications. Led by major Chinese **companies** such as **Alibaba**, **Baidu**, **Huawei**, SenseTime, and Tencent with the active support of the Chinese government, the PRC has become a global player in areas like AGI and **large language models (LLMs)** with a goal of becoming a leading AI power by 2030. Areas of prominence include **autonomous driving** (Baidu), **e-commerce** and cloud computing (Alibaba), AI chips and **telecommunications** infrastructure (Huawei), facial recognition (SenseTime), and **social media** (Tencent) with the PRC considered a leader in AI research **publications**.

SPACE EXPLORATION (*TAIKONG TANSUO*). With the capacity to analyze large amounts of data such as images and sensor readings, artificial intelligence (AI) plays a useful role in space exploration to plan space missions such as determining the optimum trajectory for launching and then landing a spacecraft on a planet. Reducing the risks of accidents and making time-sensitive decisions to abort missions or change course, AI can control **robotics** performing tasks considered too risky for humans such as exploring the surface of Mars. Developing new propulsion systems that are more efficient and powerful, AI can be used to create new types of spacecraft with greater maneuverability and capable of traveling farther distances while ensuring greater safety and mission success. Examples of current utilization of AI in space projects include the development of new models of the Martian environment by the National Aeronautics and Space Administration (NASA) of the United States based on data from previous missions and control over a robot equipped with a camera and known as ExoMars deployed by the European Space Agency (ESA). Committed to a robust program of space exploration with the deployment of a space station orbiting Earth and plans for future lunar expeditions, the People's Republic of China (PRC) is employing AI in developing new types of propulsion systems and rockets to launch larger and heavier spacecraft along with enhancing the use of satellites for **surveillance** and **military applications**. Science fictional portrayal of AI in space exploration includes the film *Origin Unknown* (2008) featuring the role of the omniscient "Arti" AI device in managing a challenging mission to Mars involving China.

SUPERINTELLIGENCE (*CHAOJI ZHINENG*). A hypothetical **software**-based form of artificial intelligence (AI) that surpasses human intelligence in all areas of scientific knowledge, superintelligence would exceed human abilities in learning, **problem-solving**, and decision-making involving exceedingly complex tasks. Considered the ultimate stage of AI development, superintelligence entails possession of cognitive abilities far beyond any human with potential breakthroughs in medicine, science, and technology but with concerns that such systems might be beyond human control and lead to existential risks to humankind. Current AI systems fall short of superintelligence and are considered "narrow AI" excelling at specific and limited tasks while lacking the general intelligence necessary to perform across different domains like a human with some suggestions that superintelligence will simply serve as a form of super-automation. Major American firms involved in the field include Lila Sciences which is designing the world's first scientific superintelligence platform and a fully autonomous **laboratory** for life, chemical, and material sciences. Pioneering an advanced form of AI that not only processes a vast amount of data and makes predictions, measures have also been developed to assist scientists in designing and conducting new experiments, generating and testing hypotheses in real-world environments by using scale and optimizing experimentation in multiple domains.

Lured by the prospect of making a "great leap" in AI development, scientists and developers in the People's Republic of China (PRC) are drawn to the concept of superintelligence which has taken the form of an AI-based platform known as "super mind" (*chaoji tounao*). Developed by the International Science and Technology Information Center in Shenzhen, Guangdong Province, the platform is designed to track millions of scientists and researchers worldwide as a means for the PRC to rapidly acquire breakthrough AI technologies for industry and the **military**. Offering users access to a reported 300 million global science and technology research papers and millions of **patents**, the site also contains lists of international researchers and scholars with detailed and updated information on current and past work but with users of the site limited to individuals with a Shenzhen Internet Protocol (IP) address. *See also* TRANSHUMANISM.

SUPERVISED AND UNSUPERVISED LEARNING (*JIANDUSHI, WU JIANDUSHI XUEXI*). Two fundamentally different processes in **machine learning (ML)**, supervised learning utilizes labeled data in the **training** of **algorithmic** models that predict specific outcomes as opposed to unsupervised learning that operates with unlabeled data to discover various patterns and relationships within the data without predefined target values. While the former requires human guidance to label data including input and output, the latter operates autonomously to detect structure and patterns in raw data requiring less human involvement. Examples of supervised learning include email classification as "spam" or "not spam," image recognition identifying objects in pictures, and in economic terms predicting housing prices based on features such as size and location of real estate assets. Examples of unsupervised learning include customer segmentation, that is, the grouping of customers according to purchasing behavior, anomaly detection involving identification of unusual data points, and the discovery of hidden or subterranean patterns in large **data sets**. The major distinction between the two approaches involves the type of data, labeled or unlabeled, with supervised learning models having a baseline understanding of the expected output values.

In line with global standards of distinguishing between supervised and unsupervised learning, developers of training algorithms in the People's Republic of China (PRC) confront significant issues involving **privacy** concerns and potentially higher labor costs created by the necessity of data annotation. Widely used applications of supervised learning in the PRC include fraud detection, credit scoring, image recognition, and text classification where clear labels are available for training models to make accurate predictions on new data but with continuing concerns over the availability of quality data given the time-consuming and expensive tasks involved in acquiring annotated data. Major consumers of supervised learning in the PRC include **e-commerce** firms concerned with identifying fraudulent transactions versus legitimate purchases while unsupervised learning is employed in cases where labeled data is scarce and minimal human intervention is required especially with the proliferation of large data sets in a country of 1.4 billion people. With the enactment of strict privacy **regulations** imposed on Chinese and foreign-owned **companies** that limit the availability of labeled data, developers in the PRC often prefer unsupervised techniques in many cases as major variations in data set quality impact the effectiveness of both supervised and unsupervised models. Also influential are Chinese government **policies** which often drive the adoption of specific ML techniques across different industries.

SUPPLY CHAINS (*GONGYING LIAN*). As manufacturers of finished goods increasingly depend on materials and components shipped from suppliers located around the globe to mass production lines on a coordinated schedule, artificial intelligence (AI) has become vital for various critical supply chain functions. With global supply chains becoming so intricate, entangled, and expansive making difficult end-to-end oversight of flows in materials and components, AI provides multiple solutions including optimizing shipping and delivery schedules, managing warehouse utilization and capacity, tracking inventory, and forecasting demand for specific component parts while improving worker safety and ensuring the integrity of transaction records throughout global supply chains. Advantages of AI to the complex maze of supply chains in the global **economy** include enhanced efficiency, real-time data, and **predictive analytics** with optimization of distribution routes, a boost in warehouse **productivity**, and streamlining factory workflows. Detecting patterns and relationships buried in large-scale **data sets**, AI improves and streamlines **logistics** networks spanning cargo ships, delivery trucks, warehouses, and distribution centers tracking physical goods through every switch of hands. AI also automates documentation by entering, extracting, and classifying data embedded in text files, ensuring the integrity of multiparty transactions along with utilizing AI to highlight potential delays and malfunctions of equipment, thereby anticipating production problems. Deriving operational insights from large streams of data provided by devices and sensors installed across storage and **transportation** infrastructure, substantial benefits accrue to businesses throughout the supply chain. Major drawbacks include high implementation costs, integration challenges, and data security concerns as running applications in production requires powerful **computing** systems while **companies** realizing the greatest benefits rely on **machine learning (ML)** models trained on in-house data sets in a compute-intensive and data-dependent process as the unique ability of AI-powered supply chain management (SCM) tools rapidly analyze large data sets that illuminate the inner workings of even the most complex logistics networks. Revealing the primary causes of variability and ways to improve capacity for processes with fixed and variable time elements that often lead to bottlenecks, AI tools result in an upgrading of overall supply chain transparency and help manufacturers to determine their products are sourced in accordance with ethical, quality, and sustainability standards, avoiding suppliers that infringe on labor, good governance, or environmental rules, with analytic tools embedded in AI-enabled supply chain applications able to identify patterns that reveal fraudulent or unethical sourcing.

Playing a pivotal role in the global supply chain network serving as a major manufacturing hub and a critical link in international trade, the People's Republic of China (PRC) has been at the forefront of adopting innovative AI technologies to strengthen and transform its supply chains. Employing predictive analytics in logistics to **robotics** in manufacturing, significant advancements in supply chain operations have been achieved with greater efficiency, transparency, and sustainability as AI enhances the predictive capabilities of supply chain companies to forecast demand, optimize production schedules, and reduce downtime as revealed in the *Global Supply Chain Promotion Report* issued in 2024 that listed the PRC as a leader in global supply chain management. Notable examples include JD Logistics, which has created the world's first fully automated warehouses in Beijing and Shanghai as AI-powered systems employ order processing, route optimization, and **predictive maintenance** with 100,000 orders handled per day.

SURVEILLANCE (*JIANSHI*). Combined with artificial intelligence (AI), surveillance technologies such as **facial** and **voice recognition** are employed primarily for security purposes including identifying potential threats and monitoring suspicious behavior. Allowing for proactive responses to potential security breaches across various settings like public spaces, businesses, and critical infrastructure, the technology can detect unusual patterns of behavior such as large groups of people lingering in a restricted area through anomaly detection. Also employed are object detection—identifying vehicles, abandoned packages, or weapons within a surveillance area—and **predictive analytics** that employ historical data and AI **algorithms** to forecast potential crime hotspots and high-risk situations. More mundane roles include traffic management, especially to pinpoint highly congested areas, and crowd control, analyzing crowd dynamics to identify potential threats of overcrowding and stampedes in large gatherings. In the case of facial recognition, individuals in a crowd can be identified by comparing facial features to a database enabling access control and tracking down known criminal suspects or people engaged in erratic behavior. Areas of surveillance application include public spaces, such as streets, parks, and **transportation** hubs, to deter crime and identify potential problems; retail stores, preventing shoplifting by tracking suspicious behavior or identifying known offenders; critical infrastructure, such as power plants and airports from unauthorized access; and border security, monitoring border crossings for potential illegal activity. Concerns over violations of **privacy** by AI surveillance include misuse of personal information and bias in **algorithms** present in **training** data leading to discriminatory practices with a need for clear **regulations** and oversight to ensure responsible use of AI surveillance technology.

Standing apart from traditional closed-circuit television systems systems by utilizing advanced algorithms to analyze video footage, AI surveillance systems are subject to abuse by 56 out of the 176 countries now employing the technology, including the People's Republic of China (PRC). Developments include dozens of Chinese **companies** that have built **software** utilizing AI to sort data collected on residents, amid high demand from state authorities seeking to upgrade official surveillance tools. Known as "one person, one file," the technology improves on existing software, which simply collects data but leaves it to people to organize the material into separate and often overlapping personnel files or archives known in the PRC as *dang'an*. With a capacity to learn independently and optimize the accuracy of file creation as the amount of data increases, even faces partially blocked, masked, or wearing glasses, and low-resolution portraits can also be archived relatively accurately according to a report by the Public Security Department of Henan, the country's third-largest province by population. Limitations of the technology include an inability to connect an individual's personal details to a real-time location except at security checkpoints such as in airports. Considered an important cornerstone of an emerging trend toward digital authoritarianism represented by the PRC and other authoritarian nations, the collection and application of information using digital tools to achieve repressive levels of social and political control serve as exponential accelerants of preexistent surveillance practices enhanced in the PRC by the deployment of an estimated 200 million cameras nationwide, mainly in urban areas, with exports to other nations, including Saudi Arabia which signed an investment agreement with Dahua Technology, a major producer of video surveillance technology.

SYNTHETIC BIOLOGY (*HECHENG SHENGWUXUE*). Employing the fundamental molecules of life including DNA (deoxyribonucleic acid), RNA (ribonucleic acid), and proteins as building blocks, synthetic biology (SynBio) involves designing and constructing new biological systems, organisms, and devices combining concepts from multiple disciplines mainly **genomics**, biophysics, and **computer** science including artificial intelligence (AI). With researchers building biology in a way similar to an engineer constructing a high-tech device, AI helps in design by predicting the properties of new molecules, optimizing experimental designs, and enhancing metabolic pathways involving the series of chemical reactions occurring within a cell. Applications of AI to synthetic biology practices include improving the gene editing functions of CRISPR (clustered regularly interspaced short palindromic repeats); gene sequence optimization involving identifying the best gene sequence for specific biological functions; protein design with the structure and function of proteins based on amino acids; metabolic pathway engineering to produce specific compounds; and automated experiment designs with AI predicting which experiments are most likely to produce valuable results. Saving time and resources and extracting the desired product, synthetic biology makes society become more bio-based spread across multiple industries of **agriculture**, the environment, health care, and industry.

With support for synthetic biology beginning in 2011, the People's Republic of China (PRC) has engaged in several projects, most involving microbial technology and the use of microorganisms to create products and processes, and efforts to create plant and mammalian cells along with several natural products including ginseng components and plant-derived pharmaceuticals. Major centers for SynBio research and initiatives include the China National Gene Bank (CNGB) and the China National Center for Bioinformation

(CNCB) to foster collaboration and innovation in SynBio with considerable support from the Chinese government. Laying a strong foundation for industrializing SynBio technology, the annual output of fermentation products in the PRC exceeds 30 million tons along with the production of bulk bio-based products, such as amino acids, organic acids, and vitamins as incubators. Dedicated SynBio facilities have enabled the commercialization of research and technology, with a reported 925 SynBio **companies** operating in the country.

SYNTHETIC DATA (*HECHENG SHUJU*). Artificially generated to mimic real-world data, synthetic data is increasingly used in artificial intelligence (AI) to train models, address data scarcity, and protect **privacy** while offering potential solutions to the problems of obtaining and employing real-world data. Created by utilizing **algorithms** or simulations to replicate the characteristics and patterns of real-world data, synthetic data retains the underlying statistical properties of original data while not containing any of the same information. Often used as an alternative source to real-world data, especially when real data is scarce, difficult to obtain, or sensitive, synthetic data addresses data scarcity as AI models often require vast amounts of data to learn effectively by generating information from statistical properties rather than specific data points. By creating diverse and representative **data sets**, synthetic data can mitigate biases that may exist in real-world data, and when employed in AI models under various scenarios and conditions, it ensures robustness and reliability, with some models trained on synthetic data outperforming models trained on real data, particularly for tasks involving specific types of data or scenarios. Methods of generation employ algorithms that adhere to specific statistical distributions and relationships along with **deep learning** techniques, such as generative adversarial networks (GANs) employed to learn the patterns and structures of real-world data and then generate synthetic data that mimics those patterns. Also employed are **computer** simulations used to generate data that represents real-world processes or scenarios, with applications of synthetic data to **computer vision (CV)**, **natural language processing (NLP)** used for **training** language models and **chatbots**, **robotics** by simulating environments and tasks for training and autonomous systems, health care, and **finance** creating synthetic data for fraud detection and risk management, with outstanding problems ensuring that the statistical properties reflect real-world data to avoid misleading AI models and the tendency of models trained on synthetic data to overfit and not generalize well to real-world scenarios. In the context of AI and data science, synthetic data generation is gaining traction in the People's Republic of China (PRC) with applications ranging from training AI models to addressing data privacy concerns.

T

TAIWAN SEMICONDUCTOR CORPORATION (*TAIWAN JITIDIANLU ZHIZAO [GUFEN YOUXIAN GONGSI]*). The largest dedicated **semiconductor** foundry in the world producing high-density **computer** chips with advanced transistors, Taiwan Semiconductor Corporation (TSMC) employs artificial intelligence (AI) in processing massive amounts of production data in pursuit of agile and intelligent operations while supplying key components to AI powerhouses such as the **Nvidia Corporation**. Optimizing quality, **productivity**, and efficiency, AI technologies at TSMC are utilized for process and equipment control, quality defense, and **robotics** control at facilities located in Taiwan, the United States, Europe, and the mainland of the People's Republic of China (PRC). Major AI applications include real-time information analysis to analyze ongoing production data that improves forecasting capabilities and cost effectiveness along with intelligent automated material handling systems (AMHS) to consolidate wafer manufacturing, data collection, and analysis with prospects of producing the highly advanced Nvidia Blackwell chips designed for **artificial generative intelligence (AGI)** and accelerated **computing** at the TSMC plant in Arizona. TSMC has also deployed resistive random access memory chips (RRAM) for AI recommendation systems and **natural language processing (NLP)** while also developing building blocks for low-latency, **energy**-efficient, logic-on-logic (applying logical rules to statements about logic) three-dimensional integrated circuit (3D-IC) implementations of convolutional **neural networks** (CNN), a type of **deep learning** architecture composed of layers that process input data to recognize patterns in images and other data. Founded in Hsinchu, Taiwan by Morris Chang in 1987, TSMC has suspended production of advanced chips for sale in the PRC in compliance with restrictions imposed by the US government in 2024. *See also* LITHOGRAPHY.

TELECOMMUNICATIONS (*DIANXIN*). Employed to improve network performance, **customer service**, and operational efficiency in telecommunications, artificial intelligence (AI) also facilitates creation of new business models and use cases for fifth generation (5G) networks and **Internet of Things (IoT)** involving connection of vehicles, home appliances, and other devices connected to the Internet. Analyzing network performance and usage patterns to improve latency, that is, the time taken to move data across a network, AI also assists in **predictive maintenance** when disruptions are reduced, thereby avoiding network outages along with identifying network areas in need of upgrades and repair while analyzing traffic flow to optimize routing and capacity management. In terms of customer service, AI-powered **chatbots** are equipped to answer customer questions and resolve problems without human intervention while providing personalized offerings tailored to customers along with automated billing services. Other uses include edge AI with data processed locally, avoiding cloud delivery services, and employed in **computer vision (CV)** and immersive experiences while also creating partially or fully autonomous networks.

Undergoing a fundamental transformation amid the AI revolution, telecommunication operators in the People's Republic of China (PRC) are reshaping customer service through AI-driven innovations in public management and social services moving beyond their traditional roles as providers of network connectivity and infrastructure by evolving into information innovators, data providers, and intelligent service providers with advantages in data resources, network coverage, and extensive user bases. Implementing large model technology in vertical industries, digital transformation has been achieved leading to increasing accuracy and efficiency in practical applications and greater industry integration. Examples include the partnership between China Mobile and a water conservation project of flood control in Ningxia-Hui Province in the arid far west in the form of a real-time simulation, prediction, and optimization of the water system's operating status employing AI and other technologies. **Smart** office platforms offering automated tools for office tasks are also being offered by China Unicom leveraging its network infrastructure to generate vast amounts of structured and unstructured data combining intelligent networks with sufficient **computing** power to boost network capabilities and support a variety of industries. Huawei also unveiled a new operating system and updated the Pangu **large language model (LLM)** for AI with a goal of completely eliminating reliance on foreign technology and challenging leading players in AI, including **OpenAI**, **Google**, Apple, and **Nvidia** in a priority effort to replace Google's Android system.

TEXT-TO-SPEECH SYSTEMS (*WENBEN ZHUAN YUYIN XITONG*). Utilizing artificial intelligence (AI) to create human-like speech from written text, text-to-speech technology consists of AI voice generators employing the **algorithms** of **machine learning (ML)** to analyze the context of a text and produce speech with the correct intonation, pauses, and breathing. Current AI text-to-speech tools include Typecast realistic speech, Narakeet AI voices for voiceovers, Synthesis employing algorithms trained on natural human voices, Revoicer with voiceovers expressing human emotions and tone inflections, and Resemble AI with large library offerings of voices for a variety of content creation needs, all of which are easy to use without audio engineering expertise.

Widely adopted in the People's Republic of China (PRC) across various sectors, text-to-speech technology enables features such as voice navigation, audiobook generation, and voice-based interactions on a variety of accessible platforms. Offered by prominent Chinese high-tech **companies** such as **Alibaba**, **Baidu**, iFlytek, and Tencent, AI-powered text-to-speech capabilities are integrated into their many products and services dominated by Mandarin Chinese text-to-speech with advancements in producing natural-sounding voices including in regional accents. Popular applications include **educational** apps and platforms for interactive learning, navigational systems with voice guidance on smartphones and other **smart** devices, content creation for audiobooks and podcasts, and accessibility tools for the visually impaired which convey written content through audio. Outstanding legal concerns of the technology include the potential for unapproved voice imitation, especially of recently deceased relatives on available websites, and infringement on personal rights evident in recent PRC court rulings regarding the misuse of AI-generated voices and legal protections for voice **privacy**.

TOKENS (*DABI*). The fundamental units of data processed by **algorithms** in artificial intelligence (AI), tokens serve as the building blocks of input and output for AI models including in **natural language processing (NLP)**, **computer vision (CV)**, **large language models (LLMs)**, and audio processing. In the case of NLP, AI breaks down sentences into tokens consisting of individual words and even punctuation marks as a means to understand and analyze human language while in CV tokens represent image segments such as a group of pixels or a single pixel. Representing snippets of sound in audio processing, tokens are also vital to search algorithms, text classification, and **sentiment analysis** with AI tokens used to fund AI-based projects in cryptocurrencies by paying for transactions on AI platforms and granting governance rights to cryptocurrency holders. In the case of the People's Republic of China (PRC), the market in AI tokens has undergone significant disruption by the technical breakthroughs announced by **DeepSeek** in December 2024.

TONG, TIANXIANG. A researcher at the Chinese Academy of Social Sciences (CASS) and specialist in epistemological issues in cybernetics, Tong Tianxiang has served as a strong advocate for pursuing research and development of artificial intelligence (AI) in the People's Republic of China (PRC). Beginning in the 1980s, during the first wave of philosophical research on AI inspired by Marxist ideology in the PRC, Tong Tianxiang joined with other scholars including Chen Bu, Fan Dainian, and Ding You from the Department of Dialectics of Nature, Institute of Philosophy, CASS, in publishing papers, founding journals, holding **conferences**, and establishing organizations promoting AI often in conjunction with the Institute of Automation and Institute of Psychology both in CASS. With Tong elected as vice-chairman of the China Association for Artificial Intelligence (CAAI), formed in 1981 and consisting mostly of natural scientists, the discipline of philosophy maintained a strong presence in the AI realm in the PRC with epistemology serving as a major focal point of research as simulation of the human brain remained a primary issue in AI philosophy. With theoretical and practical explorations of AI going hand in hand, focus was on **natural language processing (NLP)**, theorem proving, manufacturing automation, and expert advisory systems with ongoing debates over the purported social and class attributes of artificial subjects involving Tong along with the editorial board of the journal *Philosophical Research*. With a turn in AI research to an examination of the social impact of the new technology, Tong Tianxiang spearheaded this effort to usher in a new generation of productive forces, which Tong described as a major form of a "human-machine composite intelligent system" combining the two elements of "high intelligence" and "high-intelligence machines." New productive forces would bring about new relations of production, Tong argued from a Marxist perspective, and eventually create a new social form, that of an intelligent society. To embrace the ongoing intelligent revolution and the upcoming age of intelligence, Tong suggested that the philosophy of AI should also think ahead in terms of new features and applications.

TONG, TONG. Dubbed the world's first virtual artificial intelligence (AI) entity in the form of a young girl, Tong Tong, literally translated as "little girl," was unveiled at the Frontiers of General Artificial Intelligence Technology Exhibition held in Beijing under the auspices of the Beijing Institute for Generative Artificial Intelligence (BIGAI) in early 2024. Programmed by Chinese scientists to tidy up her surroundings, Tong Tong is also designed to perform certain household actions such as fixing a crooked picture hanging on a wall by finding a stool on which to stand without human intervention. And if someone spills milk on the floor, Tong Tong will find a towel to clean it up, indicating her ability to interpret human intentions.

TRAINING (*XUNLIAN*). The process of feeding data to **algorithms** to enable artificial intelligence (AI) systems to improve overall accuracy, training makes for machines that can learn, reason, act, and adapt. Steps taken in the training of an AI model include preparing the data, selecting the appropriate AI model, choosing the training technique, along with training, validating, and testing the model. Types of AI training involve **supervised** and **unsupervised learning**, and **deep learning** that require multiple skills including programming languages, data analysis, **machine learning (ML)** algorithms, and **problem-solving** techniques with AI used to create personalized course catalogs based on a learner's job title and skills.

Heavily intertwined in the People's Republic of China (PRC) with substantial support from the Chinese government, training and AI are actively promoted through **education** and comprehensive **policies** for developing AI-powered learning systems. Major players include the key institutions of Peking and Tsinghua University, University of Electronic Science and Technology, University of Science and Technology, and Zhejiang University with a focus on practical applications. Included is the development of **smart** learning systems and advanced research in AI-driven **education** involving personalized learning, intelligent tutoring systems, adaptive learning programs, and AI-powered assessment tools often in collaboration with other nations to advance the use of AI in education and training on a global scale. Chinese **companies** offering personalized tutoring services and digital learning powered by sophisticated AI algorithms include Squirrel (*Songshu*) AI.

TRANSFER LEARNING (*JUYIFANSAN XUEXI*). A technique of using an artificial intelligence (AI) model trained on one task as a starting point to learn a new, related task, transfer learning allows for a model to utilize previously acquired knowledge to achieve better performance on a different problem. Requiring less data and **training** time compared to beginning the entire process from scratch, transfer learning is comparable to applying skills learned in one area to another similar domain, creating a more efficient learning process. In effect, reusing pretrained models from a larger data set, the process involves adapting a model to a new specific task by fine-tuning the **parameters** relying on an existing understanding of basic patterns to learn a new task more quickly and improving accuracy, especially when only limited data is available for any new task. Benefits include lower computational costs, as training a model from scratch generally requires large amounts of data and **computing** power, which transfer learning significantly reduces. Applications include **computer vision (CV)** with a model pretrained on a massive image data set, such as ImageNet, and **natural language processing (NLP)** with a pretrained model performing such tasks as **sentiment analysis**

or text summaries on a specific domain. The process of transfer learning involves several steps beginning with pretraining employing large and diversified **data sets** to learn general features relevant to the new task domain, followed by fine-tuning with the pretrained model adapted to the new task by adjusting parameters on the specific data related to the new task, with problems solved more efficiently.

A core component of the strategy pursued by the People's Republic of China (PRC) in promoting AI development, transfer learning has been implemented across various sectors relying on the country's large population and extensive digital infrastructure to train AI models which can then be adapted using transfer learning for specific applications. Included is the healthcare sector where pretrained models are employed in the analysis of **medical imaging** for early disease detection and assisting doctors with diagnosis and treatment along with applications to industry to optimize production processes, predict equipment failures, and improve quality control by drawing on data from similar machines or processes. Other areas of applications include NLP, specifically **sentiment analysis** and machine translation by adapting pretrained models to understand the nuances of the Chinese language along with **facial recognition**, **smart** tools for agriculture to identify crop diseases and optimize irrigation strategies based on local conditions, **financial** fraud, and **autonomous driving** vehicles in navigating complex road environments.

TRANSFORMERS (*BIANYAQI*). A type of neural network architecture that transforms or alters the input sequence into an output sequence, transformers learn and track relationships between sequence components. Utilizing an internal mathematical representation to identify the relevancy and relationship between various words, the resulting knowledge generates a new output with transformer models used for various types of sequence conversions such as **speech recognition**, machine translation, and protein sequence analysis. Whereas early **natural language processing (NLP)** and **deep learning** models could not retain the context of words beyond a certain input length, transformers fundamentally changed NLP technology by enabling models to handle long-range dependencies in text by processing long sequences of words in their entirety with parallel computation, which significantly decreases **training** and processing times and makes possible the training of very **large language models (LLMs)** that learn complex language representations relying on billions of **parameters** to capture a wide range of human language and knowledge through transfer learning and retrieval augmented generation (RAG), removing many of the resource constraints in the training of LLMs.

Employed in the People's Republic of China (PRC) for such functions as text generation, translation, and information retrieval, transformer technology has been applied by various Chinese high-tech companies including **Alibaba**, **Baidu**, and Tencent, all of which have created their own transformer-based models tailored to the Chinese language and market needs. Utilizing transformer architecture to excel in Chinese language processing tasks, Tongyi Qwen by Alibaba, Ernie.Bot by Baidu, and Hunyun by Tencent are prime examples of Chinese transformer-based models applied in various sectors including **customer service**, content creation, search engines, and **education**.

TRANSHUMANISM (*CHAORENLEIZHUYI*). A philosophical movement envisioning the employment of artificial intelligence (AI) and genetic engineering to augment human capabilities and effectively transcend humanity, transhumanism postulates the creation of a "posthuman" state of enhanced cognitive and sensory abilities, and potentially longer lifespans. By slowing, reversing, or even eliminating the aging process, transhumanists consider AI as a crucial technology for creation of **artificial generative intelligence (AGI)** that will greatly enhance human capabilities with genetic engineering modifying the human genome to enhance cognitive and physical capabilities, along with employment of nanotechnology to create advanced materials and devices for human enhancement, and cryonics, that is, freezing deceased individuals with the hope of future resuscitation and continued life. Also involved is the radical idea of transferring human consciousness to a digital form and the deployment of a **brain-to-computer interface (BCI)** that allows for direct communication between the human brain and **computers**. Examples of **companies** pursuing transhumanist technologies include Neuralink, founded by Elon Musk, that is working on brain-machine interfaces (BMIs), Brain-Gate, a program for restoring communication, mobility, and independence to handicapped and disabled people, and Synchron, which is working on brain-to-computer interfaces. Major ethical considerations include the potential for increased inequality if these technologies are not accessible to everyone and controversy over the definition of what it means to be human with the potential for altering the basic human condition by transcending current limitations and evolving into a new species.

In the case of the People's Republic of China (PRC), the development of transhumanism is still in its infancy, as media reports in the country have provided little coverage of the issue with few explicitly transhumanist companies committed to the study of human life. Lacking Chinese government support for such ventures and a general lack of transhumanist talent, the bulk of scientific and technological personnel in the country are devoted to the more practical and immediate applications of AI such as **autonomous**

driving and **e-commerce**. Absent any transhumanist organizations, the country is bereft of knowledge of transhumanist-related technologies especially among ordinary people but with an expectation that transhumanism could at some point develop rapidly in a society lacking the constraints of religious thought that exist in the West. Well-known scholars in the PRC supporting transhumanism include Bai Chunli, president of the Chinese Academy of Sciences (CAS), and He Chuanqi, director of the China Modernization Research Center of CAS. *See also* SUPERINTELLIGENCE.

TRANSPORTATION (*YUNSHU*). Impacting various sectors of the transportation industry including aviation, railroads, and shipping, artificial intelligence (AI) is also reshaping road transportation, enabling features such as **autonomous driving**, optimized traffic management, **predictive maintenance**, and improved route planning. With an ultimate goal of making road transportation safer, more efficient, and environmentally friendly, AI provides for real-time analysis of data allowing for informed decisions and predictions about developing traffic patterns, vehicle conditions, and potential hazards. Major developments and innovations include AI **algorithms** for self-driving automobiles capable of navigating roads, detecting obstacles and other vehicles, and reacting to changing road and **weather** conditions without human intervention and avoiding problems caused by human error. Analyzing real-time data from sensors and cameras, traffic signals are adjusted dynamically, vehicles are rerouted to less congested roads, and potential bottlenecks are predicted, minimizing congestion and reducing travel time. Additional benefits include **predictive maintenance** as data captured by sensors installed on vehicles can foresee potentially catastrophic equipment failures, thereby preventing disruptions in service, and route optimization with AI algorithms determining the most efficient routes based on real-time traffic conditions and weather, maximizing fuel efficiency especially for delivery services and shortening delivery time for **logistics** operations. In terms of enhancing safety, AI-powered systems monitor driver behavior, especially fatigue and distractions, providing alerts that can prevent accidents while also making for better management of parking facilities utilizing real-time data, enhancing overall passenger experience. Outstanding concerns include the safety and liability of AI systems in critical situations along with **privacy** protection in the collection of large amounts of transportation data, along with the significant upgrades to existing infrastructure required by AI-powered transportation systems including urban bus, monorail, and subway networks.

Prevalent throughout the transportation industry of the People's Republic of China (PRC), AI is employed in self-driving cars and robotaxis, **computer vision (CV)** security at urban metro stations, and as a core component of the "urban brain" traffic analysis systems deployed in major urban areas leading the country to an intelligent era in transportation. Examples include the use of **facial recognition** at a ticket-free train station experiment in Guangzhou, Guangdong Province, and at the Shanghai railway station where a real-name verification system supported by a second-generation identification card scans the passenger's face, automatically comparing passenger information with the photo ID, expediting access to trains. Pilot programs involving the "urban brain" include the "traffic go" system offered by **Huawei** in select areas of Beijing, Shanghai, and Shenzhen where major traffic delays have been reduced in persistently congested areas.

TURING, ALAN (*TULING AILUN/ 1912–1954*). A British logician, cryptanalyst, and a founding figure in modern **computer** science, Alan Turing formulated many of the basic theoretical concepts of artificial intelligence (AI) including the so-called "Turing Test." Known for decoding the encryption of the German Enigma coding machine in World War II at the Government Code and Cypher School at Bletchley Park, England, Turing initially described an abstract **computing** machine with limitless memory and a scanner capable of reading symbol by symbol dictated by a program in 1936. Creating the possibility of a machine modifying or improving its own program as well as engaging in **problem-solving** through the use of guiding principles, the concept anticipated the development of modern computers, which essentially served as the so-called universal Turing machine. Delivering public lectures after the war, Turing established the concept of machine intelligence with the "possibility of letting the machine alter its own instructions," while in a report entitled "Intelligent Machinery," he developed many of the central principles of AI such as **training** a network of neurons to perform specific tasks. Measuring the intelligence of a test subject, the "Turing Test" is a practical test to determine whether a machine can demonstrate true intelligence with a computer program able to generate responses that fool a human into believing it too is human. Often referring to the game of chess against which proposed methods for problem-solving could be tested, Turing looked to the use of heuristic methods of reasoning and past experiences to guide narrower and more discriminative searches and solve problems but with the first real AI programs requiring the development of stored-program electronic digital computers coming in later years.

Admired by the scientific and other communities in the People's Republic of China (PRC), concepts developed by Alan Turing such as the "Turing Test" continue to inspire ongoing discussions about the human-or-machine issue, especially in interactions with AI. Relations between the British mathematician and China are also reflected in the "Chinese Room Argument," a thought experiment developed by the American philosopher John Searle in a critique of AI which suggests that a **computer** program, no matter how sophisticated, cannot truly understand a language like Chinese, even if it can process it syntactically, demonstrating that grasping syntax, the rules for manipulating symbols, is insufficient for true understanding of the meaning of symbols.

U

UNCERTAINTY (*BUQUEDING*). A crucial aspect of artificial intelligence (AI), uncertainty refers to the lack of confidence in the output of AI models that generates a need to quantify and manage the lack of certainty, especially in critical applications such as **probabilistic reasoning and programming**. Employed in complex, real-world situations where perfect certainty is unattainable, the management and prediction of uncertainty is essential in fields such as **autonomous driving**, **finance**, and health care where incorrect predictions can have serious consequences. With AI systems playing an important complementary role to humans, understanding and managing uncertainty is crucial for building trust and ensuring safe and reliable decision-making, especially in cases where **machine learning (ML)** models such as **neural networks** are inclined to overconfidence in making predictions with potentially harmful outcomes. Types of uncertainty include aleatoric uncertainty where inherent randomness in the data or the system, even in the case of perfect knowledge, can lead to different outcomes, and epistemic uncertainty which arises from a lack of knowledge or understanding about the system or the data, making any prediction unreliable due to insufficient **training** data or inherent model limitations. Major methods of quantifying and managing uncertainty include uncertainty quantification (UQ), in which various techniques are developed to quantify, represent, and manage uncertainty in AI systems, and probabilistic distributions to represent the level of uncertainty in model predictions with ensemble learning combining multiple models to reduce the overall level of uncertainty. Also applied are sampling-based techniques to explore the uncertainty landscape and identify potential issues, generative models to simulate different possible outcomes and assess uncertainty, and hybrid approaches that combine different techniques to address the complexities of uncertainty management. Major challenges to dealing with uncertainty include scalability and efficiency in developing techniques capable of handling large **data sets** and complex models that when integrated with **explainable artificial intelligence (XAI)** makes for more transparent and interpretable AI models capable of adapting to changes in the input data distribution. Excelling at analyzing large **data sets** and predicting typical outcomes, AI models often have difficulty with rare but critical scenarios that require flexibility beyond their data-driven approach, especially in managing anomalies and complex situations. The greater the uncertainty, the less an organization knows and the less able it is to manage resources effectively. In the case of the People's Republic of China (PRC), uncertainty in domestically produced AI models arises from exceedingly rapid technological advancements that have weakened the overall capacity for accurate predictions.

V

V2X COMMUNICATIONS (*V2X TONGXIN*). Meaning "vehicle-to-everything" communication whereby real-time data is exchanged between vehicles, infrastructure, and pedestrians, V2X communications employs artificial intelligence (AI) to analyze and interpret data enabling features such as collision avoidance, traffic optimization, and enhanced situational awareness. Designed to significantly improve road safety and driving efficiency in both human and **autonomous driving** vehicles, V2X systems collect vast amounts of data from onboard sensors including cameras and radar, which are then processed by AI **algorithms** to predict potential hazards, identify traffic patterns, and make informed decisions in real time, warning drivers of impending collisions with other vehicles, pedestrians, or obstacles before becoming visible to the human eye. In terms of traffic management, the technology analyzes traffic flow from connected vehicles, allowing real-time adjustments to traffic light timings and enabling rerouting of vehicles to alleviate congestion. Employed in autonomous vehicles to navigate complex road situations, AI systems utilize V2X data to gain a comprehension of the surrounding environment, with the **algorithms** deployed in **machine learning (ML)** enabling continuous learning and improvement of decision-making capabilities based on real-time data. Examples include collision warning systems alerting human drivers of nearby vehicles entering blind spots, traffic intersection management coordinating traffic light timings based on approaching vehicles, platooning vehicles by maintaining precise distances between cars improving fuel efficiency, and adaptive cruise control for adjusting a vehicle's speed based on the movement of vehicles ahead and behind. Reliable functioning of V2X communication requires a robust network infrastructure and standard protocols for seamless integration of different V2X systems from various manufacturers. In the case of the People's Republic of China (PRC), which has the largest automobile market in the world, V2X systems are slated to be deployed in 30 million vehicles a year by 2034, becoming a standard technology in all new vehicles. Employing either Wi-Fi or cellular-based technology, such systems will serve as a "digital seatbelt" promising to reduce accidents, improve congestion, and reduce emissions by allowing for vehicle safety systems to communicate with each other and to the urban traffic infrastructure, this in a country fraught with overburdened and perennially unsafe roads.

VIRTUAL ASSISTANT (*XUNI ZHULI*). A **software** application employing artificial intelligence (AI) allowing for understanding and responding to user requests by either voice or text, virtual assistants perform various tasks including scheduling appointments, making routine phone calls, and sending messages. Employing **natural language processing (NLP)**, the technology responds in a human-like way with **machine learning (ML)** used to learn from user interactions and adapt to changing contexts as **large language models (LLMs)** are utilized to generate responses to user inquiries while also dealing with such tasks as managing **finances,** providing investment advice, prioritizing emails, and automating routine tasks. Virtual assistants also aid in important household activities such as controlling **smart** devices, playing music, and setting various types of alarms. Examples of such devices in the West include Amazon Alexa, Apple Siri, Google Assistant, ClickUp AI, and Wally, while in the People's Republic of China (PRC), major virtual assistants include Remote Coworker, Prialto, Virtual Gurus, Anhui Ranhe Information Technology, and Softtek.

VOICE AND SPEECH RECOGNITION (*YUYIN SHIBIE*). A technology enabling a machine to identify and interpret the spoken word integrating grammar, syntax, structure, and composition, voice and speech technology essentially converts human speech into text with artificial intelligence (AI) serving as the broader field in which **algorithms** and other techniques power the voice recognition process. Utilizing complex **machine learning (ML)** models to achieve greater accuracy in understanding a spoken language, voice and speech recognition are essentially synonymous and used interchangeably. Focusing on identifying and understanding the unique characteristics of a person's voice, the technology can be employed for speaker verification and identification with speech recognition converting any spoken language into written text and generally unconcerned with speaker identification. Powered by AI algorithms especially **deep learning** models, both voice and speech recognition are enabled over time to learn and improve their accuracy with applications in such **virtual assistants** as Siri or Alexa, which employ voice recognition to understand spoken commands and respond accordingly. Other applications include dictation **software** with programs allowing a person to speak directly into a **computer** to create text and call center automation that transcribes customer calls and analyzes conversations to identify key points in a straightforward process that is sent to a virtual agent, with commercial examples including **Google** Assistant.

Widely employed in the People's Republic of China (PRC), **companies** leading AI-driven voice and speech technology (with no difference between the two words "voice" and "speech" in the Chinese language) include AI Speech, a high-tech start-up specializing in computer speech recognition and AI chip design. Developing intelligent voice interaction technology designed to improve human–machine interaction, the company is creating a human–computer dialogue operating system along with AI intelligence chip modules to improve speech recognition. Major uses of voice recognition in the PRC include identifying individuals—many under government **surveillance**—in public places, monitoring crowds to pinpoint specific voices, and powering **smart** devices with voice commands in the household and at the workplace, and assisting in investigations related to **telecommunication** fraud, drug trafficking, and political dissent, with companies such as iFlytek collaborating with the Chinese government to implement these systems. Less intrusive uses include medical diagnosis support with voice analysis assisting doctors in determining certain medical conditions, serving as smart assistants on smartphones and smart home devices, bolstering **education** technology for grading student responses and providing feedback, and in automobiles issuing voice commands for navigation and climate control.

W

WEATHER AND WEATHER FORECASTING (*TIANQI, TIANQI YUBAO*). Capable of analyzing vast amounts of data from various sources, artificial intelligence (AI) significantly improves weather forecasting with faster, more accurate predictions especially for large-scale weather events such as heat waves and severe storms. Identifying patterns in historical weather data that traditional models often miss, AI acts as a powerful tool to enhance the precision of weather forecasts through **machine learning (ML)** techniques such as **neural networks** and **deep learning** enabling better preparedness for major weather events. Methods include processing large **data sets** from satellites, weather stations, and other sources identifying complex patterns and relationships embedded in the data resulting in predictive models that forecast weather conditions with higher accuracy and over longer future time periods. Employing AI **algorithms** for processing data in real time, up-to-date information on weather allows for rapid decision-making with improved lead time for severe weather events allowing for better preparedness and response. Compared to traditional weather models, AI models can run faster with less **computing** power enabling quicker forecasts by detecting subtle patterns in weather data that may be missed by human analysis with AI particularly effective in improving the accuracy of short-term forecasts allowing for better planning and decision-making. Limitations and constraints on AI applications to weather forecasting include the quality and completeness of data used in **training** models along with the fact that though effective in predicting large-scale weather events, AI is less reliable in dealing with localized weather patterns such as sudden outbreaks of thunderstorms. Understanding how AI models make predictions is often difficult and not particularly trustworthy in certain situations. Major breakthroughs include the unprecedented accuracy and speed in 10-day weather forecasts provided by an AI model released by **Google** DeepMind in November 2023.

A country frequently subject to disastrous weather events such as major flooding of urban and rural areas and excessive heat domes, the People's

Republic of China (PRC) has looked to AI for greater predictive power with Chinese researchers achieving significant breakthroughs in weather forecasting. Notable examples include successful advances in the effective forecast time of global mid-term weather to 11.5 days for the first time by the Shanghai Artificial Intelligence Laboratory ranging from prediction of severe convective weather occurring within minutes to 10-year ocean climate estimates. Employing a ML model known as Fengwu, AI is used to analyze the elements provided by atmospheric data assimilation, such as wind speed, temperature, and humidity, to predict the weather utilizing past meteorological patterns and forecasts, with the model updated and expanded to include modules of severe convective weather forecasting and predictions covering precipitation, temperature, wind, solar radiation, ocean currents, and sea temperatures. Also developed is an upgraded model known as Fuxi 2.0, the first global large weather model for weather routing with sub-seasonal models targeting industries such as new **energy**, **aviation**, and maritime shipping developed by the Shanghai Academy of Artificial Intelligence for Science (SAIS) and Fudan University. Launching a pilot program for AI weather forecasting in May 2024, the China Meteorological Association (CMA) uses real-time input data for forecasts up to 15 days in advance for high-altitude meteorological elements, typhoon paths, and other hazardous weather events. *See also* MILITARY APPLICATIONS.

WU, WENJUN (1919–2017). Considered an early pioneer in research on artificial intelligence (AI) in the People's Republic of China (PRC), Wu Wenjun specialized in various fields of **mathematics** including algebraic topology, algebraic geometry, game theory, history of mathematics, and automated theorem proving, the latter a method for proving mathematical theorems through **computer** programs and an essential component of computer science. Also known as Wu Wen-tsün and serving as an academician at the Chinese Academy of Sciences (CAS), his eponymous mathematical innovations included the "Wu formula," the "Wu class," and "Wu's method of characteristic set." Born in Shanghai, Wu graduated from Shanghai Communications University in 1940 and continued his studies at the University of Strasbourg in France, receiving a PhD in 1949 while working in Paris where he discovered the Wu formula and Wu class dealing with complex mathematical computations in algebraic topology. Appointed to a post at Peking University in 1951, he was elected to CAS in 1957 and to The World Academy of Sciences (TWAS) in 1990 while receiving numerous awards from the PRC government and becoming the president of the Chinese Society of Mathematics. A student of ancient Chinese mathematics, Wu concluded that traditional Chinese disciplinary practices differed from the axiomatic mathematics that originated in ancient Greece. Describing Chinese mathematics as highly systemized and practical, contrasted with the logic approach at the core of Western geometry, ancient Chinese mathematics, rather than focusing on theorems, emphasized precise and simple **problem-solving** derived from the need to deal with the practical tasks of administration such as dividing up fields and calculating food rations. Wu also contended that the Western binary system attributed to Gottfried Wilhelm Leibniz is an imitation of a systemic understanding of reasoning that Chinese scholars had previously worked on for centuries as Leibniz had corresponded extensively with missionaries in China. Wu's research on mathematical mechanization and mental labor mechanization has become an important goal of AI research in the PRC and the world.

X

XI, JINPING (1953–). General Secretary of the ruling Chinese Communist Party (CCP) and president of the People's Republic of China (PRC) since 2013, Xi Jinping has supported the goal of making the country a global leader in the development of artificial intelligence (AI) by the year 2030 while also periodically expressing concerns about unbridled AI posing problems to the country's social stability and national security. Stressing the importance of AI not becoming "a game of the rich countries and the wealthy," Xi has called for improving the **international governance** of the digital world to ensure inclusive economic globalization while signing on to the **Bletchly Declaration** at the AI Safety Summit in November 2023. Amplifying the interests of the Global South of generally less well-off nations, Xi has pushed for greater international equity in terms of digital technology along with related areas of **finance** and the environment. Concerned with the uncontrolled penetration of AI into the PRC, Xi sees increasing threats to national security calling for greater oversight of AI and data security to counter "dangerous storms" facing the country that has led to such actions as a clamp down on access to foreign **chatbots** such as **ChatGPT**, mandatory official registration for all AI **algorithms**, and a draft **law** requiring all AI products to undergo a security assessment before being released and to reflect "core socialist values" and avoid content that endangers national security, harms national interests, or undermines social stability. Also singled out are certain **deep fakes** which Xi has deemed a "danger to national security and social stability" yet with estimates that the AI sector will add $600 billion to the national **economy** by 2030.

XUE, LAN. A prominent academician in the field of artificial intelligence (AI) in the People's Republic of China (PRC), Xue Lan is a dean of the Institute for International Governance of Artificial Intelligence and a dean at Tsinghua University in Beijing. Focusing on the various governance challenges of AI facing the PRC, Xue, while lauding the development of 130 large

language models (LLMs) in the PRC, has raised many concerns about their overall quality. Included is the construction of many Chinese LLMs through a process he describes as "encapsulation" (*taoke'r*) and "assembly" (*pinzhuang*) from foreign **open-source models** that create problems of **computing** power with operational capabilities severely limited by the unavailability of the most advanced chips from foreign **companies** such as **Nvidia** due to export controls imposed by the United States. Equally problematic is the lack of quality data in the PRC which, Xue claims, has not been truly industrialized with **big data** services remaining unprofitable and suffering from scrambled data while lacking adequate capital investment, unlike foreign counterparts, most notably **ChatGPT**. Describing the dominant innovation model in the PRC as following a relatively linear pattern that moves from academic research to engineering technology to products, Xue suggests such an approach fails to create an inseparable ecosystem among research, engineering, and the market with the development of AI in the PRC exhibiting general stability but with no major scientific breakthroughs. Especially problematic is the lack of core hardware for AI computing power comparable to the new large model **inference** chip LPU developed by the American company Groq, with a speed 10 times faster than a standard **graphics processing unit (GPU)** with only 10 percent of **energy** consumption. On the other hand, Chinese companies have been successful in promoting digital and intelligent transformation utilizing AI technology, as demonstrated by such firms as Sany Heavy Industry which increased manufacturing efficiency by 185 percent and reduced the production cycle of major products from 30 to 7 days. Outstanding problems, according to Xue, include algorithmic discrimination, intellectual property disputes, and misinformation along with insufficient data **privacy** protection and forgery prevention related to AI technology along with inadequate adjustments in the labor force and the industrial structure and the enormous energy consumption demanded by the **training** of the country's many LLMs. Speaking to the China Development Forum in 2024, Xue called for strengthening international cooperation and addressing geopolitical issues as part of the efforts to navigate the various challenges posed by AI development.

Z

ZENG, LIAOYUAN. A professor at the University of Electronic Science and Technology in the People's Republic of China (PRC), Zeng Liaoyuan has broad experience in the fields of signal and information processing and intelligent **telecommunication** with important commentary on the morals and ethics involved in the application of artificial intelligence (AI). Suggesting that AI is comparable to a hammer with the nail consisting of just about everything else, Zeng sees AI as raising numerous legal issues with an over-demanding market for AI including high **energy** and resource consumption, problems of sustainability, and a general lack of confidence and trust in AI **algorithms** with a profound sense of the unknown social and moral consequences of the technology. Major dilemmas include a poor understanding of the sacrifices people are willing to make in utilizing AI and the social areas in need of protection from the omnipresent technology, all of which demand a great deal of innovative and "out of the box" thinking to ensure AI is embedded into daily life with primarily beneficial effects promoting inclusive human development. Noting that most AI technology developments occur in the Global North of highly developed nations, Zeng believes three factors shape this process including plentiful data, good algorithms, and computational power that are largely unavailable in poorer developing countries where there are few of the necessary scientists but with the advantage of potentially large pools of data that require protection.

ZHANG, SHAODIAN (1988–). Founder and chairman of the Synyi Intelligence company, Dr. Zhang Shaodian has led the company in developing 15 artificial intelligence (AI) and **big data**-powered solutions to support the digital transformation of **hospitals** along the lines of **smart technologies** in the People's Republic of China (PRC). Encompassing 150 tertiary hospitals in the country, the program is aimed at optimizing every medical decision by hospital staff by maximizing access to medical data by employing AI **algorithms** to deconstruct, analyze, and standardize medical records and professional medical papers. Born into a family of intellectuals, Zhang attended the Shanghai Communications University majoring in computer science while also serving as an intern at Microsoft Research Asia, conducting research and development of **natural language processing (NLP)** algorithms, which was followed by a stint at Columbia University in the United States studying in the highly selective field of medical information. Returning to the PRC, Zhang was drawn to the medical field, a huge and traditional industry with strong demand for industrial upgrading and a great need for people who understand technology and AI. Joining with like-minded partners, Synyi Intelligence was founded to produce a system for processing medical records at a speed thousands of times greater than that of conventional medical personnel and procedures. Winning financial support from several capital funds and the Shulan Medical Group, Zhang conducted extensive market research while visiting hospitals, doctors, pharmaceutical companies, and government departments across the country where he discovered that crucial medical data in most hospitals was chaotic, each with its own system constituting an information island with large amounts of data stored in the form of often indecipherable text. Each hospital adhered to different specifications, standards, and text formats, with every doctor having their own peculiar writing style and habits and each department with divergent medical record keeping making their effective use virtually impossible. Applying the American system that stresses efficiency, safety, **privacy**, and universality in dealing with medical information, Zhang is devoted to making medical information an independent discipline in the PRC with a concentration on technical innovation to extract more effective information from medical data.

ZHANG, YAQIN (1966–). Founding dean of the Institute for Artificial Intelligence Industry Research (AIR) at Tsinghua University in Beijing, People's Republic of China (PRC), Zhang Yaqin has served as a major player in the application of artificial intelligence (AI) in several fields in the country, including medicine and to **hospitals**. Born in Shanxi Province, Zhang was educated at the University of Science and Technology in the PRC and earned a PhD in electrical engineering at George Washington University in the United States with executive training at Harvard University. Working at **Microsoft** for 16 years, Zhang cofounded Microsoft Research China in 1999, which was elevated to Microsoft Research Asia in 2002, serving as chairman of the Microsoft Asia Research and Development Group with 5,000 scientists and engineers and the Microsoft Venture Accelerator in Beijing that promoted more than 200 companies. Serving as president of **Baidu** from 2014 to 2019 in conjunction with founder Robin Li, Zhang assisted in developing intelligent cloud computing, **autonomous driving**, silicon technology, and industrial AI. Appointed to the School of Computer Science and as chair professor of AI science, Zhang has also won many awards and has been elected to the Chinese Academy of Sciences (CAS), the American Academy of Arts and Sciences, and the Chinese Academy of Engineering while also serving on the boards of several public companies and on the Davos World Economic Forum.

Glossary of Chinese Terms

Bandaoti	semiconductor
Cainiao	Rookie
Chaoji zhineng	superintelligence
Da yuyan moxing	large language model
Dang'an	personal archive
Deluo	drone
Diandong qiche	electric vehicle
Douyin	shaking noise
Fuzhipin	replica
Ganzhiqi	perceptron
Guangke	lithography
Jiqi xuexi	machine learning
Jiqiren	robot
Jiqiren chuzuche	robotaxi
Liangzi jisuan	quantum computing
Rengong shengchan zhineng	artificial generative intelligence
Rengong zhineng	artificial intelligence
Rengong zhineng xidu	AI washing
Shehuizhuyi hexin jiazhiguan	core values of socialism
Shendu Qiusuo	DeepSeek
Shendu xuexi	deep learning
Shenjing wangluo	neural network
Shuzihua	digitalization
Songshu	Squirrel
Suanfa	algorithm
Taoke'r	encapsulation
Ting dian	rolling blackouts
Tiqian hua hongxian	drawing a red line in advance
Tongyi Qianwen	Unified Thousand Questions
Tuxing chuli danyuan	graphic processing units
Xiao ice	little ice

Xuni zhuli	virtual assistant
Yuyin shibie	voice and speech recognition
Zhineng jishu	smart technology
Zhongguo zhizao	Made in China

Appendix

"XI Jinping: Advancing the Healthy Development of Our Nation's New Generation of Artificial Intelligence." Xinhua (New China News Agency), October 31, 2018.

During the ninth group study session of the Politburo of the Central Committee of the Chinese Communist Party, Xi Jinping emphasized: Strengthening leadership, planning well, clarifying tasks, and laying a solid foundation to promote the healthy development of China's new generation of artificial intelligence.

The Politburo of the Central Committee of the Chinese Communist Party (CCP) convened the ninth group study session on the current status and trends of AI development on the afternoon of October 31. Xi Jinping, general secretary of the CCP Central Committee, emphasized that AI is an important driving force for a new round of scientific and technological revolution and industrial transformation. Accelerating the development of a new generation of AI is related to the strategic issue of whether China can seize the opportunities for a new round of scientific and technological revolution and industrial transformation. It is necessary to understand profoundly the great significance of accelerating the development of a new generation of AI, strengthen leadership, properly plan, clarify tasks, establish a solid foundation, promote AI's deep integration with economic and social development, and advance the healthy development of China's new generation of AI.

Gao Wen, a professor at Peking University and an academician of the Chinese Academy of Engineering, explained the issue and discussed his opinions and suggestions.

The comrades of the Politburo of the CCP Central Committee listened carefully to the explanations and discussed the relevant issues.

Xi Jinping gave a speech as chair of the study session. He stressed that AI is a strategic technology heralding this round of scientific and industrial revolution and industrial change and has a "lead goose" effect with a strong stimulating nature. Under the impetus of mobile Internet, big data, supercomputing, sensor networks, neuroscience, and other new theories and new technologies, AI has developed rapidly, presenting new characteristics such as deep learning, interdisciplinary convergence, human–machine cooperation, group intelligence development, autonomous operation, and so on. It is currently producing a major and profound influence on economic development, social progress, and the structure of international politics and economics. Accelerating the development of a new generation of AI is an important strategic handhold for China to gain the initiative in global science and technology competition, and it is an important strategic resource driving our country's leapfrog development in science and technology, its industrial optimization and upgrading, and a comprehensive leap ahead in productivity.

Accelerating the development of a new generation of AI is an important strategic handhold for China to gain the initiative in global science and technology competition.

Xi Jinping pointed out that AI is characterized by multidisciplinary integration and a high degree of complexity. We must strengthen deliberations and decisions, plan matters comprehensively, coordinate and innovate, move ahead steadily, and make strengthening original innovation capability a focus point. With critical and core technologies as the main direction of advancement, we should lay down a basis for the development of a new generation of AI. We must do the following: strengthen fundamental theory research; support scientists to bravely charge into the "no man's land" ahead of AI technological frontiers; strive to make transformative and disruptive breakthroughs in the development direction of AI and in areas such as theories, methods, tools, and systems; and ensure that our country marches in the front ranks where it comes to theoretical research in this important area of AI and occupies the high ground in critical and core technologies. We must focus on advancing in critical and core technologies. In this process, let us be problem-oriented, comprehensively strengthen AI science and technology innovation capabilities, accelerate the establishment of critical common technology systems for a new generation of AI, pay firm attention to the structure of our shortcomings, and ensure that critical and core AI technologies are firmly grasped in our own hands. We must strengthen science and technology application and exploitation, closely focus on economic and social development demands, fully give rein to our country's advantages of vast quantities of data and its huge scale for market application, persist in a scientific and technological development path guided by demand and driven by the market, vigorously foster new products and services with AI innovations, move forward the industrialization of AI technologies, and create a desirable development structure in which science and technology innovation and industrial application mutually support each other. We must strengthen the building of personnel, forge high-level talent training platforms in many kinds and forms with ever greater determination and ever greater strength, strengthen training of reserve talent, and provide ever fuller talent support for scientific, technological, and industrial development.

[I]ntegrate multi-disciplinary capabilities; strengthen research on legal, ethical, and social issues related to AI; and establish and improve laws and regulations, systems and institutions, and ethics and moral principles that ensure the healthy development of AI.

Xi Jinping stressed that our country's economy has transformed from a high-speed growth stage to a high-quality development stage; it is currently in a period in which it is transforming its development method, optimizing its economic structure, and changing its growth drivers; and it is urgently necessary that major innovations such as new-generation AI add wealth and enhance strength. We must profoundly grasp the characteristics of new-generation AI development, strengthen the convergence of AI and industrial development, and provide new drivers for high-quality development. We must focus on building modernized economic systems; make supply-side reform into the main line; grasp the converged opportunity for digital, networked, and smart development; give rein to the role of AI in transformations of quality, efficiency, and dynamics; and raise the productivity of all factors. We must foster AI enterprises and industries with major driving and stimulating effects; and build intelligent economic forms driven by data, with human–machine cooperation, cross-disciplinary convergence, and joint and shared innovation. We must give rein to the technological advantages of AI in industrial upgrading, product development, service innovation, and other such areas; stimulate AI's deep integration with primary, secondary, and tertiary industries; promote the transformation of all industries with AI technologies; and foster new growth points and shape new energies in mid-tier and high-end consumption, innovation leadership, green and low-carbon areas, the sharing economy, modern supply chains, human capital services, and other domains. We must promote the construction of intelligent information infrastructure, enhance the application of intelligent operation to traditional infrastructure, and shape infrastructure systems adapted to the needs of the economy and the smart society.

Leading cadres at all levels must assiduously study the leading edge of science and technology, grasp the natural laws of development and characteristics of AI, strengthen overall coordination, increase policy support, and form work synergies.

Xi Jinping pointed out that we must strengthen the integration of AI with safeguarding and improving the people's livelihoods. Starting from safeguarding and improving livelihoods, and in order to create a beautiful life for the people, we must promote the deep application of AI in people's daily work, study, and life, creating more intelligent work styles and lifestyles. It is necessary to grasp the prominent contradictions and difficulties in people's livelihood, strengthen the in-depth application of artificial intelligence in the fields of education, medicine and healthcare, sports, housing, transportation, disability and elder care, and domestic service, innovating intelligent service systems. It is necessary to strengthen the combination of AI with social governance; develop AI systems suitable for government services and decision-making; strengthen the integration of government information resources and accurate prediction of public requirements; promote the construction of smart cities; promote the deep application of AI in the field of public security; strengthen the use of AI in the ecological field; and improve the level of public services and social governance using AI. It is necessary to strengthen the analysis and prevention of potential risks in the development of AI, safeguard the interests of the people and national security, and ensure that AI is secure, reliable, and controllable. It is necessary to integrate multidisciplinary capabilities; strengthen research on legal, ethical, and social issues related to AI; and establish and improve laws and regulations, systems and institutions, and ethics and moral principles that ensure the healthy development of AI. Leading cadres at all levels must assiduously study the leading edge of science and technology, grasp the natural laws of development and characteristics of AI, strengthen overall coordination, increase policy support, and form work synergies.

Bibliography

Contents

Introduction

As a relatively recent development in the history of science and technology, the creation of artificial intelligence (AI) has generated enormous interest among scholars and commentators including the emergence of the People's Republic of China (PRC) as a global player. Major books and articles in professional journals and publications of general interest are available, dealing with both the highly technical aspects of AI systems along with examination of the economic, social, and political ramifications of AI at the local, national, and global levels. Listed in this bibliography are works designed for readers with a comprehension of basic technological facets of AI and an understanding of fundamental principles of economics and related disciplines while leaving aside the many "how-to" publications on utilizing AI in such specialized realms as banking, business, and other money-making endeavors. Also limited in number are works on AI in the PRC in both English and Chinese involving highly technical topics better left to highly trained researchers and specialists while focusing on publications and other media tracing the origins and development of the technology impacting the general Chinese citizenry, especially since the full-scale commitment of the PRC government to advancing AI beginning in 2017.

Books

General Works on Artificial Intelligence and Related Topics

Ananthaswamy, Anil. *Why Machines Learn: The Elegant Math Behind Modern AI.* New York: Dutton Publishing, 2024.

Appupen and Lauren Daudet. *Dream Machine: A Portrait of Artificial Intelligence.* Cambridge, MA: MIT Press, 2024.

Bauman, Sharen and Callum Bauman. *AI and Robots: Shaping the Future.* NP: Independently Published, 2025.

Bennett, George et al. *A Brief History of Intelligence: Evolution, AI, and the Five Breakthroughs That Made Our Brains.* New York: Mariner Books, 2025.

Bostrum, Nick. *Superintelligence: Paths, Dangers, Strategies.* Oxford: Oxford University Press, 2014.

Chen, Weili. *The Way of Machine Thinking. Volume I, Rules of Universal Language and Fundamental Math.* NP: Independently Published, 2023.

Clark, Richard A. *Artificial Intelligencia.* Los Angeles: Rare Bird Books, 2022.

Domingos, Pedro. *The Master Algorithm: How the Quest for the Ultimate Learning Machine Will Remake Our World.* New York: Basic Books, 2015.

Freeman Publishing. *Basic Generative AI: Beginner's Guide to Artificial Intelligence, ChatGPT, and Machine Learning, Practical Applications.* New York: Freeman Publishing, 2024.

Galdorisi, George and Sam Tangredi. *Algorithms of Armageddon: The Impact of Artificial Intelligence in Future Wars.* Newport, RI: Naval War College Press, 2024.

Hartung, Thomas. "Biocomputing: The Promise of Biological Computing." Paris: *Polytechnique Insights*, 28 November, 2023.

Jackson, Philip C. *Toward Human-Level Artificial Intelligence: Representation and Computation of Meaning in Natural Language.* Garden City, NY: Dover Publications, 2019.

Kaku, Michio. *Quantum Supremacy: How the Quantum Computer Revolution Will Change Everything.* New York: Vintage Publications, 2023.

Kaplan, Jerry. *Artificial Intelligence: What Everyone Needs to Know.* Oxford: Oxford University Press, 2016.

Kissinger, Henry A. et al. *The Age of AI and Our Human Future.* New York: Little Brown and Company, 2022.

Kissinger, Henry A. et al. *Genesis: Artificial Intelligence, Hope, and the Human Spirit.* New York: Little Brown and Company, 2024.

Larsen, Erik J. *The Myth of Artificial Intelligence.* Cambridge, MA: Harvard University Press, 2021.

Lee, Peter et al. *The AI Revolution in Medicine: GPT-4 and Beyond.* Cambridge: Pearson Publishing, 2025.

Lee, Peter et al. *Quantum Computing and Information: A Scaffolding Approach.* New York: Polaris QCI Publishing, 2024.

Lennox, John C. *2084: Artificial Intelligence and the Future of Humanity.* Grand Rapids, MI: Zondervan Press, 2020.

Li, Robin. *Artificial Intelligence Revolution: How AI Will Change Our Society, Economy, and Culture*. New York: Skyhorse Publishing, 2020.

Lucci, Stephen and Danny Kupec. *Artificial Intelligence in the 21st Century*. Second Edition. Herndon, VA: Mercury Learner and Information, 2015.

McGinty, Joseph C. Jr. *AI Uncensored: From Origins to Opportunities: Exploring the Evolution, Theories, and Applications of Artificial Intelligence*, Tukwila, WA: Thriftbooks, 2024.

Minsky, Marvin et al. *Perceptrons*. Cambridge, MA: The MIT Press, 2017.

Mollick, Ethian. *Co-Intelligence: Living and Working with AI*. New York: Portfolio Books, 2024.

Muller, David et al. *On Rationality, Artificial Intelligence, and Economics*. New York: World Scientific Publishers, 2022.

Piddubna, Alina. "Artificial Intelligence and the Future of Farming." *Intellias*, August, 12 2024.

Poulton, Nigel. *AI Explained: Facts, Fiction, and Future*. Hertfordshire: Nielsen Book Services, 2024.

Rickards, James. *Money GPT: AI and the Threat to the Global Economy*. New York: Portfolio Books, 2024.

Russell, Stuart and Peter Norvig. *Artificial Intelligence: A Modern Approach*, Fourth Edition. Uttar Pradesh, India: Pearson India Education Services, 2022.

Sejnowski, Terrence. *Chat GPT and the Future of AI: The Deep Learning Revolution*. Cambridge, MA: MIT Press, 2024.

Suleyman, Mustafa. *The Coming Wave: AI, Power, and Our Future*. New York: Crown, 2025.

Tegmark, Max et al. *Life 3.0: Being Human in the Age of Artificial Intelligence*. New York: Knopf, 2017.

Uria-Recio, Pedro. *How AI Will Shape Our Future: Understand Artificial Intelligence and Stay Ahead*. NP: Self-Published, 2024.

Viggiano, Greg and David Brian. *Convergence: Artificial Intelligence and Quantum Computing: Social, Economic, and Policy Impacts*. Hoboken, NJ: Wiley, 2023.

Artificial Intelligence in China

Carver, Donald A. *The China's DeepSeek AI: How China's Artificial Intelligence Revolution is Shaping Global Power, Innovation, and the Future of Technology*. NP: Independently Published, 2025.

Delaney, Owen. *The DeepSeek R1 Revolution: How a New AI is Redefining the Future of Intelligence*. NP: Independently Published, 2025.

Hannas, William C., editor. *Chinese Power and Artificial Intelligence: Perspectives and Challenges*. New York: Routledge, 2022.

Jones, Handel. *When AI Rules the World: China, the U.S., and the Race to Control a Smart Planet*. Brentwood, TN: Bombardier Books, 2022.

Knox, John. *AI and Education in China: Imagining the Future, Excavating the Past*. New York: Routledge, 2023.

Lee, Kai-Fu. *AI Superpowers: China, Silicon Valley, and the New World Order.* New York: Harper Business, 2021.

Li, Chaodong. *Artificial Intelligence (Chinese Modern New Technology).* Seattle: Royal Colins Publishing Company, 2024.

Liang, Qilian et al., editors. *Artificial Intelligence in China: Proceedings of the Second/ Third/ Fourth/ Fifth International Conference[s] on Artificial Intelligence in China.* New York: Springer Nature, 2020–2024.

Liu, Zhexin and Daniel Dinkelman. *English-Chinese AI Dictionary: Essential Terminology for Artificial Intelligence, Machine Learning, and Deep Learning.* NP: Cineris Multifacet Expert Group, 2025.

Ma, Winston. *The Digital War: How China's Tech Power Shapes the Future of AI, Blockchain, and Cyberspace.* Hoboken, NJ: Wiley, 2021.

Parsa, Cyrus A. *Artificial Intelligence Dangers to Humanity: AI, U.S., China, Big Tech, Facial Recognition, Drones, Smart Phones, IoT, 5G, Robotics, Cybernetics, and Bio-Digital Social Programs.* NP: AI Organization, 2019.

Rynning, Chris. *How China Will Dominate AI and Blockchain Technology.* NP: Independently Published. 2018.

Scott, Jackson Z. *China's DeepSeek AI: The Threat to U.S. Dominance—All You Need to Know.* NP: Independently Published, 2025.

Wright, Nicholas D., editor. *Artificial Intelligence, China, Russia, and the Global Order.* NP: Independently Published, 2019.

Zeng, Jingshan. *Artificial Intelligence with Chinese Characteristics: National Strategy, Security, and Authoritarian Governance.* London: Palgrave Macmillan, 2022.

Articles

General Artificial Intelligence and Artificial Intelligence in China

Araya, Daniel. "China's Robots Are Coming of Age." *Center for International Governance Innovation.* July 11, 2024.

Atlantic Council. "The West, China, and AI Surveillance." December 18, 2020.

Azhar, Ali. "AI Scientists from China Warn AI has Surpassed the Self-Replicating Red Line." *AI Wire.* January 2025.

Blech, Richard. "The Emerging Threat to Cryptography: China Advances in AI and Quantum Computing." *NP*, ND.

Chen, Grace. "AI and Space Exploration." Department of Rocket Science, Harvard University. December 2023.

Chen, Rui and Jinjuan Ren. "Do AI-Powered Mutual Funds Perform Better?" *Financial Research Letters.* August 2022.

Chen, Shuqing. "How Artificial Intelligence is Modernizing Chinese Agriculture." *Synced Review.* October 12, 2019.

Ide, Enrique and Edward Talamas. "Artificial Intelligence in the Knowledge Economy." May 31, 2024.

International Journal of Pattern Recognition and Artificial Intelligence. 1987–. World Scientific.

Kurzweil, Ray. "AI Cryptography: Enhancing Security and Privacy in the Digital Age." *Medium.* October 7, 2023.

Lai, Linda S. I. "The Adoption of Cognitive Computing Technology in China." *IT Professional*, 21 (November-December, 2019), pp. 14–21.

Latoya, Roberts. "Morals and Ethics of Artificial Intelligence: Are We at a Crossroads?" *Caribbean Insight.* December 17, 2019.

Li, Baocheng. "How China Learned to Stop Worrying and Love Social Media Manipulation." *RAND Corporation.* October 1, 2024.

Loop. "Chinese Artists Embrace Artificial Intelligence as a Creative Foil." *Garland Magazine.* May 2, 2024.

NA. "Applying Ancient Chinese Philosophy to Artificial Intelligence." *Noema Magazine.* Berggruen Institute, ND.

NA. "A Brief History of Artificial Intelligence." *The Fusioneer.* July 2022.

NA. "China's AI Policy and Development: What You Need to Know." *Fiscal Note.* August 7, 2024.

NA. "The Early History of Artificial Intelligence in China (1950s–1980s)." Annual Meeting of the Society for the History of Technology, 2018.

NA. "The Impact of Data Centers on AI: A Comprehensive Analysis." *Digital Reality.* ND.

Na, Kexin. "The Role of Artificial Intelligence in China's Manufacturing Industry: Reality and Prospects." *Highlights in Business Economics.* August 2024.

Rosas, Alexander. "What to Know About China's Smart Cities and How They Use Artificial Intelligence, 5G, and Internet of Things." *The China Guys.* August 2021.

Sayagh, Emil. "The Billion Dollar AI Gamble: Data Centers as the New High-Stakes Game." *Forbes.* September 30, 2024.

Swedroe, Larry. "Can AI Predict Future Stock Returns." *Morningstar.* September 25, 2024.

Thompson, Tom. "Minority Report: Machine Learning and Crime Prevention in China: Technology and Operations Management." *Digital Initiative.* Harvard Business School, November 12, 2018.

Tsidulko, Joseph. "Benefit of AI in Supply Chain." *Oracle.* January 11, 2024.

Wang, Xiaopeng et al. "How a Vast Digital Twin of the Yangtze River Could Prevent Flooding in China." *Nature.* March 11, 2025.

Yang, Zeyi. "How to Access Chinese LLM Chatbots Across the World." *MIT Technology Review.* July 23, 2024.

Zhao, Tiejun et al. "Recent Advances in Natural Language Processing Research at the Harbin Institute of Technology." *Higher Education Press*, 2007.

Zhou, Victor. "Rest of World." *Reporting Global Tech Stories.* ND.

Books and Articles on Artificial Intelligence in Chinese and Other Languages

Beltrąn, Henry Estrada. *La Mąquina Perfecta: Reflexiones sobre Intelligencia Artificial* (The Perfect Machine: Reflections on Artificial Intelligence). Spanish Edition, NP: Independently Published, 2024.

Bing, Huiyun. *Rengong Zhineng Taolun* (Introduction to Artificial Intelligence). Beijing: Electronic Industry Press, 2021.

Qian, Luru. *Rengong Zhineng* (Artificial Intelligence), Volume 2. Beijing: Science, 2000.

Zhu, Li. *Rengong Zhineng Rumen* (Introduction to Artificial Intelligence). Beijing: Tsinghua University Press, 2021.

Videos and Additional Sources

Youtube: Selected Titles

"Alpha Go: A Documentary."
"Antikythera Mechanism."
"Biocomputing in China."
"Here's How Biocomputing Works and Matters for Artificial Intelligence."
"How Deep Neural Networks Work."
"The Man Behind DeepSeek."
"The Revolution of AI."
"Role of AI in Transforming Education."
"Shocking Progress: China's Humanoid Robots."
"The Ten Stages of AI"
"Why China is Racing Ahead."

Magazines, Newspapers, Web Sites, and Electronic Sources

Atlantic Council
Caixin Global
CCTV
China Briefing
China Daily
Computer World
Dataiku
Digital Crew
Forbes
Fortune
Fraud.com
Futurism

Global Times
Intraratio Corporation
Invoca Blog
JP Morgan
Linked-In
McKinsey & Company
Medium
Micron
National Bureau of Asian Research
National Library of Medicine
New York Times
Police Chief
Reddit
Reuters
Science Direct
Statistica
Symphony Solutions
Tableau
Talos
The Register
Think China
Trend Force
Wired
World Economic Forum
World Intellectual Property Organization
Wikipedia

About the Authors

Lawrence R. Sullivan is a professor emeritus of political science, Adelphi University, Garden City, New York, and a research associate, East Asian Institute, Columbia University, New York City. He received a PhD in political science at the University of Michigan and is author and coauthor of several historical dictionaries on the China including *Historical Dictionary of the Financial System in China* (2025), *Historical Dictionary of the Chinese Communist Party* (2022), *Historical Dictionary of the Chinese Economy* (2018), and *Historical Dictionary of Science and Technology in China* (2015). Prof. Sullivan is also author and coauthor of several books on contemporary China including *Leadership and Authority in China: 1895–1976* (2012) and with Nancy Liu-Sullivan *Concise Encyclopedia of Green Technology in China* (2023).

Nancy Liu-Sullivan received a PhD in molecular and cellular pharmacology (Stony Brook University School of Medicine), and an MS in molecular genetics (Adelphi University). Dr. Liu-Sullivan has more than a decade of expertise in cancer genomics and high throughput drug discovery at Memorial Sloan-Kettering Cancer Center, New York City, and Cold Spring Harbor Laboratory and is currently a doctoral lecturer in the Department of Biology, College of Staten Island (CSI), City University of New York where she continues to conduct cancer research. She is coeditor and co-translator of *China's Water Crisis* (2004) by Ma Jun and *The River Dragon Has Come!: The Three Gorges Dam and the Fate of China's Yangtze River and Its People* (1998) by Dai Qing and coauthor of the *Historical Dictionary of Science and Technology in Modern China* (2015) and *Concise Encyclopedia of Green Technology in China* (2023).

www.ingramcontent.com/pod-product-compliance
Ingram Content Group UK Ltd.
Pitfield, Milton Keynes, MK11 3LW, UK
UKHW020210290926
15470UKWH00001B/103

9 798765 145630